MAN & THE AUTOMOBILE
A TWENTIETH-CENTURY LOVE AFFAIR

Covered Phaeton

MAN & THE AUTOMOBILE
A TWENTIETH-CENTURY LOVE AFFAIR

Judith Jackson

Technical Author   Graham Robson
Foreword by Henry Ford II

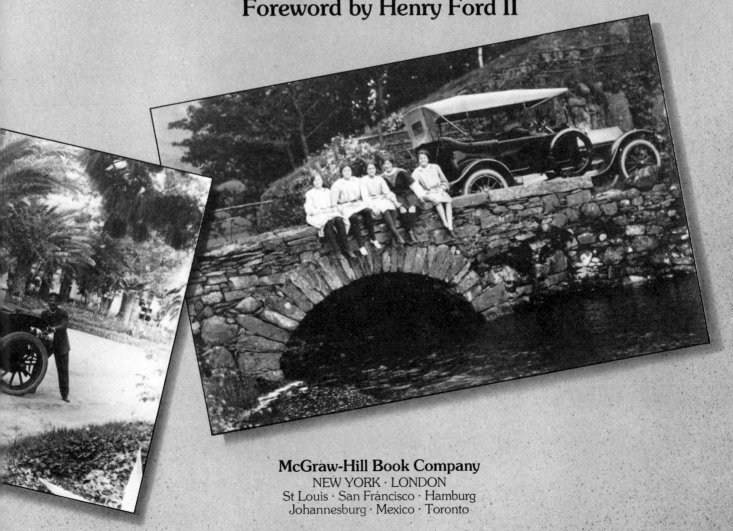

McGraw-Hill Book Company
NEW YORK · LONDON
St Louis · San Francisco · Hamburg
Johannesburg · Mexico · Toronto

First published in the United States of America, 1979,
by McGraw–Hill Book Company
1221 Avenue of the Americas, New York.

First published in the United Kingdom, 1979,
by McGraw–Hill Book Company (UK) Limited,
Maidenhead, Berkshire, England.

Man and the Automobile was conceived, edited and
designed by Harrow House Editions Limited, London.

Editorial consultant Victor Stevenson
Edited by Gill Rowley
Designed by Mike Rose and Bob Lamb with assistance
from John Pallot and Jonathan Gill–Skelton
Research by Ethel Hurwicz and Sunny Albert
Picture research by Maggie Colbeck, Pam Hepburn
and Liz Rudoff

Editorial Director   Martyn Bramwell
Art Director   Nicholas Eddison
Production   Kenneth Cowan
Reader   Fred Gill

Typeset in Souvenir Light
by William Caple & Company, Leicester, England.
Illustrations originated
by Reprocolor Llovet, Barcelona, Spain.
Printed and bound by Artes Graficas, Toledo, Spain

Library of Congress Cataloging in Publication Data
Jackson, Judith, 1938–
    Man and the automobile.

    1.   Automobiles – History.   I.   Robson, Graham,
joint author. – II.   Title.
TL15.J24 1979 388.34'22'09   79–14104
ISBN 0–07–032119–1
Depósito legal: To. 517-79

Contents

Foreword

The long and continuing relationship between man and the automobile has now become so much a part of our lives that it is perhaps now more akin to a marriage than a love affair. The story of the motor car in the United States began in 1893, when the Duryea brothers built the first successful petrol–powered vehicle. Ford Motor Company was founded just a few years later, in 1903, and in the three–quarters of a century since then, Ford alone has built nearly 150 million vehicles in plants all over the world. The "love affair" has become something much more permanent.

The motor car has its devotees and its critics, and manufacturers are now facing the most crucial challenge of their lives. The demands on their resources, their technology and their ingenuity have never been greater and occasionally, in the heat of the commercial battle, it is good to linger over books like *Man and the Automobile* and remind ourselves of just how much the motor car has contributed to life, leisure and happiness. It has created mobility and brought people and places closer together. It serves as a vital tool of business and industry and remains man's infinitely obliging servant.

From the challenging days of the 1960s when, for the first time, more cars were sold outside North America than inside, the world's motor industry has come closer together in concepts, ideas and products. The choice facing the buyer is greater than at any time in the past; the people working on present and future designs have never been so many in number or so varied in their talents.

This book sets out to remind us that our pioneers – some of them still youthful – have created much more than mere machines: they have created mobility itself. The growth of motorised transport has probably given more pleasure and freedom to the individual, and provided a greater spur to industrial productivity, than any other single invention.

Henry Ford II
Chairman of the Board
Ford Motor Company

Introduction

For many people their relationship with the motor car has been a love affair right from the start; others view the motor car with very mixed feelings, but, love it or hate it, nobody can deny that the automobile is here to stay.

When I started work on this book, a car was very much an integral part of my everyday life – a functional if sophisticated machine which enabled me to cope with a busy domestic and social day, and to earn my living. Like countless other people I took the car for granted and yet, if it were to disappear overnight, at least half of us would have to change our jobs or move house and many of us would find our social lives drastically reduced.

There are many, however, who do not think of the motor car as just another machine but who derive an enormous amount of fun from it – usually by asking it to attempt all manner of extraordinary feats. At the other end of the scale there are people who regard the motor car as one of the evils of our society. It can be argued – and frequently is by the

environmental lobby – that the motor car is a polluter and destroyer of the environment and that it desecrates the quality of life. As a journalist, these are arguments which often confront me and give me cause for thought. But no matter which view one takes of the car, one fact is beyond dispute: its development has brought about some of the most profound social and technological changes of this or any other century.

The extent of the technological change is illustrated in the last section of the book, which is concerned solely with the engineering "milestones" in the history of the car. Social change, on the other hand, is more diffuse and difficult to formulate. For this reason I have drawn very extensively on people – on their memories, their writings, their family albums. Contemporary newspapers and magazines, and particularly the advertising they carried, provided a fascinating insight into the way previous generations have felt about the motor car. I also found a wealth of material in the Public Records Office, which houses a vast number of reports, including those of Select Committees, on road–building programmes and other motoring legislation.

One aspect of the motor car which had eluded me in the

past was that of the enthusiast – the man or woman who has been touched by the magic of motoring and whose eyes light up at the very mention of a Mors or a Bugatti. Because my approach to the motor car has always been a somewhat pragmatic one, I used to find this attitude surprising, but as our work on the book progressed I found my own attitudes changing – and changing very largely because of the remarkable pictures which were gathering round me. For this reason I am particularly grateful to the picture researchers who worked with me on the project with such enthusiasm, skill and imagination. Somehow they persuaded people to turn out their attics and emerge with a wealth of unique pictures which tell their own story – the story of the close and varied relationship man has had with the motor car during the past hundred years: how he invented it, built it, bought it, sold it, loved it – and made it a part of his life.

The history of the car has been well recorded. What I have tried to do is to bring people back into the story. Obviously no book can include everything and I can only apologise if I have left out your own particular favourites: I have had to leave out several of my own. The difficulty is that although the motor car is very young, with scarcely a hundred years of history behind it, an astonishing amount has happened in that time.

Many people helped and encouraged me while the book was in progress and to all of them I am extremely grateful. Two people in particular deserve my thanks for their patience and understanding. John Bolster, whose book *The Upper Crust* was a constant source of inspiration and amusement, has a special feeling for the early days of motoring which he was always prepared to share, and Cyril Posthumus has an encyclopaedic knowledge of the motoring world, past and present, from which he unfailingly produced answers to even the most obscure questions. My sons Fraser and Lincoln, who suffered with me through the gestation period of the book, also deserve my thanks.

Here then is a book that seeks to portray man's changing relationship with the motor car over the years. From its early days as a toy of the rich and status symbol of the powerful it has now become the ubiquitous tool of tradesmen and travellers, sportsmen and adventurers the world over. Perhaps no other machine has come to mean so many things to so many people or proved so indispensable to everyday life.

Judith Jackson

The Rattletrap Ancestors

For those of us born in the twentieth century it is almost impossible to imagine what life was like before the advent of the internal combustion engine and the motor vehicle which it now powers. That bygone age in which horses outnumbered powered vehicles by hundreds, if not thousands, to one can exist only in our dreams and our imagination. It is unlikely that those days were really as peaceful as we now imagine – for horses are demanding creatures needing constant care and attention, albeit producing noises and smells of a milder sort than the motor car.

In more than eighty years of motoring, both the motor car and the society in which it exists have seen great changes. But the changes have been gradual, almost imperceptible – an evolving part of our way of life. In the late nineteenth century, roads, such as they were, carried only horse–drawn traffic and most journeys were of only a few miles. Our ancestors would have regarded a journey to a neighbouring market town in much the same way as the traveller of today would regard a transcontinental journey – something to be carefully considered and planned in every detail: even, perhaps, something to be undertaken with a certain amount of trepidation.

A major change in this attitude toward travel came about largely as a result of the rapid growth of the railway system, which, in Britain and in many other countries, received great support both from private and government sources. But despite the changes in attitude, and the acceptance of long–distance travel as part of a way of life, the motor car remained for many years the province of the wealthy enthusiast, whose treasured and fragile machine was brought out only in fine weather and even then to the consternation of neighbours and friends, many of whom just could not bring themselves to take this new–fangled invention seriously.

THE RATTLETRAP ANCESTORS
The Age of Steam

By the end of the eighteenth century, Britain was using about one and a half million animals of one sort and another to provide what was regarded as essential transport. Passenger transport was virtually non–existent and, even for the moderately affluent, stage coach fares were high at sixpence a mile – at a time when labourers were paid about five shillings a week. Clearly there was a need for some form of cheaper, faster and mechanised transport. There had been many experiments. A Dutchman had built, and experimented with, a sailing wagon; clockwork was thought by some to be a possibility; and Isaac Newton had produced a design for a steam–jet–propelled coach as far back as the 1680s. But the first successful attempt was probably that of Nicholas–Joseph Cugnot, who, in 1771, produced a steam–driven truck which puffed its way around the Paris Arsenal. This vehicle, built by a French farmer's son, is generally regarded as the world's first practical road vehicle which was not propelled by men or animals, and as such the steam truck marked the beginning of the horseless carriage.

The Cugnot steam truck heralded a hundred years of devotion to steam power, although the development of steam–driven vehicles between 1770 and 1870 took place almost entirely in Britain. The first full–scale steam vehicle to run on British roads was the brainchild of Richard Trevithick, and made its first run on Christmas Eve 1801. It was more like a railway engine designed for use on the road than anything which we would recognise today as a motor car. It was capable of 10 mph and ran spasmodically between the City and the West End of London. But although steam engines were widely used in ships, railways and in heavy industry, on the road they proved cumbersome and unreliable.

Nevertheless the enthusiasts persevered. In 1836 Walter Hancock ran a passenger service in London involving three steam vehicles, which went some way towards showing that they might be a serious proposition. Perhaps rather surprisingly their most attractive feature was their modest running cost. Records of a regular service between Cheltenham and Gloucester show that the cost of coke was nine shillings a day while the equivalent cost of horses was forty–five shillings a day – five times as much.

Popular though steam was in Britain, the major break–through in steam engineering for the road finally came, once again, from France. The Paris Exposition of 1889 featured a steam–powered carriage built by Leon Serpollet. Together with his playboy friend Ernest Archdeacon he drove the carriage from Paris to Lyon. Archdeacon, according to contemporary reports, dressed as though for a formal social occasion, with pearl–grey waistcoat, bowler hat and spats. The 300–mile trip lasted two weeks and during that time almost everything on the vehicle which could break did so. Far from discouraged, Serpollet went on to build lighter and smaller steam cars and tricycles, as well as lorries, tractors and buses. Some of the vehicles were capable of 14 mph, which was faster than any other mechanical vehicle, but they were still left far behind by a good horse. It is reported that the Prince of Wales ordered one of the Serpollet light steam cars, although there is no record of what he thought of it.

Steam was also gaining popularity in America, due to the efforts of the Stanley brothers, whose first steam car was completed in 1897. The Stanleys knew little about the internal combustion engine but, being farmers, had a very practical attitude to mechanical matters. Stanley steamers were extremely successful and even appeared on the track at Daytona, where, on 25 January 1907, a Steamer Special,

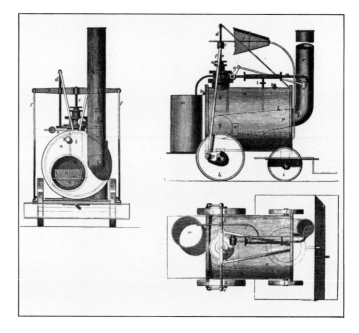

Steam–driven vehicles became a practical reality with Nicholas–Joseph Cugnot's *fardier à vapeur* in 1771. Trials of an earlier prototype *(top)* had so impressed the French Minister of War that Cugnot was authorised to construct another, larger version, which was built at the Paris Arsenal. Despite contemporary reports that this new *fardier* had run amok and crashed into a wall, it may still be seen in Paris.

Richard Trevithick published technical drawings *(above)* of his passenger–carrying steam locomotive in the first issue of *The Practical Magazine*. On Christmas Eve 1801, the vehicle climbed Camborne Beacon in Cornwall with several men clinging to the engineer's platform at the rear. The single–cylinder engine of the locomotive was recessed into the boiler and a slender handle was used for steering.

driven by one Fred Marriott, claimed a speed of 197 mph before hitting a rut, leaving the ground and blowing itself, though fortunately not the driver, to pieces. Details of the incident are uncertain. What is certain, however, is that the steam engine had by this time been overtaken by the internal combustion petrol engine. Ingenious though the steam vehicles had been they had neither the stamina nor the performance to compete commercially with the faster, more powerful and more flexible petrol–driven cars, although steam enthusiasts hope for a revival to this day.

Steam tractor with carriage trailer *(left)* driven by the Comte de Dion with M. Bouton as his passenger. It was in this combination that the Comte de Dion finished first in the 1894 Paris–Rouen trials, but failed to be awarded a prize because the judges did not consider the vehicle to be a true car.

Gardner–Serpollet steam car *(below left)* being driven by its owners Mr and Mrs H. F. Compton at their home, Minstead Manor, in the New Forest, in Hampshire, England.

Delivery van powered by a Serpollet steam engine *(below)* which took part in the 1894 Paris–Rouen trials, driven by M. Étienne le Blant. The vehicle was by no means a great success: it crashed during the practice sessions and managed to get no farther than Mantes in the actual trials.

The Innovators

The real history of the motor car as we know it today begins with Karl Benz and Gottlieb Daimler. Although the names of these two great German engineers are inextricably linked, they never met each other, and the merger of their companies did not take place until 1926, long after Daimler's death. They were by no means the only pioneers in the field, but their influence on the petrol–engined motor car is indisputable – and widely recognised.

Gottlieb Daimler was born in Schorndorf in 1834, the son of a baker. As a student of Stuttgart Polytechnic, he studied engineering. After receiving his degree, he went to England to observe the development of the steam car and returned to Germany to work at Gasmotoren–Fabrik Deutz – a company specialising in internal combustion engines. While at Deutz, Daimler designed the first practical four–stroke petrol engine, and in 1882, with his friend Wilhelm Maybach, founded his own business. Their first vehicle was actually a motor bicycle with a wooden frame and a single–cylinder petrol engine, but the first car, a four–wheeled vehicle built in 1886, was a

traditional carriage – lacking only the shafts and the horse – to which Daimler had fitted a slightly larger version of the single–cylinder engine. Although the body of this vehicle was extremely basic the engine was relatively advanced and it was on engines that Daimler preferred to concentrate.

Karl Benz was the son of an engine driver who died in a railway accident when his son was two. In 1874, after several engineering jobs, Benz set up his own small business to make two–stroke engines that ran on coal–gas, but with help and financial encouragement from friends he started to work on the development of an engine that would run on a more adaptable fuel than gas or steam.

Petrol, or benzine, was also known as ligroin and was usually bought at chemists' shops for use as a cleaning fluid. The engine Benz built roughly followed the pattern of his gas engines and he completed his first petrol–driven tricar in October 1885, a few months ahead of Daimler. But whereas Daimler fitted his relatively advanced engine to a chassis that looked as though someone had forgotten the horse, Benz used a specially built three–wheeled chassis with the single front wheel steered by a handle which also operated the brake.

The first trial run of the tricar was not a conspicuous success. The steering proved inadequate and Benz hit a wall within the first few yards. On his second run he managed about a

Gottlieb Daimler, 1834–1900 *(above),* the German experimental engineer whose petrol engine, produced in 1893, is the true ancestor of the modern car engine.

Karl Benz, 1844–1929 *(below),* was probably the first man to realise the commercial potential of the horseless carriage. Unlike Daimler, he concentrated on proven designs rather than experimenting.

Daimler's first car *(left),* built in 1886, on a trial run at Bad Canstatt near Stuttgart. In the driving seat is Wilhelm Maybach, Daimler's partner, with Paul Daimler, eldest of Daimler's children, by his side. The body follows the traditional design of the horse–drawn carriage, with the engine mounted under the feet of the rear passengers. The engine was capable of 900 rpm and the car's top speed was almost 10 mph.

A prototype 1895 Daimler *(right)* powered by a 2–cylinder, 4 hp engine. Driving in the grounds of the Daimler factory is Wilhelm Maybach, with Daimler sitting beside him, and two potential customers.

An 1897 Daimler *(far right)* that has been lovingly restored.

Karl Benz *(left)* pictured in one of his early petrol–driven cars, an 1886 three–wheeler. This picture was taken in Munich in 1925, four years before Benz's death.

An 1893 "Viktoria" *(right),* Benz's first four–wheeled car and the world's first production car. In its first year, sales reached forty–five. The car had double rack–and–pinion steering and a maximum speed of 11 mph.

A 15 hp Benz "Spider" *(far right).* This is an open–bodied version of the 1902 model.

hundred yards, but it was some time before he completed his first non-stop mile. His wife, Berta, impatient with her husband's slow progress, "borrowed" the car one morning and set off with their sons, Eugen and Richard, to make the sixty-two-mile trip from Mannheim to Pforzheim. The trip was not without its problems, with one or both boys having to push the car up hills, but they finally arrived at their destination, having completed the world's first journey by car. But although the car was shown with great success at exhibitions in Paris and Munich, there were few buyers either for it or for a slightly larger version with four seats. It was suggested to Benz by his French agent, Émile Roger, who planned to sell the cars in Britain and America, that having only three wheels the tricar was both unstable and uncomfortable. Thus Benz was persuaded to build a four-wheeled car.

The four-wheeled Benz was an important breakthrough. Launched in 1893, it was called the Viktoria and was powered by a more advanced version of the original Benz engine, which now developed 3 hp and had a top speed of 11 mph. Roger had been right – the four-wheeler was an immediate success and forty-five cars were sold in 1893.

Daimler was also having considerable success. Several manufacturers, including Panhard-Levassor, were building cars and engines based on Daimler designs, but Gottlieb Daimler was reluctant to build bigger and faster cars – believing that there was no need to go any faster on the roads and that drivers would be unable to handle more powerful engines. He preferred to see Daimler-powered buses, ambulances, fire engines and tractors. However, he was a sick man, so in 1898 he handed over the management of the company to his sons, just two years before he died.

Karl Benz lived until 1929, and by the end of 1901 his company had built and sold 2702 vehicles. But in the following year, a sensational car swept the motoring world, decimating Benz sales. The revolutionary newcomer was the Mercedes, built by the Daimler company and named after the eleven-year-old daughter of Émile Jellinek, a wealthy Czech diplomat with a passion for cars. Jellinek had run an 1899 Cannstatt-Daimler, but following the fatal crash of a similar car on the La Turbie hill climb in France, he suggested that there should be a lighter car with a more powerful engine. He promised Wilhelm Maybach, now running the Daimler company, that he would buy thirty-six cars if the first was delivered by October 1900, and if the car was named after his daughter. Maybach could not meet the deadline, but Jellinek kept his promise and the first Mercedes was delivered in 1901, completing the trio of famous names which are still synonymous with cars of the highest quality.

THE RATTLETRAP ANCESTORS

"C'est brutal, mais ça marche"

For many years the Paris firm of Panhard et Levassor had maintained a thriving business making wood– and metal–working bandsaws, but in 1888 Mme Louise Sarazin, the widow of a close friend of Gottlieb Daimler, persuaded Émile Levassor to build the Daimler 1·6 hp petrol engine: a modest beginning which was to herald the age of the motor car. Three years later, in January 1891, the Panhard–Levassor made its debut with a return trip of six and a quarter miles, and in 1894 won the world's first organised motoring event – the Paris–Rouen Reliability Trial.

The car featured a front–mounted engine, a foot–operated friction clutch and a sliding–pinion gear change about which M Levassor is alleged to have said: "C'est brutal, mais ça marche" (It's crude, but it works). It certainly worked well enough for Levassor to win the first real motor race on 11 June 1895 – a prodigious feat in which Levassor drove the 732 miles from Paris to Bordeaux and back at an average speed of 11 mph. Although he was accompanied by his mechanic d'Hostingue (who considered a bowler hat suitable garb for the occasion), Levassor drove the entire distance

One of the earliest catalogues from a car manufacturer *(above left)* was published by Panhard–Levassor in 1892. Like modern counterparts it contained details of the car's speed, fuel consumption and specifications.

The Hon Evelyn Ellis *(left)* in his 1895 Panhard–Levassor, generally believed to be the first imported car in Britain. In October 1895 the car appeared at Britain's first motor show, which was organised to draw attention to the restrictive traffic laws that made motoring in Britain almost impossible.

"Nouveau type" of Panhard–Levassor *(top)*, built in 1894, which finished seventh in the Paris–Rouen Trial.

1896 Panhard–Levassor *(above)* on display outside a London garage.

The Emancipation Run *(right)* was held in November 1896 to celebrate the revision of the "Locomotives on Highways" Act, after which cars no longer had to be preceded by a man carrying a red flag, and the speed limit was raised from 4 to 12 mph. The run is commemorated each year in the modern London–Brighton Run.

himself. Ironically, even the world's first motor race was marred by a dispute over the regulations and Levassor was disqualified on a technical point: his car had only two seats. Nevertheless, he won a prize of 12,600 francs and had a monument erected in his honour at the Porte Maillot in Paris.

By 1896, when Levassor had put his gears in a box "to keep out the dirt", and developed a four–cylinder engine to give improved performance, the Panhard–Levassor had become the form of transport most coveted by the upper–class French, and those who were able to procure a specimen of P–L's limited production were regarded as extremely fortunate.

One of the fortunate few was the Hon Evelyn Ellis, son of Lord Howard de Walden and a pioneer motorist who brought a Panhard–Levassor to Britain in 1895. The elderly father did not share his son's enthusiasm for this new–fangled motoring and, following a visit, wrote him a stern note: "If you must bring that infernal thing here, kindly bring a little pan to put under it to catch the filthy oil it drips." To which his son gave the spirited if irreverent reply, "Certainly, father, if you'll bring a big pan for your carriage horses when you visit me."

Oil drips notwithstanding, Panhard–Levassor had established a format for the front–engined passenger car which has changed very little since it was first introduced.

These, however, were not the days of speedy production. Panhard–Levassor built only five cars between October and December 1891, but one of them was destined to become one of the most celebrated examples of the marque. In 1894, when the car was three years old, it was sold to the Abbé Gavois, a parish priest in Rainville, Picardy, whose dearest wish was to own such a car. For eighteen years it was in daily use as transport for the Abbé, and it became an object of great curiosity among motoring experts, who found it hard to believe that a car could last so long.

Although Rainville was in a battle zone, the old Panhard–Levassor trundled around the parish unscathed throughout the war. But after the Armistice, the Abbé decided that the time had come to sell it and use the proceeds to help the needy of his parish. He climbed into the car, drove it the ninety miles to Paris and sold it back to the firm who made it. For many years thereafter it was exhibited with pride by Panhard–Levassor.

THE RATTLETRAP ANCESTORS
American Debut

All significant developments in the automotive world had, until the 1870s, taken place in Europe – the cradle of the internal combustion engine. But America could not be expected to remain dormant for long. Nor did she. Curiously, however, the first significant move did not actually involve a car. In 1877 a devious solicitor from Rochester, New York, called George Selden, made a provisional patent application for a horseless carriage driven by a Brayton–type two–stroke gas engine. Although it now seems certain that no such vehicle existed, the provisional patent was granted to Selden – an act that was to have considerable repercussions.

Meanwhile there were other men in America with a more practical approach to the forthcoming motoring age. In 1888 Ellwood Haynes built a petrol–engined vehicle with a wick–type carburettor and a Mr Connolly gave public demonstrations of a petrol–engined tram. A vehicle built by one E. Pennington succeeded in completing a mile in fifty–eight seconds, although the car nearly exploded in the process. But none of these early vehicles was a practical proposition. That could not be said, however, of the petrol–engined cycle–car built in 1893 by the Duryea brothers, Frank and Charles. Although their very first attempt was not a great success, their second vehicle undoubtedly was. Powered by a 1½ hp engine with two cylinders, it came first in America's first motor race, from Chicago to Evanston and back, a distance of fifty–four miles, which took place in a blizzard in November 1895. At an average speed of 7·6 mph, the Duryea managed to beat an

Charles E. Duryea *(left)* at the wheel of his 1895 car, in which he won the gruelling Chicago–Evanston race. Although thirty–four cars were entered, only six started and the route included some steep hills where the competitors had to get out and push. This car was the prototype for Duryea's 1896 production car, for which the manufacturer was constantly seeking publicity. He appeared with it as an act in Barnum and Bailey's circus, sandwiched between an elephant act and the wild man from Borneo. He also took the car to England to take part in the Emancipation Run.

Crossing America *(below)* from San Francisco to New York in an Oldsmobile in 1903. Endurance events of this sort were well publicised by newspapers and there were three such crossings in the same year along the same route. This car, driven by Messrs Whitman and Hammond, took fifty–three days.

"Old Steady" *(below right)* competing in a cross–country event staged by Oldsmobile along a route from New York to Portland, Oregon. The race was won by a similar car nicknamed "Old Scout", which completed the journey in 44 days.

imported Benz by one and a half hours, but only after the Benz driver had succumbed to the cold and another driver had been found to replace him.

Spurred on by their success, the Duryea brothers set up the Duryea Wagon Company, the first motor company in America, but although the company actually made eighteen cars, the brothers fell out with each other and the company collapsed. Its demise was scarcely noticed in the rash of new companies springing up. Only a year after the birth of the Duryea company, Henry Ford made his debut on the motoring scene, with Ransom Ely Olds, James Packard and David Buick in his wake.

It was Henry Ford who finally challenged the stranglehold that George Selden had gained on the American motor industry. Having completed the patent in 1895, Selden was entitled to 1¼ per cent of the retail price of all the cars, domestic and imported, sold in America. In 1899 he sold the controlling interest in the patent rights to the Columbia company (while retaining a percentage for himself), which attempted to form a "closed shop" of manufacturers and importers and to exclude all those who did not conform. But led by Henry Ford, the independent manufacturers, of whom there were now more than thirty, demanded that the claims of Selden's patent be proved in court. Eventually, in 1905, a vehicle was produced. Despite the date 1877 that was painted on the side, it had been constructed more recently, and with great difficulty, by Selden's son and an engineer who, perhaps understandably, preferred to remain anonymous. This vehicle was persuaded to cover 500 yards without stopping, but the court was not impressed and the patent was broken, allowing the other manufacturers total freedom to operate.

Ransom Olds, who is alleged to have become an engineer because he couldn't stand the smell of horses, had made several experimental vehicles with steam and electric engines before he produced his first petrol-engined car. The Curved Dash was extremely simple, good looking and effective. It had a 1·6 litre water-cooled engine which lay under the passenger compartment, and boasted a top speed of 20 mph. It nearly came to a premature end when fire destroyed all the development work on the car, but the vehicle itself survived to become one of the most popular models in America in the early 1900s, 5000 being made in 1904.

David Buick had already made a fortune out of making baths before he turned his hand to cars in 1903. His first production car had a 2·6 litre engine, also lying under the seats, and it too became extremely popular. Buick was not able to meet the unexpectedly high demand for the vehicle and by 1909 both Buick and Oldsmobile had become part of the rapidly growing General Motors Corporation.

In retrospect it seems inevitable that the motor car would grow rapidly in America. Distances were great, and the pioneering spirit was still strong. Not surprisingly there were strange vehicles of all sorts on the roads – farm vehicles, buggies, buckboards, roadsters, runabouts and luxury European imports. In 1901 there were 4000 cars in America and by 1905 there were 24,000. The Americans promoted the motor car with motor shows, motor sport and copious advertising. In 1900 alone there were four motor shows in America, two of them combining the show with motor racing events. The biggest show of the year, held in Madison Square Garden, New York, boasted thirty-four makes, half of them having petrol engines, the others steam or electric.

The show was such a success with the public that the organisers extended its run and built a special pavilion in which stood ten so-called "veteran" cars, including the 1893 Duryea, which was already considered to be outdated.

THE RATTLETRAP ANCESTORS

Motorists at Large

In the latter part of the nineteenth century, roads in Britain were peaceful places – their quiet only occasionally shattered by the clattering hooves of a runaway horse. As most journeys of any length (which in those days meant about fifty miles) were made by train, roads were the natural habitat of farmers, tradesmen and local residents. Signposts were few and far between: apart from the fact that they were unnecessary for local people, who knew the area well, large numbers of people would have been unable to read them. The roads themselves consisted of mud and stones, compacted by years of use by horses and horsedrawn vehicles. These first roads wound from village to village, often following pathways and traditional boundaries that had been in existence for centuries.

The advent of the motor car did not disturb this calm overnight. But it took no longer than twenty years to change almost totally a way of life which had been the result of long and gradual evolution. It is not difficult to imagine the impact which the early motor cars had on English rural life. The inevitable noise, smell and general commotion caused great hostility on the part of country–dwellers, whose horses had to learn to live with the strange objects that had come to share their roads.

THE RATTLETRAP ANCESTORS

The Joys of the Open Road

The traditional dominance of the horse on the open road gave way only gradually to the internal combustion engine. In Britain particularly, the process was hampered by punitive traffic laws that were so restrictive as to make motoring virtually illegal. In France, however, which in 1903 boasted the most active motor industry in the world, the upper classes took to the motor car with great enthusiasm. Would–be British motorists who imported expensive machines from the Continent also imported a mechanic to look after the car – a practice which often caused considerable friction between the resident domestic staff and the newcomer, who usually felt himself of somewhat higher status.

But although Britain got off to a slow start, the industry was soon to catch up. By 1907, with the help of such men as F. H. Royce and William Morris, the motor car was widely available in Britain even to the middle–class professional. A West Country doctor who imported a 10 hp Peugeot recounted his motoring experiences in a letter to his wife.

"I am just wild with delight. This car is an event in our life and I am sure we will enjoy it amazingly."

He goes on to tell how the salesman had told him that it would do twenty miles to the gallon (petrol then costing one shilling and fourpence a gallon), the tyres would last for 8000 miles, the car licence cost two pounds ten shillings, and insurance ten pounds. Drivers' licences for himself and his chauffeur (whose role had been converted from that of groom overnight) cost five shillings each. Although the speed limit was 20 mph he drove the Peugeot around Devon at 40 mph and christened it "Bird" because in his view it flew like one.

The less affluent took to the motor bus or charabanc, which was starting to replace the horse–drawn bus, and although at the beginning of 1905 there were only twenty motor buses in London, four years later, in 1909, the number had risen to well over 1000.

In a world in which people were divided into motorists and anti–motorists, the motor car finally received the ultimate accolade when King Edward VII gave this new way of life his seal of approval by purchasing the first of the royal Daimlers.

Apart from traffic regulations, the principal enemy of the motorist was dust. Roads, which had been constructed to carry slow–moving horse–drawn traffic, quickly disintegrated under the speeding wheels of the new motorised vehicles. Over–taking was virtually impossible and the only sensible motoring dress of the day was tight at wrists and ankles, with veils and goggles protecting the head from the pervasive dust and flying stones. Garages were few and far between and any motorist out for a drive needed to be his own mechanic. Punctures in the early pneumatic tyres caused by sharp flints on the roads were frequent, and overheating was a constant cause of breakdown. Nevertheless, the motor car became more and more sought after. Soon, motorists were demanding that the Government pay for wide–ranging road improvements, including tar spraying to lay the dust. They also campaigned for the abolition of the speed limit.

The motorist was still, however, barely acceptable socially and was the object of much criticism – some of it very bitter. In 1908 the *Economist* pointed out:

"Here public expenditure is calmly suggested in order to please the richest class of pleasure seekers."

There was also a definite feeling among the upper classes that the actual mechanics of motoring were somewhat unsavoury. Writing in *Happy Motorists* in 1906, Filson Young said, "To be absorbed in the mechanical details of motor cars, unless such absorption be a condition of one's profession or business; to spend one's time on them, to think, talk, read about them to the exclusion of real and vital matters – this is to put oneself on a level with stablemen and jockeys."

More realistically, leading figures in the motoring world argued that cars were here to stay and that roads should be made safe for them, though they were unable to suggest how this might be achieved.

Running repairs to a 1925 Horstmann *(above)* in a Sussex lane. This car belonged to the gentleman in plus–fours, Mr Percy Mager. The Horstmann was built at Bath, in Somerset, and featured among other innovations a kick starter. This device, which the manufacturers claimed to be "of a simple arrangement", was also capable of inflicting bruises on the unwary operator.

Kingsway, London (*above*), in about 1911. Horse–drawn vehicles, favoured by tradesmen, shared the already crowded road with motorised vehicles and pedestrians.

Aunt Peggy and chauffeur (*above*) enjoying a day out in the park in 1906.

A miscreant driver in a 1910 Packard (*left*) has an altercation with a traffic policeman in downtown Manhattan. The battle of Motorists *v.* The Law has raged without interruption almost since the day the motor car was invented and shows no sign of abating.

A Splendid Carriage

When the motor car emerged from its infancy as a fully–fledged status symbol of the Edwardian era, motoring was a pastime for the privileged and wealthy enthusiast. Yet despite the novelty of the activity, customers still demanded value for money. Silence, smoothness and high performance were the qualities most sought after, and reliability was considered equally important.

Writing in *Motors and Motoring* in 1902, Sir Henry Thompson Bt, FRCS, MB London, blithely described the new–found pleasures of motoring:

"No effort is necessary to the owner of a motor car who has a trustworthy driver to relieve him of the mental labour of watching the road, since he need have no fixed time for departure. A drive behind a horse scarcely amounts to a recreation after the turmoils and worry of his work. In the automobile he finds ample sources of interest, amounting sometimes to a gentle and healthy excitement with complete rest and absence of fatigue from muscular exertion; without the bustle, noise and sense of confinement which accompany railway travelling; together with the refreshment of novelty and suggested ideas occasioned by the contemplation of a continually changing panorama or scenery, at the same time enjoying the recuperative effect of breathing the fresh country air."

Motoring continued to be a dry–weather pastime, and very much a leisure activity, though the practical advantages of motor cars were certainly recognised by one Edwardian writer, the Hon John Scott–Montagu, writing on "The Utility of Motor Vehicles": "For fetching guests from the station in the country I would recommend – and I am supposing myself writing for those who have a stable of some half a dozen horses – a covered as well as an open motor, or perhaps a motor which can have a top fitted on when the weather is bad. Ladies do not like arriving at teatime with their fringes out of curl or the feathers of their hats drooping or facing the wrong way."

A SPLENDID CARRIAGE
Mighty Mercedes

Right from the start Mercedes built only the very highest-quality cars and, having taken on their new identity with the name Mercedes, the cars went from strength to strength. The first Mercedes was exhibited with great acclaim at the Week of Nice in 1901 and won its first race at an average speed of 35 mph. This first Mercedes had a honeycomb radiator, a foot-operated throttle and a magnetic electric ignition system. The public loved it, although it cost about £2000. Two years later came an even better car. The engine had been enlarged to 60 hp and, with the "Roi des Belges" body, made every other motor car look old-fashioned. The curved bodywork was named after King Leopold II of Belgium, who had bought a 1901 Mercedes. His close friend Cleo de Mérode had helped the King to decide on the shape of the bodywork by putting two curved buttoned chairs side by side and suggesting that the body should be similarly shaped. The design development was carried out by the famous Paris firm of coachbuilders, Rothschild et Cie, although many others were to copy it.

The 60 hp Mercedes had enormous success in competition. In it, Camille Jenatzy won the Gordon Bennett race in Ireland in 1903: it was the first international motor race to be held in Britain – and needed a special Act of Parliament to allow it to be run on public roads. Jenatzy averaged 49·2 mph over the 367-mile course and won easily. He was fortunate to have been taking part at all, for the cars which the factory had built for the race had been destroyed in a fire. At the last minute Mercedes modified a number of road cars belonging to customers so that they could take part in the race, and it says a great deal for the durability of the road cars that they survived the experience.

The only problem that customers encountered with the Mercedes was that it was difficult to start when cold. It took a chauffeur with good muscles to turn the 9 litre engine when it was full of cold, thick oil, and very few ladies could manage it. Nevertheless, the car was a best-seller at £2500 and motoring historians are generally agreed that it was one of the greatest cars of the era.

In his book *The Upper Crust*, John Bolster describes the 60 hp Mercedes with total admiration.

"To appreciate how immense the performance of the Sixty was, it is necessary to recall how slowly other cars went in 1903. A typical small car would have a maximum speed no higher than 30 mph and would climb a 1–in–10 gradient at five to seven mph in bottom gear; hills steeper than 1–in–8 requiring the passengers to dismount. A proud automobilist would claim he had surmounted Westerham Hill 'without shedding'. A medium–sized four–cylinder car would attain 40 to 45 mph and 'romp up Westerham with power in hand'.

"The 60 hp Mercedes, when stripped for racing, would attain 80 mph and hold it for as long as the road permitted. With a large open touring body, mudguards and lamps, a maximum around 65 mph would be realistic. It took hills at a higher speed than many cars . . . would reach on the level and with none of the gear noise and vibrations of lesser breeds.

"Having driven the Sixty I am almost at a loss to put the experience into words. As the engine idles, the whole car rocks with the power impulses of the four great cylinders, but the engine is surprisingly quiet, in spite of all those exposed gears and pushrods. The sensation on moving off is quite unlike that given by any other car. . . . Even now this is a great car and in 1903 it must have been beyond belief."

Without doubt the 1903 Mercedes opened up new vistas for the motoring enthusiast who wanted speed and refinement, and set the standard for a new era of motoring.

A 1903 Mercedes Simplex 18/22 *(above)*, one of the most important early cars to come from the Daimler factory after the name Mercedes had been adopted for passenger cars. Commercial vehicles were still called Daimlers. Daimler's chief designer and partner, Wilhelm Maybach, wearing a light suit, is seated beside the driver.

The King of Bulgaria and his aides *(above right)* being driven in a 1905 Mercedes Simplex. This was the 40/45 version of the car, which boasted a top speed of 50 mph.

Mercedes Simplex 40/45 *(right)* being driven by the Duchess of Sutherland, on her way to a special Ladies' Automobile Meet in London in 1904. It was extremely chic at that time for ladies to be seen driving cars. The Duchess is dressed most elegantly in white and her chauffeur is riding behind her, so it is unlikely that she would have been prepared to attempt any running adjustments.

The earliest Mercedes racing car *(below)*, built in 1901. It won its first race at Nice in the same year at an average speed of 35 mph.

The Silver Ghost

See illustration overleaf

The story of the Silver Ghost began in 1903, when F. H. Royce, an electrical engineer with a business in Manchester, modified a secondhand 10 hp Decauville for his own use. Encouraged by the result, Royce went on to build two more prototypes, one of which was sold to Henry Edmunds, a director of Royce's firm and a friend of the Hon C. S. Rolls. Rolls, who had a business selling Panhard–Levassor and Minerva cars, liked the Royce so much that he agreed to take all the cars made by Royce, and to call all the cars by the name Rolls–Royce. Rolls' partner, Claude Johnson, would promote and sell the cars – a job for which he was eminently suited, having been secretary of the Automobile Club of Great Britain and Ireland (now the RAC).

The market Rolls and Royce set out to capture was that of the wealthy motorists who needed a large car to carry luggage and servants as well as passengers. Rolls' requirements were as follows:

"In appearance and dimensions, the Rolls–Royce landaulet should resemble the best electric carriages in use in London . . . the engine should be removed as far as possible from the carriage proper. The engine must be vibrationless. The motion of the car must be absolutely silent. The car must be free from the objectionable rattling and buzzing and inconvenience of chains. . . . The engine must be smokeless and odourless."

In addition to fulfilling these stipulations, the car had to be powerful enough to cope with the combined weight of the car's own body and a full complement of passengers and luggage.

At London's Olympia Motor Show in November 1906, Rolls–Royce showed a new chassis. It had a six–cylinder, 7 litre engine attached with special mountings that allowed the chassis to flex – a major innovation at a time when most engines were bolted straight onto the chassis – and was known as the 40/50. The name "Silver Ghost" was coined by Claude Johnson: "silver" because the metal parts were silver–plated and the body finished in aluminium paint, and "ghost" because of the car's remarkable silence. Theoretically, the car shown at Olympia was the only Silver Ghost, although the name was eventually used for all the 40/50 cars of the period to avoid confusion with the New Phantom, a 40/50 model launched in 1925.

The car, fitted with a Roi de Belges body built by Barker and Company, was offered to *The Autocar* for road test. The testers were clearly impressed: "At whatever speed this car is being driven on its direct third there is *no* engine vibration so far as sensation goes, nor are one's auditory nerves troubled, driving or standing, by a fuller sound than emanates from an eight–day clock. There is no feeling of driving propulsion; the feeling as the passenger sits either at front or back of the vehicle, is one of being wafted through the landscape."

A series of reliability trials followed in which the car performed admirably, showing modest petrol consumption and needing little mechanical attention. It was indeed a car to be proud of.

The Silver Ghost

Royce's creation, the Silver Ghost, was a stupendous success even at the price of £985 for the chassis alone. It set a new standard in luxury motoring which has never been surpassed, and has become the hallmark of the rich, the powerful and the famous throughout the world.

A SPLENDID CARRIAGE
Rivals in Luxury

Although Rolls–Royce and Mercedes certainly dominated the quality car market of the Edwardian era there were plenty of other car–builders who helped to provide the wealthy with their preferred transport. The range of cars available ran from extreme luxury at one end of the scale to the mass–produced, small cars at the other. For the luxury car buyer anything was possible. To a certain extent, the car he bought was his own creation. Every detail was available, at a price, and the future owner could choose his own coachbuilder, his own individual fitments and effectively his own unique car.

One of the most important rivals to Rolls–Royce was Napier. Montague Napier was the owner of a long–established firm making small presses for coin and printing when, in 1899, he was asked by the well–known motoring figure Selwyn F. Edge if he would modify an 1896 6 hp Panhard from tiller to wheel steering, and fit a tubular radiator and pneumatic tyres. Intrigued by the task, Napier went on to suggest other possible modifications, finally coming up with a new engine, so that in effect the first Napier was a highly modified Panhard. The car was completed just before the Thousand Miles Trial of 1900 – a most ambitious event involving sixty–five vehicles of which only twenty–three finished. Selwyn Edge finished second overall and, impressed by the car, finalised a deal with Napier in which Edge would drive, publicise and be sole distributor for Napier cars. The first Napiers were sporting vehicles – a 40 hp car, with Edge at the wheel, winning the Gordon Bennett Cup race from Paris to Innsbruck.

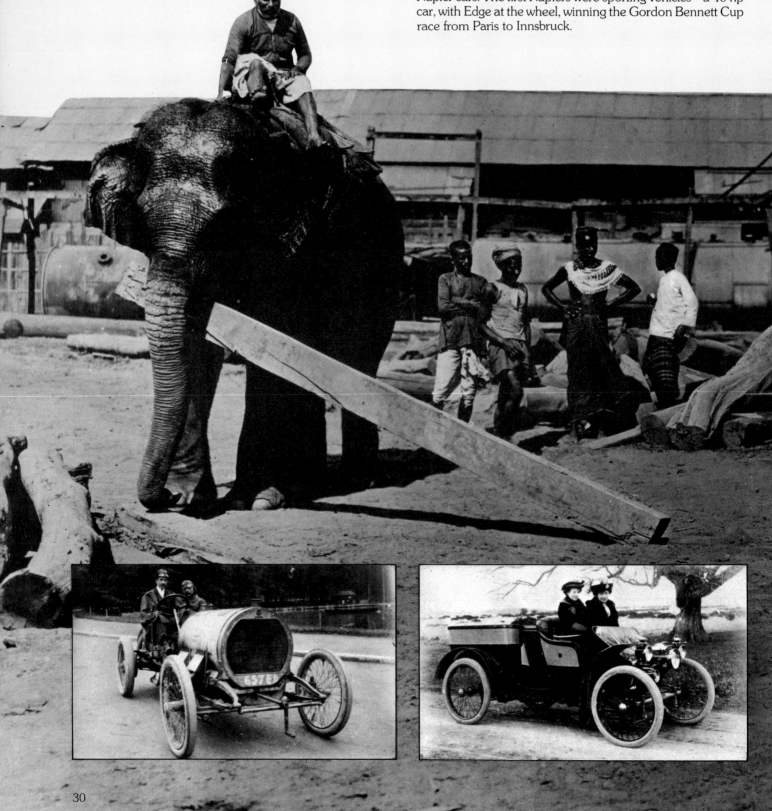

Edge and Napier quickly recognised the potential for a top-class luxury car and its development was to prove one of their most successful ventures. The chassis price alone, for the 90 hp Napier of 1907, was £2500 and the marque so appealed to the very wealthy Maharajas that one of them ordered a version which was twenty-one feet long and carried eleven passengers in comfort on four rows of seats.

Another famous name of the period was Hotchkiss. Benjamin Berkeley Hotchkiss was an American gun-maker with a factory at St Denis near Paris. When the demand for guns receded, he turned his attention to car-building, concentrating on cars with engines of up to 18 litres, which were particularly successful on the American market, where they were sold by advertising which claimed that they were "built like a gun by gun-makers".

A car which also appealed to wealthy enthusiasts was the Lanchester, although by comparison with some other makes the cars were somewhat old-fashioned. The first production Lanchester, which appeared in 1900, had tiller steering, and it was not for several years that Frederick Lanchester was persuaded to replace it by the more advanced steering wheel. On the other hand he could not be persuaded to adopt the long bonnet line which was *de rigueur* on luxury cars, and despite the Lanchester's excellent performance, customers increasingly showed a preference for the more elegant lines of the Rolls-Royce and the Napier.

The car which made its name by being the first motorised vehicle owned by Queen Wilhelmina of the Netherlands was the Spyker – a car which made its debut in 1900. The Spijker family, whose name was changed to make the spelling simpler on the cars, set up in business as coachbuilders in 1880, but soon turned to cars. Their first prototype had a 5 hp engine and was shaft driven, but it was a commercial disaster. Undeterred, the Spijkers went on to experiment with, and produce, larger-engined vehicles and the Queen's car was a 40 hp landaulette which they built in 1911. Equipped with a roof rack, wide running-boards and buttoned leather upholstery, it was an extremely elegant machine.

African import (*above*), a 1914 Napier Colonial Tourer. Another import is the elephant: African elephants are unwilling to carry wood, so Indian elephants were imported with their *mahouts* (keepers) to help out.

Fitch-Shepard (*far left*), an American amateur driver, in his 1906 Hotchkiss racing car.

A 1903 Lanchester (*centre left*) carrying two ladies out for a summer time spree.

C. J. Glidden in his Napier (*left*) fitted with flanged wheels. These interchangeable wheels enabled Glidden to complete a 50,000-mile world tour, using railway tracks where roads were too bad or frequently non-existent.

A SPLENDID CARRIAGE
"La Petite Voiture"

The name of de Dion Bouton was one of the earliest to make an impact on the automotive world, yet sadly, even though the name lives on today, few people appreciate the important and innovative role played by the company in the early days of the motor car. In its day the de Dion Bouton was the most sophisticated machine produced. Marketed by an aristocrat and driven by the chic ladies of Paris, it rapidly became one of the most sought–after European cars. Part of its success stemmed from the fact that it shunned the trend towards bigger, more powerful and more costly cars and chose instead to remain small and practical.

The name came about as the result of a liaison between the Comte de Dion and a small manufacturer of steam engines, Messrs Trépardoux et Bouton. The Comte had been passionately interested in engineering since his childhood and became a partner in the Trépardoux et Bouton firm in 1881. The Comte's father, the Marquis, was gravely concerned by his heir's involvement in what he considered to be a lower–class pursuit, but he need not have worried; the firm made and sold steam vehicles with great success. The Comte, however, had his eye on bigger fish – "nasty explosion engines" – and it was on this matter of petrol versus water–powered engines that the Comte and Trépardoux failed to agree. Trépardoux finally left the firm as a result of this conflict, but not before he had played a major part in the design of the rear suspension layout which carries the de Dion name to this day.

Backed by success with steam vehicles, de Dion Bouton had sufficient confidence to delay the launch of their first petrol–engined car until it had been thoroughly tested. It was not released for general sale until 1899, although a prototype appeared in 1898 at the first Motor Show to be held at Boston, Massachusetts. "La Petite Voiture" had the engine mounted at the rear and the seats positioned face to face. It was an immediate success, largely because it was extremely easy to drive – a feature that was particularly appealing to new motorists. The business grew rapidly: by 1900 "La Petite Voiture" was the world's best–selling motor car and could be seen as far afield as India, Malaya, China, Australia and Bolivia. The production rate was then about one hundred cars a month.

The $3\frac{1}{2}$ hp car was succeeded by a $4\frac{1}{2}$ hp model with the same configuration. Although the backward–facing seat was the most comfortable of the three, it also made a useful luggage carrier when not being used for passengers, and the space below it housed such essentials as the radiator and a tool box. Although the de Dion Bouton was not cheap, it was excellent value for money by comparison with the big Mercedes and Panhard–Levassors, which were the ultimate in contemporary motoring. But by far the most important feature of the de Dion Bouton was its reliability. One typical de Dion Bouton owner was a country doctor, the late Dr Frederick Lewis of Henfield, who recalled his delight with his $3\frac{1}{2}$ hp car with these words:

"The little fellow was the one I liked because it was so light and handy in the narrow lanes. It wasn't very fast, but it never gave any trouble. Every Sunday afternoon, while the garden boy washed the car and filled all the greasers, I saw to the inlet valve, cleaned the petrol filter and checked over the ignition and wires. I could do it all in a quarter of an hour and that little car always started on the second turn, even in the coldest weather, and never once let me down on the road. Of course I mostly used her on my rounds but I used to go up to London once a month and I went to Inverness and back in the autumn of 1902, without touching a thing. Rich neighbours with their

Count Albert de Dion *(top)*, one of the founders of the de Dion Bouton empire, posing astride his petrol–engine–assisted tricycle – an early forerunner of the modern moped. The hat and moustache give him a distinct resemblance to his partner Georges Bouton.

Vis–à–vis *(above)* built by de Dion in 1900 and believed to be the first car imported into Australia, by William Elliot in 1901. The driver is A. J. Penier, seen here with his wife and family.

Proud owner Mr Urridge *(right)* taking delivery of his brand–new 1905 4–cylinder de Dion, from Creasey's, the south–east London coachbuilders.

60 hp Mercedes or big de Dietrichs used to say, 'Here comes old Toto still driving his little de Dion'. But I had the last laugh. I don't think he *ever* took that Mercedes more than twenty miles without bursting a tyre and it was always in dock for some trouble or other. Of course it was a grand car, and it would do seventy, but in those days if you wanted to keep out of trouble you could never get into fourth speed at all with a car like that; no woman could drive it and not many men could start it. The worst thing de Dion ever did was to stop making their single–cylinder cars."

An advertisement in *The Autocar* in 1910 gave more unsolicited testimonials couched in terms which would delight a modern manufacturer. "I have nothing but praise for the little de Dion car. After six months' very hard work, it is running more sweetly and powerfully than upon the day I took it from your agent." Such publicity paid dividends. So popular were

the little "Ding dongs", as they had been nicknamed, that R. J. Mecredy's book *De Dion Motor Carriages and how to drive them* went into three editions.

An important part of de Dion's business, and the one which ultimately led to its downfall, was its sale of engines to other car–makers. By 1906 nearly 50,000 units, out of a total production of 60,000, had been sold to other manufacturers. The growing competition signalled the eclipse of the de Dion Bouton company. In retrospect, however, it can be said that supplies of the single–cylinder engines gave a useful beginning to more than 200 other makes.

The single was followed by a wide variety of other engines and models, and although most of them were designed for the middle–class motorist, de Dion Bouton did not entirely neglect the "quality" market. The Marquis de Dion (formerly the Comte), who was something of an eccentric as well as

being one of the most successful duellists of his day, even appeared in a car fitted with electric lights, roof ventilators, swivelling armchairs, disappearing tables, a writing cabinet and an inflatable day–bed big enough for him to lie on during long journeys.

But although de Dion survived the First World War by judicious and sometimes bizarre modification of its products for military use, it could not survive the ensuing developments in European motoring. By the late 1920s, passenger cars had either to be in the luxury class, and very highly priced, or produced in large numbers by the latest mass–production techniques. De Dion fell between the two. Both the Marquis and Bouton were elderly men, resistant to change, and although the commercial vehicle part of the firm continued for a while, the Second World War finally put the finishing touches to the demise of a great marque.

A SPLENDID CARRIAGE
Royal Patronage

By 1908 the Delaunay–Belleville was the make of car most sought after by kings, emperors and heads of state. It was known as "The Car Magnificent" and was widely regarded, by those fortunate few in a position to compare the two, as a vastly superior car to the Rolls–Royce. Delaunay–Belleville were originally specialists in steam machinery. Queen Victoria's yacht had Delaunay–Belleville boilers and the company's name was synonymous with high quality and reliability. When the firm started to make cars, in 1904, their vehicles were less technically advanced than some of their competitors, but were of a standard of construction that was second to none.

Probably the most famous Delaunay–Bellevilles of all were the three magnificent machines built for His Imperial Majesty Nicholas II, Czar of all the Russias. These huge cars had 11·8 litre, six–cylinder engines with capacious luxury bodies, capable of carrying the Czar and his large family. The cars were fitted with compressed air starters which were so powerful that the enormously heavy cars could be started in gear – apparently so that they could make a quick getaway in the event of an assassination attempt. The bodywork of the Delaunay–Belleville was always dominated by the circular radiator and bonnet – a hangover, it was believed, from the shape of the steam boilers that had gone before.

While the Delaunay–Belleville was the preferred transport of the Czar of all the Russias, the crowned heads of Britain chose the Daimler to travel in. The Daimler Motor Company had been founded in Britain by an engineer and businessman, F. R. Simms, who had imported a Daimler–engined Panhard–Levassor into Britain for the Hon Evelyn Ellis in 1895 and subsequently arranged to buy the Daimler patents outright. After considerable ramifications, the first British–built vehicle made its debut in mid–1897 and quickly endeared itself to the Royal Family. It was a powerful, chain–driven, four–cylinder machine which clearly appealed to King Edward VII. King George V was equally enthusiastic about the later large Daimlers, which had 9·5 litre, six–cylinder engines, and ordered the cars in various shapes, including limousines, landaulettes and station wagons.

In the early 1900s several other firms were in a position to compete for the title of "Best Car in the World" and, more

The proud owner (*left*) of a 1910 Delaunay–Belleville, pictured with his chauffeur outside Artillery Mansions, London.

A 1915 Daimler (*below*) built for an Indian prince. Unlike most quality–car makers of the time, Daimler often built their own bodies. This one features a seat and foot–rest on the running board for a servant, as well as electric lighting.

importantly, for the customers who could afford to buy such vehicles. But most of the competition fell by the wayside. Of the great makes, Napier had fallen sadly behind their great rival Rolls–Royce. Napier had made their name largely due to some epic drives by S. F. Edge, who won the 1902 Gordon Bennett race by default when everyone else dropped out. He also drove his Napier for twenty–four hours at Brooklands at an average speed of 25 mph. But publicity was not enough, and although Napiers sold well when Mr Edge was in charge, the 60 hp, six–cylinder cars gradually faded from the scene.

Connoisseurs of the luxury automobile preferred the Lanchester to the Napier. Dr Frederick Lanchester was certainly one of the most innovative automotive engineers of the period, and did a great deal of work privately for Daimler. The cars which bore his name, however, although capable of excellent performance, looked very unlike their rivals. The styling fashion of the era was that of the long, low bonnet. The Lanchesters, in direct contrast, had the engine positioned between the driver and the front–seat passenger, thereby depriving the designer of the need for a great deal of bonnet space and the customer of the familiar long, elegant profile. Sadly, the Lanchester lost customers to its more stylish com-petitors despite its loyal following.

HH The Jansaheb *(above)* being driven in his 1907 28 hp Lanchester. The European chauffeur, steering with the lever at the side, was probably imported from England with the car, as was normal practice at the time.

A SPLENDID CARRIAGE
The American Aristocrats

In America, as in Europe, car ownership boomed in the early years of the twentieth century. In 1900 there were 8000 private cars in the United States; by 1915 there were 2,300,000. Much of the credit for this enormous increase must go to Henry Ford, who made a substantial personal contribution to the automotive revolution; but he was by no means wholly responsible. Although American manufacturers pioneered the techniques of mass production, there were also many famous names amongst the smaller manufacturers who produced expensive, elegant machines.

Outstanding in this category was Pierce, later to become Pierce–Arrow, whose factory in Buffalo, New York, had first made bicycles and then light cars. In 1905 Pierce produced its first 4 litre, four–cylinder car – a 32 hp vehicle called the Great Arrow. Technically the Great Arrow was far in advance of the domestic competition. Its three–speed gearbox was controlled by a lever on the steering column and the car incorporated drive shafts instead of the more usual chain–drive mechanism.

The fact that wealthy Americans were prepared to pay large sums to import European luxury cars did not mean that there were no expensive American products but rather that the European cars had a snob–appeal which the American cars lacked. In an attempt to combat this attitude, an American designer, Lee Chadwick, produced one of the most costly of all American cars, the Great Chadwick Six – a monster 11·5 litre car with a four–speed gearbox and a chain drive. Chadwick, who was a motor sport enthusiast like so many of his compatriots, devised the first effective supercharger in an attempt to get more power from his engine for road races and hill climbs.

The name of Cadillac also emerged at this time, as synonymous with luxury motoring. In 1912 the firm turned from producing a small single–cylinder vehicle to a much larger 20/30 hp car. The engine had a capacity of 5·5 litres and a top speed of 60 mph, and the bodywork was similar in style to the European cars of the period, with a long, low bonnet and distinctive radiator grille. This Cadillac was, moreover, the first production car to have electric lights and an electric starter as standard equipment and it was hoped that the latter would be sufficiently reliable for the starting handle to be unnecessary. The manufacturer showed faith in his product by not supplying a starting handle with the car.

However, there was no electric starter on the Simplex 50 hp Roadster, launched in the same year. This was another vast machine, powered by a 9·8 litre engine with the gearbox and differential housed in the centre of the car. It was by no means an object of great beauty, but its top speed of 80 mph endeared it to motor sport enthusiasts, of which there were plenty. In fact the tendency amongst the American–built cars of the period was definitely towards speed rather than elegance, whereas the manufacturers of expensive European cars scorned the sporting image. They preferred selling to crowned heads to winning races, so the American manufac–turers catered for their own domestic market.

The Great Arrow, the Great Chadwick Six and the Simplex Roadster put speed before elegance. The Hupmobile had neither, but nevertheless was an extremely popular car in America in the pre–1914 era and will long be remembered for its name if nothing else. The brothers Hupp had begun to make cars in 1908 in various body styles, including a seven–seater, and almost all of them were powered by a 2·8 litre engine. Although usually conventional, the Hupp brothers

pioneered a steel–bodied car in 1913, and brought in electric lights and starting a year later – still some years ahead of several better–known manufacturers.

American manufacturers were fortunate that their efforts were uninterrupted by the initial stages of the First World War. Competition between them was fierce and the search for technical improvements continuous. It was equally fortunate that the shortage of European–built cars provided them with a healthy export market and that while Europe was busy on the battlefield, America was able to take the lead in the field of automotive engineering.

One of the most significant developments was that of the V8 engine. American motorists were demanding smoother, quieter cars than they had been offered and at the 1915 Motor Show in New York, Cadillac unveiled their first V8–engined car. The design of the engine was not original, having been based on a de Dion Bouton V8 engine that had first appeared in France in 1909. But Cadillac improved and extended the design to give it increased flexibility with the help of a British engineer, Mr D. M. White, who had previously worked with the Napier company. This extremely popular car sold nearly thirteen thousand in its first year, excluding many more which were sold to the US Army.

Nonetheless, the most elegant carriage to be produced in America at this time was probably the Packard Twin–Six – a remarkable machine whose 7 litre, twelve–cylinder engine was so flexible that it would pull away from 3 mph in top gear. The Twin–Six set new standards in effortless, luxury transport from which, despite the Depression, the American motor industry never looked back.

A 1906 Pierce–Arrow *(top left)* in Massachusetts. The driver, in a contemporary driving costume, including goggles, sits on the right–hand side. Pierce–Arrow continued this custom until 1918, long after other American manufacturers had moved their steering wheels to the left.

Willy Haupt *(above left)* charging his Chadwick Great Six up the "Great Despair" hill climb in Pennsylvania, in 1907. The car had an 11·2 litre engine and was very successful in competition. In 1908 a bigger, supercharged version was entered in the Vanderbilt Cup race and the American Grand Prix.

A 1914 Cadillac *(top right)* being given attention by Miss Jacqueline Boston. Miss Boston was co–driver to Charles Jarrott in the Austrian Trials in 1914, when his car was prevented from slipping off the edge of a cliff only by a large stone which happened to get in the way. Jarrott's motto was "Always finish."

Packard Six *(above)* used by officials at an Independence Day Fair in 1915. Electric lights and starter were standard on the 4/48 model, but the front bumper on this car is a distinctly homemade addition. The car was also equipped with non–skid tyres on the rear wheels and a power pump.

Adventure on Four Wheels

The first great challenge faced by the motor car was that of the elements. Could these strange new machines prove the equal of the camel in desert travel, follow Hannibal's elephants across the Alps or compete with the faithful horse for stamina, reliability or speed? Man was quick to attempt the seemingly impossible – using four wheels instead of four legs. Competition between the rival marques was intense: the publicity value was enormous and there were fortunes to be made.

Even more important was the challenge which the early long–distance events offered to the drivers. Not only were cars in their infancy, so too were roads and maps. There was no need to look for difficulties, but a hero's welcome awaited the driver with the courage and skill – and luck – to win. This was a field in which no wealth or class barriers existed, attracting people from every walk of life – including royalty, students and garage mechanics.

Rapidly advancing technology was soon to change the face of adventure. By the 1960s the pioneering journeys had all been done and in the search for adventure enthusiasts devised a series of highly commercialised trans–world events. Car manufacturers invested vast sums of money to prove their vehicles faster, tougher and more reliable than those of their rivals. Competing cars were soon covered with sponsors' publicity stickers and back–up teams of professional mechanics were strategi–cally positioned along the routes.

Trans–world events are no longer uncharted voyages into the unknown. Quite the contrary. Navigators plot every twist and turn of the road, every pot–hole, water–splash, ascent and descent. To the genuine regret of many, the private entrant stands little chance in these latter–day crusades. Adventure has been commercialised.

ADVENTURE ON FOUR WHEELS
Race to Disaster

Serious competition motoring began in 1894 with the Paris–Rouen Reliability Trial. Makers and owners of the early cars were eager to show the world what these new–fangled machines could achieve and there followed a series of capital–to–capital races. That most of these started in Paris was no coincidence. The French manufacturers were highly competitive – and they had a good deal with which to be competitive. After the first recognised motor race, the Paris–Bordeaux race in 1895, which was won by Panhard–Levassor, motor racing entered a boom era. The cars got bigger and much faster – the most powerful being capable of speeds up to 90 mph. But in 1903, road racing came to an abrupt, albeit temporary, end.

The event that brought about its demise was the Paris–Madrid race, organised jointly by the French and Spanish Automobile Clubs. There were three stages – Paris to Bordeaux, Bordeaux to Vittoria and Vittoria to Madrid. For the first time there were strict regulations governing the speed at which competitors could drive through towns on the route. On entering each town competitors were stopped and their time of arrival recorded. Then each car was escorted through the town by a man on a bicycle to a point where the car's departure time was also recorded. Despite these precautions the race was destined to be a disaster.

There were 275 starters at the "Place d'Eau Suisse" in Versailles on 24 May 1903 and, according to contemporary newspaper reports, more than 100,000 spectators. Many of the competitors were private owners, but there were several "works" teams. Panhard entered fifteen cars, Mors fourteen, de Dietrich twelve and Renault four – two of them driven by the Renault brothers Louis and Marcel. There were even three women drivers. The vehicles ranged from the powerful 70 hp Mors to virtually obsolescent steam cars. The flag dropped at 3.30 am and the first car away was a 45 hp de Dietrich driven by the famous Englishman Charles Jarrott. He had drawn the coveted first place in a ballot for starting places and his car had an important innovation, an electric headlamp. Louis Renault started in sixth place, but by the time the cars had reached Chartres he had overtaken Jarrott by maintaining an average speed of 70 mph.

There were three major hazards. The first was the dust thrown up by the leading cars, which blinded the following drivers and made it important to be at the head of the queue. The second was a lack of adequate brakes, for although manufacturers had spent much time and effort on making their cars go faster, they had not paid the same attention to making them stop. The third hazard was the huge mass of spectators which lined the route, crowding the bends and roadside banks and spilling onto the roadway in many places.

Louis Renault in his 6·3 litre, 30 hp Renault was the first to arrive in Bordeaux, although the race leader at that stage was Fernand Gabriel driving a Mors, who had started in 86th place and arrived fourth at Bordeaux. Soon after Bordeaux the drama commenced. The first casualty was a spectator at Albi, who was hit by a car and badly injured. A few miles south of Poitiers Marcel Renault, driving a similar car to that of his brother, was blinded by dust as he entered a sharp right–hand bend on entering the little village of Couche–Verac. The car left the road and tumbled down a steep slope. Marcel Renault was fatally injured and his mechanic, Vautier, suffered severe head injuries. There followed a series of accidents killing both drivers and spectators. On hearing of his brother's death, Louis Renault retired from motor racing and withdrew the Renault team.

Faced with the possibility of still more deaths – the final tally was ten dead and many more injured – the French Prime Minister, Émile Combes, took drastic action. He ordered the race to be abandoned by signing a decree which not only stopped the race but also banned the cars from returning to Paris under their own power. The surviving cars were towed from Bordeaux to the railway station, where they were loaded onto trucks and ignominiously returned to Paris.

As the race was officially abandoned at Bordeaux, the placings there became the final results. Fernand Gabriel was declared the winner, with Louis Renault second. Of Gabriel little more was ever heard. Although he continued to race up until the outbreak of the Second World War, he never managed to repeat his epic drive on the Paris–Madrid. He died during a bombing raid on Garenne, near Paris, in 1943.

Although the abandonment of the Paris–Madrid marked the effective end of road racing in France, enthusiasm for the sport moved to Italy, where the first Mille Miglia took place in 1927. But after the 1957 event, this too had to be abandoned for precisely the same reasons as sealed the fate of the Paris–Madrid. Road racing was simply too dangerous.

A Mercedes 70 hp (*right*) driven by Baron de Caters taking the corner at Pétignac. De Caters finished twenty–seventh overall.

Hopes ran high at the start of the race. Here, competitor Lt–Col Mark Mayhew (*far right*) is seen setting off in his 35 hp Napier. The race ended for him when he crashed into a tree near Libourne.

ADVENTURE ON FOUR WHEELS
Lunacy on Wheels

The Peking to Paris race which took place in 1907 has been described as the maddest motor race of all time. Certainly it was the most adventurous sixty days in the history of the motor car. Strictly speaking it was not a motor race at all, but as an endurance event it was unparalleled.

Its story began with an announcement on the front page of the Paris newspaper *Le Matin*, "Will anyone agree to go, this summer, from Peking to Paris, in a motor car?" There were plenty of replies and a great deal of sceptical comment on the project. There were no rules. All that was required of entrants was that they should leave Peking for Paris in a motor car and arrive at their destination. The Chinese authorities were not keen on the idea, believing it to be part of a devious Western plot which would bring about the collapse of the Chinese railway company that had already laid a line as far as Nankow. It was inconceivable to the Chinese that anyone would want to make the journey from Peking to Paris in a *chi–cho* (literally a fuel chariot) purely for the achievement. They raised countless objections and solemnly refused visas, but were finally pre-empted by the arrival in Peking of the competing cars.

Prince Scipione Borghese

Despite plenty of applications, there were only five starters – a 6 hp Contal tricycle, two 10 hp de Dion Boutons, a 15 hp Stryker and a 40 hp Itala powered by a 7433 cc engine which had a fuel consumption of 8 mpg and weighed more than 3000 lb. The Itala, owned and driven by Prince Scipione Borghese and crewed by Luigi Barzini, an Italian journalist, and Ettore Guizzardi, a mechanic, would go on to make motoring history.

Prince Scipione Borghese and his wife Princess Anna–Maria were already well known as motoring adventurers. They had made lengthy and hazardous treks across Asia Minor as early as 1900. More importantly, the Prince had the necessary and considerable financial resources to make the Peking to Paris attempt a possibility. Having arrived in Peking with his car, the Prince set about his final preparations. The Chinese, now that the foreigners had arrived, were only too keen to get rid of them. The cars disturbed the sacred peace of Peking, and in the words of Barzini "would cause an upheaval in the popular mind. They would spread everywhere the fatal germs of Western corruption, call forth the resentment of ghostly powers, the vengeance of ancestors, the wrath of the gods. Better by far, to speed their departure." So visas were issued.

Meanwhile the Prince and his wife covered 300 miles on horseback measuring the roads between Peking and Kalgan to make sure that they were wide enough for the big Itala to get through. But he found that in places no road existed and that the cars would have to be towed and manhandled over rough ground. He engaged twenty–five men and four mules for the purpose, but the car still had to be lightened considerably. The body was dismantled and a wooden packing–case seat installed. Tool boxes were strapped to the running–board and pickaxes and shovels were fastened to the steel strips which replaced the mudguards. The Prince also managed to arrange fuel supplies every 250 kilometres and somehow procured military maps of the route.

The cars left Peking in a blaze of glory on 10 June on the first leg of the journey. Princess Anna–Maria and the Italian Chargé d'Affaires accompanied the car as far as Nankow and the Itala took the lead almost immediately, blazing a trail for the smaller vehicles. The first casualty was the tricycle, which proved useless on the uneven road and which arrived in Nankow by train. The Peking Traction Company, which had undertaken to supply the four mules, had sent only one mule, an old horse and a small white donkey and it was with this menagerie as well as a band of coolies and a small detachment of marines that the Itala set off for Russia. It took sixty days and their adventures have become legendary. The huge car was towed for miles across narrow mountain passes and carried across rivers. It survived being overturned on broken bridges and half–drowning in muddy paddy–fields. That it ran at all was largely due to the efforts of Guizzardi, of whom Barzini wrote: "At night, when we arrived at our halting–places, he never ate or slept until he had finished seeing to the machine; and he would sometimes spend long hours lying in absurd positions under the hot body of the car with burning oil dripping onto him. At times he would get up from his bed at the most incredible hours, seized by a sudden fear, and then we would hear him undoing nuts, taking apart bits and pieces in order to observe the most delicate organs of the engine, and putting everything back. By dawn he was invariably ready to start."

Once in Russia, the route ran alongside the Trans–Siberian railway, and frequently along the track itself, but in the Ural mountains the Itala suffered its most severe setback. A wheel which had been damaged by a chain, fitted to give added traction in the heavy mud, finally threatened to collapse completely. It was given emergency treatment in the bathing pool of a local watering place in the hope that the water would swell the wood sufficiently to tighten the spokes in the rim. But the following day, in a remote area, the wheel finally disintegrated. The resourceful crew were searching for a remedy when an old mujik appeared from nowhere driving a calf. Miraculously, the wheel had broken only a few kilometres from the best, and probably the only, cart–maker in the province. Within hours a new wheel was made and the Itala was on its way again.

As the route approached Moscow, the going became easier, the roads more civilised and food and signposts easier to find. The Itala reached Moscow on 25 July, six weeks after leaving Peking, but still 2500 miles from Paris. Amazingly, the Itala needed little attention in Moscow. Apart from the home–made wheel, which had to be changed, a good wash was all that was necessary before the car set off on the last stage of the journey, which was completed in fine style and amidst lavish receptions along the route. On 10 August, the Prince brought the Itala across the Place de la République to the offices of *Le Matin*. He had covered 10,000 miles in sixty days. The two de Dion Boutons and the Stryker arrived together, three weeks later – the de Dion Boutons having suffered no mechanical failure whatever.

The Itala stands today in the Turin Motor Museum. After the trip it was abandoned in a disused warehouse, but was fortunately rediscovered in 1923. Now it is completely restored – a fitting monument to an epic motoring event.

Rescuing the Itala (*above*) from the ruins of a wooden bridge which collapsed as the car was crossing it. The accident happened in eastern Siberia, exactly twenty days after the convoy had left Peking. As the car hung vertically over the water, twenty Siberian railway workers, armed with ropes and hatchets, demolished the bridge so that the car was standing on its wheels in the stream. Miraculously, no–one was seriously injured, and the car started with the second turn of the starting handle.

In trouble again (*above*) on a Siberian "road". The black earth had been turned into a slippery pulp by torrential rain, making it almost impossible for the heavy, powerful car to get any grip with the wheels.

On the banks of the Hun–ho (*below*), moving the car along the edge of the paddy–fields with the help of mules and Chinese coolies. Under these conditions, a speed of one mile an hour was exceptional.

PARIS
Berlin
Kovno
St Petersburg
Moscow
Kazan
Perm
Omsk
Tomsk
Krasnojarsk
Irkutsk
Kiakhta
Udde
Kalgan
PEKING

Peking to Paris: the route that crossed two continents for the mad motor race of 1907.

Desert Contest

During the early 1920s a fierce commercial battle developed between the two great French car manufacturers André Citroën and Louis Renault. In the inhospitable terrain of the African deserts, each in turn tried to prove his vehicles faster, sturdier and more reliable than those of the opposition.

Not to be outdone by a Citroën marathon which covered the 12,500 miles from Morocco to Mozambique, Louis Renault decided to attempt the first motorised crossing of the Sahara desert from north to south. Three special vehicles were built for the expedition, each powered by a 13·9 hp engine and equipped with six twin–tyred wheel assemblies and a powerful winch.

The journey started at Colomb–Béchar, the most southerly railhead in Algeria, on 10 September 1924 and finished in Bouréma in northern Niger seven days later. For a distance of 1500 miles, the speed of the trip, made under the fierce heat of day and the bitter cold of the desert night, was remarkable.

ADVENTURE ON FOUR WHEELS
South American Road Racers

Without doubt, the name of Juan Manuel Fangio (far right) is the most evocative in the history of motor sport. Even those who have never been within a thousand miles of a racing car recognise that Fangio stands for what is best in the sport. That he is alive today is something of a miracle for he came from a breed of men to whom life was exciting, dangerous and frequently expendable. Yet never in his racing career did he appear to take the risks so often associated with his European counterparts. Son of a house painter in Balcarce, Juan Manuel Fangio had been fanatically interested in cars as a child. He took part in a minor race when he was seventeen, but it was not until 1938, when he was twenty–seven and had a garage business of his own, that he began to race in earnest. That year he took part in his first Gran Premio as co–driver with Finochietti, and only two years later he achieved his first major victory driving a Chevrolet in the Gran Premio Internacional del Norte – a 5856–mile race from Buenos Aires to Lima and back. The event took thirteen days, driving north into the mountains, across the Bolivian plateau, on to La Paz and finally Lima. His win established Fangio as a first–class driver and his name dominated Argentinian motor sport long after he had gone to seek his fortune in Europe. His principal rivals were the brothers Oscar and Juan Galvez. There was intense rivalry between the drivers, but even more intense was the rivalry between their supporters – the opposing factions being known as "Fangistas" or "Galvistas". The Galvez brothers, who continued to race well into the 1960s, were not only good drivers; they represented a highly efficient organisation whose cars were extremely well prepared. There were roll–over bars in the cars, the drivers wore crash helmets and the service crew drove cars identical to the competing cars which could be cannibalised for spares if necessary. All this seems commonplace now, but in Argentina in 1941 such innovations were little short of revolutionary.

It is remarkable that South America, at the turn of the century a continent with few major roads, little sophisticated industry and a large proportion of poor inhabitants, should have taken motor racing so much to its heart. The South Americans' love of motor sport began in 1891, when a wealthy Brazilian coffee–grower on a trip to Paris bought a Peugeot with a Daimler engine and took it back to South America as a gift for his son. It was probably the first car on that continent. Since then South America, and predominantly Argentina, has been a fertile breeding ground for motor sport. There are records of motor sport events taking place in Buenos Aires as far back as 1904, but because of the appalling road conditions these events were mainly on short circuits.

An Automobile Club Argentino was founded in 1907. Amongst other things, it was keen to encourage all sorts of road transport, but particularly touring by car. In 1908 a popular Argentinian figure, Jean Cassoulet, set off in his de Dion Bouton to drive the 465 miles from Buenos Aires to Cordoba. He was generally considered to be mad – the roads were totally unmade and the car would almost certainly not be able to stand the strain. Cassoulet's critics were wrong. The car completed the journey, but at an average speed of 5·3 mph – substantially slower than a horse would have been. His trip, however, helped Cassoulet to persuade the ACA to stage the first Gran Premio Nacional in 1910, an event which was to lead to a series of classic road races which are still being run on the same roads.

There were seven starters in the first Gran Premio Nacional,

ADVENTURE ON FOUR WHEELS

namely, a 50 hp Panhard–Levassor, a Delaunay–Belleville, a Ford, a Mercedes, a Fiat, a Panhard and a de Dion Bouton owned and driven by Jean Cassoulet. One of the few recorded facts about the race is that although there were only seven competing cars on 465 miles of road, the Delaunay–Belleville and the Ford managed to hit each other.

The race was won by Cassoulet, whose earlier trip had given him warning of the conditions he would encounter. The ditches alongside the route were the major hazards and the locals enjoyed the sight of ditch–bound cars to such an extent that if there were no suitable ditch they would dig one, wait for a car to get stuck in it and then charge the unfortunate driver for pulling him out.

The Gran Premio Nacional became an important annual event. Its special feature was the condition of the roads, and this varied with the weather. Most of the route was on long, straight roads through the *pampas*. If the season was dry, these roads would be very fast and dusty, but torrential rain would instantly transform them into deeply rutted tracks. The cars were modified touring cars and the drivers had to be good mechanics in order to keep their vehicles intact during the long races.

In 1933 the Gran Premio route was altered and lengthened to 1024 miles, but that year the race was a disaster. Only one of the twenty–eight starters finished – an unknown driver called Roberto Lorenzo driving a Model A Ford – the others having been bogged down in heavy mud on the route from Buenos Aires to Bahia Blanca. On a Gran Premio route, drivers could expect to encounter every sort of weather condition from deep snow to searing heat. Even today the roads are extremely rough and the altitude makes the going tough for both men and machines.

Colourful racing of this sort inevitably breeds colourful characters. One such was a determined but impecunious driver, Domingo Bucci, who was alleged to carry a gun in the car so that he could shoot anyone or anything that did not get out of his way. Another was Domingo Marimon, by profession an undertaker, who financed his motor racing by smuggling corpses across the State line. South America was clearly a fertile breeding ground for racing drivers, many of whom were prepared to seek their fortunes in Europe. Fangio, Gonzales and Marimon were just three of the top–class drivers who gave the Europeans a run for their money.

European drivers and manufacturers had always been reluctant to take up the challenge of the Gran Premio races, but as South America began to emerge as an important market for the passenger car, European manufacturers could ignore the races no longer. In 1959 European drivers made an inauspicious debut in the 750 cc class of the Gran Premio Standard. Both driving NSUs, Paul Frère and Edgar Barth were soundly beaten. But in 1960 European fortunes changed and a Volvo, driven by Gunnar Andersson, won the race by more than an hour. By now Mercedes were in full cry – their most resounding victory being that of the all–woman crew of Ewy Rosqvist and Ursula Wirth, who not only won the race outright but set the fastest times in all six stages.

Apart from Argentina, almost every country in South and Central America has, or has had, its own road races. The famous Caminos del Incas in Peru has a 1500–mile route which climbs up to 16,000 feet, and in the fifties the Carrera Panamericana attracted teams of drivers from all over Europe. But the event which causes the most excitement today is the Baja 1000 – a race down the Mexican Baja Peninsula giving adventure–starved enthusiasts a unique opportunity to prove themselves and show off their cars.

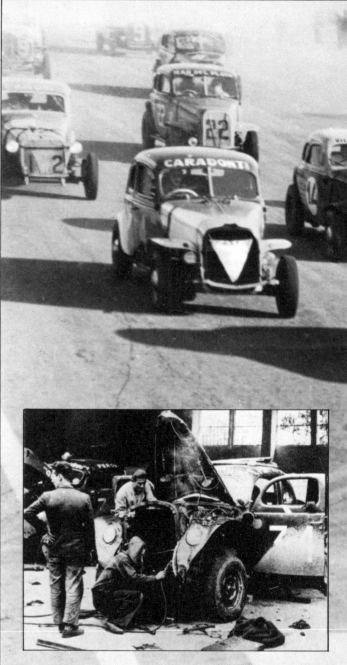

The start of a race *(top)* at the Buenos Aires Autodrome in 1955. Juan Galvez drives car Number One.

Speedy repairs *(above centre)* to a car during a Gran Premio.

Triumphant Mercedes team *(above)* at the end of the 1952 Carrera Panamericana de Mexico. Left, the famous team manager Alfred Neubauer, with winning drivers Karl Kling and Hermann Klenk in the centre.

Upside down at Santa Fe *(above)*. The race is over for this competitor.

Fangio *(above right)* on his way to his first major victory, at the 1940 Gran Premio.

Ladies tackle the 1962 Gran Premio *(right)*. Ewy Rosqvist and Ursula Wirth winning the event with ease in their Mercedes 220 SE. Ewy Rosqvist also finished third in the 1963 and 1964 Gran Premio races.

ADVENTURE ON FOUR WHEELS

Ordeal of the Unsung Heroes

While much four-wheeled adventure comes from the competition of car against car and driver against driver, the greatest adventure still comes from the combination of car and driver pitted against the elements. On 9 October 1958 Jean-Claude Baudot and Jacques Seguela left Paris in a Citroën 2CV. They got back to Paris on 12 November 1959. In little more than a year they had driven 62,500 miles round the world, crossed eight deserts and visited fifty countries. They had spent 350 nights in the open and driven for 2247 hours.

Baudot and Seguela, two young French students, wanted to see the world and their adventure began when they placed an advertisement in a Paris newspaper: "We have a proposition for unusual world-wide publicity for a new enterprise or an expanding big business."

About fifty firms became interested in their trip and, encouraged by this, the adventure-seekers set about meticulous preparations. Their choice of vehicle was governed by the need for a very light car which would be economical on petrol and oil, and preferably with an air-cooled engine. They chose the Citroën 2CV PO, which had a strengthened chassis, and

approached Citroën in the hope that the manufacturer would provide the car in return for publicity. Citroën declined the opportunity and so Baudot and Seguela bought the car themselves and set about equipping it. For two years they had asked every 2CV owner they came across to give them a list of the principal defects of the car. As a result of their research they compiled a list of spares to take with them. The spares weighed 30 lb and they hardly needed any of them.

The car itself was extensively modified. They fitted two supplementary petrol tanks, fog lamps, radio, thermometer, altimeter, interior light, insulating panels, thick floor mats, and fittings for vacuum flasks. They removed the rear seat and fitted an hermetically sealed cupboard at one side, in which to hang their few clothes. The upper halves of the door panels were removed to provide extra storage space, and racks were fitted under the front seats to stop things sliding around the floor. Apart from acquiring maps and visas, Baudot and Seguela completed their preparations by having their appendixes taken out.

Their route was to take them from Paris, through North, Central and South Africa; South, Central and North America; the Far, Middle and Near East, and back to Paris. They hoped to average 150 miles a day. Money was to be a constant problem, despite their commercial sponsors, but they planned to work when necessary in the countries they visited. The crossing of the Sahara gave the first taste of things to come, although by comparison with other deserts of the world the

Sahara is comparatively civilised. All traffic in the Sahara is highly organised. Vehicles leaving Tamanrasset must carry enough petrol for 625 miles, two spare tyres, provisions for a week and 15½ gallons of water. The Army send out a signal giving the expected time of arrival of each car, and should the vehicle not appear a search party is sent out. Baudot and Seguela arrived in Nigeria with nothing worse than severe backache caused by jolting over the rutted and corrugated surfaces of the desert tracks.

From the Niger their route took them across Rhodesia to South Africa, where they were to embark for Rio de Janeiro. Their first serious misfortune struck in Johannesburg, where the car was broken into and the contents stolen. Left with their pyjamas, two pounds sterling and a tourist guide book which opened with the words "South African hospitality is legendary and everywhere you will find a warm welcome", they finally persuaded the French Consul to refund the £100 in travellers' cheques in time for them to get to Capetown and collect a new set of tyres – the old ones having done 10,000 miles – before their boat sailed.

Punctures were to prove one of their biggest problems. Between Paris and Panama they totalled 72. Their adventure nearly came to a complete stop in Chile as they drove along a track skirting the Cordillera. Investigating a nasty noise from the engine, they discovered that the drain plug had parted company with the gearbox and all the oil had drained out. Because they were carrying no spare oil, they resigned themselves to a wait of several days for another vehicle to rescue them, when an aged Chilean appeared carrying a sack. With sign language they demonstrated their problem, whereupon the Chilean opened his sack to reveal bananas – which he solemnly peeled and stuffed into the gearbox. Those twelve bananas enabled them to drive another 190 miles and to change gear without difficulty.

Despite the devastating road conditions, and their lack of money, Baudot and Seguela nursed the 2CV across America and into the Far East. To keep the car on the road they reground the engine valves in a hotel bedroom, became shoe-shine boys in San Francisco and won $600 in a marathon gambling session on the boat to Tokyo. They were rescued by elephants from a swamp in Thailand, captured by Burmese guerillas and drove the car from outside through flooded Pakistan by pressing on the accelerator with a sand shovel. In the middle of the Sind Desert they met a man on a bicycle on a trip around the world in the opposite direction and, when their tyres finally expired, ran for forty-five miles with the punctured ones filled with sand.

In their faithful 2CV, which never let them down, they drove gently along the Côte d'Azur on the last leg of their journey from Istanbul. There was no hero's welcome for them when, exhausted, they at last reached Paris. Few people knew that they had set out and fewer still that they had returned. Despite that, they said they were glad to be home because "the best thing about France is that everybody speaks French".

A pause in the midday sun (left) beside the graves of gold prospectors in Chile's Atacama desert. This area is totally devoid of flowers, insects – and gold.

Pygmies in the equatorial rain forests of Zaire (right) perform a ritual dance around the car. Their fee for this service was 500 francs.

Crossing from Argentina into Chile (below) at 13,000 feet, over the pass of Christ the Redeemer.

ADVENTURE ON FOUR WHEELS
London-to-Sydney: an Unruly Marathon

With the decline of road racing in the post–war years, the competitive driver was faced with a choice between conventional circuit motor racing and the growing sport of rallying, and during the late 1950s and 1960s the latter came into its own, with events like the Monte Carlo, Tulip, Alpine and Acropolis becoming household names and attracting long entry lists of both amateur and professional drivers. More significantly, manufacturers were using these events as a means of publicising their cars and the competition between the rival marques was intense. Then, in 1968, a new event appeared on the international racing calendar: the London–Sydney Marathon.

For some time enthusiasts had been trying to revive the old-style events like the Peking to Paris race. With road racing banned in many countries, and political troubles rife, it had hitherto proved impossible. But the idea of a marathon run half–way round the world captured the imagination of a group of experienced rally men. More importantly, it captured the commercial imaginations of sponsors who were prepared to invest considerable sums of money in such an event. The 10,000–mile Marathon was to be sponsored by the London *Daily Express* and the Sydney *Daily Telegraph*, thus ensuring maximum publicity world–wide. There were literally hundreds of applications for entries, but the organisers limited the number of starters to 100.

The route was in two parts. There were to be seven days and nights of non–stop driving from London to Bombay, where the first seventy cars would be loaded onto a ship bound for Perth. The second section started in Perth and ended in Sydney. The Marathon was scheduled to start on 24 November in London and end in Sydney in time for Christmas. There was more than £20,000 in prize money: the first prize alone was worth £10,000 with the additional promise of substantial bonuses from manufacturer and sponsors of the winning car.

There were some rather bizarre starters at Crystal Palace on 24 November. They included a 1930 Bentley Sports Tourer, a team of three girl secretaries in a standard Morris 1100 and even an MG Midget. There were entries from fifteen countries, including the Soviet Union, whose team was led by a tank commander, and some well–known motor racing names, including ex–Grand Prix driver Innes Ireland, and Lucien Bianchi, who had won Le Mans earlier in the year.

But all eyes were on the works teams. Bookmakers gave Roger Clark, driving one of a team of specially prepared Ford Lotus Cortinas, the best odds, although the Australian team of "Gelignite" Jack Murray and Evan Green was strongly fancied in a BMC 1800. No expense had been spared by these teams, nor by Citroën – all of whom sought commercial success.

As events turned out, the Marathon was very nearly a commercial disaster for the favourites. Roger Clark led throughout the first section – through Turkey, Iran, Afghanistan, over the Khyber Pass and through India, where, according to one of the organisers, "villagers' reaction time to a car is about five minutes and cows have priority", and on to Bombay. Seventy–two cars qualified at Bombay with Clark holding a comfortable lead.

However, conditions in Australia shattered expectations. Freak weather turned the Nullabor Plain into a quagmire and an outstanding year for kangaroo breeding turned the route into a game park. One by one the favourites succumbed to the appalling road conditions, and to the fatigue which inevitably

Competitor Tony Fall (*above*) in a BMC 1800 gets a wave from a tribesman on his way through the Khyber Pass.

Porsche 911 (*below*) at the start of the London–to–Sydney Marathon. Driven by Terry Hunter of Great Britain, the car is well protected by a "cage" of steel bars and wire mesh.

—— London–to–Mexico World Cup
—— London–to–Sydney Marathon

overtook both men and machines. The Ford team had gone out with burned–out pistons, their best placing being tenth for Clark, leaving the lead to Lucien Bianchi in a Citroën. Then, less than 200 miles from the finish at Warwick Park, Sydney, Bianchi's car collided head–on with a truck, which broke his leg and put him completely out of the running. His unfortunate accident made Andrew Cowan, a 25–1 outsider driving one of the two works Rootes Hillman Hunters, the outright winner. Rootes officials could hardly believe their ears. Not only had they nearly decided not to compete in the event for financial reasons, but only two days before the finish a car mechanically similar to the winning car had been launched in Australia. For some manufacturers at least, marathons looked like a very good idea.

ADVENTURE ON FOUR WHEELS
London-to-Mexico: the World Cup

The World Cup Rally, which started at Wembley Stadium on 19 April 1970, was probably the most ambitious event of its kind ever organised. It was certainly the most expensive.

Following the success of the London–Sydney Marathon in 1968 the London *Daily Mirror* agreed to sponsor an event, the end of which would coincide with the opening match of the World Cup Football series in Mexico City. It was the toughest route ever devised: 16,000 miles of the roughest roads the organisers could find, including sections in Bolivia and Peru where armed bandits operated, and sections in the Andes where oxygen is as scarce as petrol. The prize money totalled £40,000 with incalculable publicity value for the winner. After the London–Sydney Marathon, Rootes claimed that the publicity which surrounded their win had sold an extra 1000 cars. So the World Cup Rally had substantial attraction both for private entrants and for manufacturers, even though it was estimated that it would cost a private entrant at least £6000 to take part and at least ten times as much for a manufacturer.

Ninety–six cars left Wembley on the first 4000–mile leg of the event, which would take them from London to Belgrade and back to Lisbon, where they would sail for Rio de Janeiro. There were entries from sixteen countries, the cream of international rally driving talent – and some surprises. To get maximum publicity from the event, Ford had signed inter–national footballer Jimmy Greaves to compete in one of their team Escorts. He turned out to be a more than adequate driver and finished sixth overall, despite hitting a horse in Guatemala.

British Leyland enlisted the aid of Prince Michael of Kent in an Austin Maxi, and Paddy Hopkirk, veteran of the London–Sydney Marathon, started 10–1 favourite in a Triumph 2·5. Regulations for the event were stringent and included the use of colour coding on the engine, gearbox and axle–casing to ensure that these were not changed during the event. The regulations also carried dire warnings: "Some sections of the route between Santiago and Lima are at altitudes in excess of 10,000 feet. Competitors are warned that lack of oxygen can cause one or more of the following unpleasant effects: nausea, headaches, difficulty in breathing, difficulty in making decisions, euphoria. Of these, the last is possibly the most dangerous, as the unfounded self–confidence which builds up after a continuous period of oxygen starvation could lead to a serious accident. . . . "

The event had its share of serious accidents, though none of them could be attributed to altitude. Andrew Cowan, winner of the London–Sydney Marathon, plunged down an incline on an Argentinian road, and veteran French driver Ido Marang was killed when his Citroën hit a private car in Panama. Nevertheless, twenty–three cars reached Mexico City. The winning car was a Ford Escort driven by the professional rally driver Hannu Mikkola, and it was not really surprising that Ford had won. Their investment in the World Cup Rally was little short of £100,000. However, it will probably never be known just how much the Rally cost the organisers. At the end of the event, as the cars left the Aztec Stadium to make way for the footballers, one of the officials said, "This must have been the most expensive event in the history of motor sport. The final bill will frighten the organisers so much that nobody will ever attempt another like it."

Challenges like that rarely go unanswered. Already the London–Sydney has been repeated, and it is only a question of time before someone goes rallying round the world.

Loading a Citroën DS *(below)* onto the SS *Derwent* at Lisbon en route for Rio de Janeiro. The next stage of the rally was an 11,500–mile ordeal through deserts, jungles and mountain passes. Seventy–one cars were left from the ninety–eight starters when the convoy arrived at Lisbon, and only twenty–three reached Mexico City.

Outright winners Hannu Mikkola and Gunnar Palm *(bottom)* speeding towards Mexico in their Ford Escort.

The Car at War

When the First World War broke out in 1914, the motor car gained a new lease of life. Although the Germans already had several specialised army vehicles in production, and the French had been equipping cars with machine-guns since 1905, the British Army still did not possess a single item of mechanised transport. When the emergency came and war was declared, it was not only men that were needed to serve King and Country; their cars, of all shapes and sizes, came too. Hastily painted khaki, this motley collection of vehicles was sent to France to battle in conditions for which they were never designed. But even the more reactionary cavalry officers were forced to admit that for speed and convenience, if not always for reliability, the car had distinct advantages over its predecessor, the horse.

In the early stages of the war there was still a feeling that it was "unsporting" to use cars in battle – it was rather like riding to hounds on a motor bike – and their use was largely restricted to carrying troops and weapons to the front line. After that, the traditional infantry and cavalry took over the fighting.

Nevertheless, London buses carried the Expeditionary Force to the front line at Mons, the taxis of Paris were pressed into military service, and staff cars were widely used by high-ranking officers on both sides. The armoured fighting vehicle had yet to come into its own, but the tank was on the way. By the outbreak of the Second World War, the opposing armies were equipped with all manner of tracked and wheeled vehicles. The motor car had come of age, and had become established as part of the machinery of modern warfare.

ALL CLEAR

T 4718

N·18045

B·5057

THE CAR AT WAR
Limousines in Uniform

The first week of August 1914 was gloriously sunny and those Europeans who could afford it were on holiday. The Archduke Ferdinand, heir to the Austro–Hungarian Empire, and his wife were inspecting the Imperial Army at Sarajevo when a Serbian student stepped onto the running–board of their car and shot them both. That incident marked the effective beginning of the world's first mechanised war.

The American Civil War had revealed the appalling possibilities of the machine–gun, and the Boer War had produced the first armoured train and even an armoured car – a Fowler Steam Tractor, which pulled armoured wagons – but the First World War was the first conflict to be decided by the use of machines. Prominent were the naval machines – the big battleships, destroyers and, most significantly, submarines. In aviation, too, there were great technical advances, but on the ground the war began in the traditional way, with men and horses. The motor car played virtually no role at all, except as transport for senior officers.

It is not surprising that, when war broke out, the car most in demand as personal transport for senior officers of the Allied Command was the Rolls–Royce. One of the fortunate few recipients was Sir John French, Commander–in–Chief of the British Expeditionary Force, whose Rolls–Royce limousine had been ordered by the War Office on 13 December 1913, and the records show that the completed car was delivered on 5 August 1914 at a cost to the country of £1400.

Part of the lengthy specification of the car was that the body, painted green with black mouldings, was made by Barkers. The car was fitted with "special pewter Cast India satin wood

His Majesty King George V *(top)* reviewing a battalion of the Royal Scots in a 25 hp Vauxhall – the standard model frequently used by the War Office. With the King are General Sir Arthur Paget, KCB, and General Stephenson.

An armoured 1920 Rolls–Royce Silver Ghost *(left)*, which saw service in Northern Ireland, Shanghai and Egypt and was used on security duty in the United Kingdom. The vehicle was one of a large fleet, each equipped with one Vickers ·303 machine–gun. This one carried the unlikely nickname "Wedding Bells II".

A 1916 Austin *(above)* covered with armour plating. Searchlights are mounted on the cylindrical gun turrets, each of which is equipped with a Hotchkiss ·303 machine–gun. The twin rear wheels carry chains for traversing rough ground and a hinged flap protects the headlights. Identical bodies were also fitted to Peerless vehicles, which makes it difficult to identify the make of chassis. The earliest armoured car was a 1902 Simms War Car, with a machine–gun mounted on a powered chassis. Turreted armoured cars, based on standard car or lorry chassis and engines, came later.

to doors and windows, cabinet in inlaid satin wood and rugs for the interior". Sir John, later General, French and his car both survived the war and at the end of hostilities both retired to Ireland.

While it is no surprise that General French and Sir Douglas Haig used Rolls–Royces, it is rather more surprising to discover that General Joffre, Commander–in–Chief of the French Army, also had a Rolls for his personal use. His vehicle had a cabriolet body and twin tyres on the rear wheels. How much use the famous French General actually made of his British car is not recorded, but it is unlikely that the French motor industry, led by Renault, viewed the acquisition with any great favour.

The second most popular car for use by British officers was a version of the Vauxhall Prince Henry, which had first appeared in 1910. Its four–cylinder engine, which developed 75 hp and gave the Prince Henry a top speed of 85 mph, had proved itself capable of sustained high speeds. Its road–holding, engineered by Laurence H. Pomeroy, was far in advance of anything else in its class and even before the war it was a highly desirable machine. In peacetime it was in demand as a sports car and as a long–distance tourer. In wartime it was widely used by the British Army as a staff car, carrying officers over appalling roads with impressive reliability.

Except as personal transport, however, the motor car took a long time to gain acceptance as a fighting machine. The motor cycle had proved its usefulness in the early stages of the war. The German Army mounted its troops on motor cycles, and although the soldiers had to get off their machines in order to fire their guns they were still more than a match for the horse–mounted opposition. The motor cyclist dispatch rider was also a familiar sight behind the front lines – the more traditional field telephone having been rendered useless by the constant shelling, which destroyed its land–lines.

The Belgian Army seems to have been the first to armour its cars against the enemy, using – to the horror of the cognoscenti – a Rolls–Royce Silver Ghost which was surmounted by a machine–gun turret. In achieving this, the Belgians had been helped, albeit unwittingly, by a Mr Frank Trehearne–Thomas, a partner in a South Wales steel and tin-plate firm, who in 1911 had ordered a Rolls–Royce 40/50 Limousine with twin tyres on the rear wheels. Rolls–Royce were much opposed to this and argued vigorously against it, but Mr Thomas insisted. He intended to use the car extensively for long–distance touring and believed that twin tyres at the rear would be an advantage to a car loaded with heavy luggage. Rolls–Royce finally built the car and when war broke out the company was able to apply the experience thus gained to the modification of cars for less peaceful purposes.

One of the main reasons why cars had failed to gain favour as war machines was that their use was, for obvious reasons, incompatible with trench warfare. Once its path was crossed by a trench, the car had no apparent advantage over a horse–drawn vehicle. In January 1915, a young man at the Admiralty called Winston Churchill suggested that the use of caterpillar–style tracks would enable vehicles to cross ditches with ease. He wrote to Lord Asquith, "It would be quite easy in a short time to fit up a number of steam tractors with small armoured shelters in which men and machine–guns would be placed, and which would be bullet–proof. The caterpillar system would enable trenches to be crossed quite easily and the weight of these machines would destroy all barbed wire entanglements."

Ignored by Prime Minister Asquith, and by the War Office, Winston Churchill persuaded Major Hetherington of the Dunkirk naval armoured car squadron to have some prototypes built. His theory proved correct and the tank was born. At last the motor car was at war, though not in a form anyone had previously imagined.

Fatal Journey

Had the Archduke Franz Ferdinand and his wife driven to their civic reception at the Town Hall, Sarajevo, in a closed car instead of an open Gräf & Stift on 28 June 1914, the course of European history might have been different. After the reception, the Archduke and Duchess resumed their journey through the city streets little knowing that a student called Gavrilo Princip was waiting for their car with a revolver at the ready. As the car travelled along the banks of the picturesque River Miljacka, the student ran alongside and shot both its royal passengers. His action virtually put an end to the Hapsburg dynasty and precipitated the outbreak of the First World War.

The Sarajevo assassination had the additional effect of

causing a change of emphasis in the world's motor industry. Until October 1914 the motor car was an image–builder, a status symbol with romantic overtones. Almost overnight, the car became an instrument of combat, a fighting vehicle, a practical and before long indispensable workhorse. In Europe, particularly, the car never really regained its former glamour. By the 1920s, the proportion of closed cars produced had risen dramatically. The saloon car provided both privacy and security, neither of which were afforded by the open car. Saloons were also cheaper and easier to make, for which reasons they appealed to the manufacturers. But there was one lesson which was never learned from the Sarajevo incident. Slow–moving open cars make prime targets, and fifty years later President John F. Kennedy, perhaps the best–loved American president of recent times, was to suffer a similar fate in Dallas, Texas.

Home Front, 1914-18

When the First World War broke out, the motor car was in the process of becoming an important social issue in Britain. Light cars had begun to establish themselves, making motorised transport available to many more people, while substantial imports from America were to reduce the price of a car still further. Nevertheless there was still a vigorous anti–motoring lobby, in which Lloyd George was prominent, demanding that the car be suppressed. *The Economist* commented in 1913, "The vehicles of the rich still kill and maim far more people than the vehicles of the poor ... but then nearly all politicians and officials drive constantly at an excessive speed them– selves." The speed limit at that time was 20 mph.

There was already a tax of threepence a gallon on imported oil (commercial vehicles getting half of this back in rebate) and a horsepower tax rising from three pounds a year, for vehicles from 6½ to 12 hp, to forty–two pounds for vehicles of more than 60 hp. This went some way towards mollifying the anti– motorists. The proceeds of the horsepower tax went into a road fund, which was to be spent on replacing the old mud and dust roads with tarred surfaces: as the dust settled, so too did many of the objections. But the Road Fund, which collected far more than it spent, created an unfortunate fiscal precedent which subsequent governments have prolonged.

There was also a 33 per cent tax on imported luxury items – of which the car was considered to be one. This was brought in soon after the outbreak of war as a result of pressure from the British motor industry, which feared the threat of American imports. British manufacturers were busy fulfilling Govern– ment wartime contracts and could not supply the growing domestic demand for passenger cars.

No restriction had been placed on the use of the private car after the outbreak of war, probably because of the high social status of the car–owning population. There was no petrol rationing, and until well into the war at least one car manufacturer, Napier, used Cabinet ministers to endorse their products in advertisements. There was, however, a certain amount of feeling that to run a motor car was unpatriotic, and in 1916 the National Organising Committee for War Savings chose to refer to private motoring as "a form of selfish or thoughtless extravagance". But it made no appreciable difference. Using a motor car to go horse racing was a particularly contentious issue. The Government had agreed to allow horse racing to continue on the somewhat tenuous grounds that an adequate supply of bloodstock was necessary if Britain was to have sufficient horses for defence purposes. But as the Government had appealed to the public not to use the trains because this interfered with troop movement, the only way the punters could see their horses run was by using motor cars. In what they evidently believed to be a patriotic gesture, the racecourse owners promptly raised their admis– sion charges, thus making horse racing the prerogative of the moneyed and the motorised. To counter criticism, the Government proposed a further tax of sixpence a gallon on petrol. The motoring lobby, led by William Joynson Hicks, later Viscount Brentford, attacked the proposal saying that pleasure motoring had entirely given way to motoring for the war effort. His critics pointed out that it was still possible to see large crowds of private cars at race meetings. There was only one possible solution and eventually the Government took it. In September 1916 the Jockey Club suspended all race meetings for the duration. In one area at least, the car had proved its supremacy over the horse.

Increasing use of the motor car in this period had a number of unexpected effects on social habits and fashions. In 1916 the length of women's skirts rose permanently above the ankles. At various times this has been considered as highly significant – one social historian describing it as "an indication of woman's liberation from her subordinate role". A more likely explanation seems to be that, with the absence abroad of the majority of able–bodied males, women were required to replace them in jobs which would have been awkward in a skirt which trailed along the ground – notably such jobs as driving ambulances and dust–carts and repairing and servicing the vehicles they drove.

The war was nearly over before the Government decided that it disapproved of the "extravagant use of motor cars". In January 1918 it made an order defining the purposes for which petrol might be used, which included taking children to school, going to the doctor, dentist, the lawyer or a bank and performing any other public duty (including appearing at a court of law). As this list encompassed many of the uses to which the moneyed classes would normally put their private

Women war workers *(right)* building a lorry chassis in 1917. Lack of able–bodied men transformed women, previously regarded as fragile and impractical, into engineers. They also turned their hands to stoking boilers and worked on assembly lines. But their principal task was in the munitions factories, where they were trained to fill fuses for bomb detonators.

cars, the new order made remarkably little difference to the overall consumption of petrol. It appeared to mean to many in the social set that at least one dinner party guest should be a professional man and that there was certainly no reason why the chauffeur should be sacked. But, at the same time, the Select Committee on Luxury Duty put the motor car firmly in what it believed to be its place by including it on a list of goods which ought to be subject to a luxury tax, irrespective of cost. These included many of the essentials of high living such as feather boas, fans, perfumes, yachts and pleasure boats, billiard tables and cocktail shakers.

Although the car was still considered a toy of the idle rich by many of those who could not afford one, its appeal to the masses was undiminished on both sides of the Atlantic. The Ford Motor Company had opened an assembly plant at Trafford Park, Manchester, in 1911 and in the first year of operation built 3000 cars – establishing Ford as the market leader in Britain. By 1915 production had increased to one hundred vehicles a day, most of which were adapted for military use as trucks and light vans. But even the anti–motorist lobby was forced to admit that Britain needed the internal combustion engine, for practical as well as pleasure purposes, and, in particular, if Britain was to eat, for agricultural purposes. So while the transatlantic threat was resisted by the British motor industry, it was nevertheless forced to accept the import of thousands of Fordson tractors from Dearborn, Michigan. War was declared on the commercial front even as it was settled on the battlefield.

An ambulance built onto a Vauxhall 30 hp chassis *(below)*. This one was used by the New Zealand division of the "Anzacs" – the Australian and New Zealand Army Corps.

The first gas–powered car in France, 1917 *(bottom)*. The gas was contained in the balloon structure on the roof – a system developed from pre–war British experiments on buses.

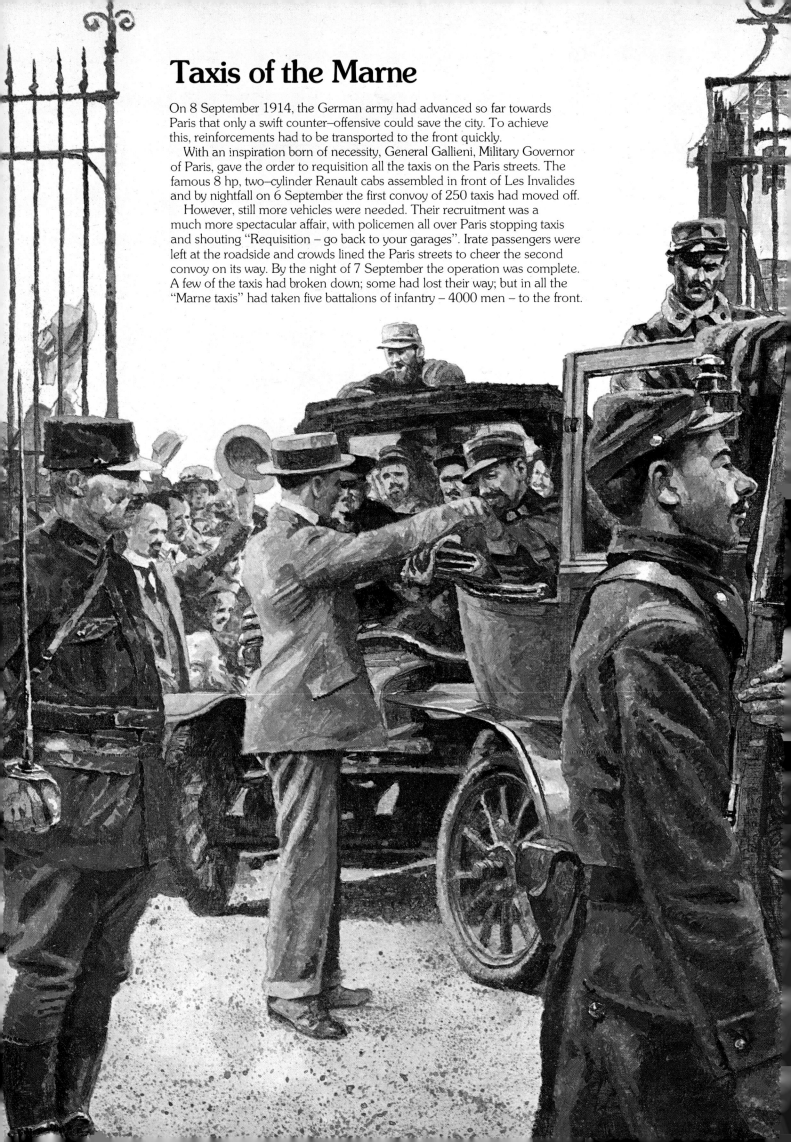

Taxis of the Marne

On 8 September 1914, the German army had advanced so far towards
Paris that only a swift counter–offensive could save the city. To achieve
this, reinforcements had to be transported to the front quickly.

With an inspiration born of necessity, General Gallieni, Military Governor
of Paris, gave the order to requisition all the taxis on the Paris streets. The
famous 8 hp, two–cylinder Renault cabs assembled in front of Les Invalides
and by nightfall on 6 September the first convoy of 250 taxis had moved off.

However, still more vehicles were needed. Their recruitment was a
much more spectacular affair, with policemen all over Paris stopping taxis
and shouting "Requisition – go back to your garages". Irate passengers were
left at the roadside and crowds lined the Paris streets to cheer the second
convoy on its way. By the night of 7 September the operation was complete.
A few of the taxis had broken down; some had lost their way; but in all the
"Marne taxis" had taken five battalions of infantry – 4000 men – to the front.

2068-G7

A chauffeur–driven Austin Six
(top) leaves a London gas depot in Hyde Park in April 1940 with a gas–filled bag on its roof. The gas bag was an alternative to petrol for some motorists, but in general gas was not a practical fuel: modifications to the car were expensive and complicated, and depots were infrequent. Rural experiments with methane gas obtained from rotting chicken manure, and wood–burning

stoves, also proved unsatisfactory. The nearside headlamp of the Austin carries a cover that allowed just enough light through for the driver to see where he was going, in order to comply with wartime blackout restrictions.

Tearing up petrol coupons
(above) to celebrate the end of petrol rationing in May 1950. Rationing was introduced on 16 September 1939 and motorists

were allocated fuel according to the importance of their war effort and the size of their car's engine. The average allowance was 150 miles of motoring a month.

Volunteer ambulance drivers
(above) being given night–driving training in Battersea Park in March 1939. Women volunteers drove the ambulances without lights and wearing gas masks. The pilot on the running board watched the

kerb and directed the driver.

Air–raid precautions *(right)*. Patrolmen from the Automobile Association put up warning signs for motorists of impending blackout restrictions in January 1940. A month later a night–time speed limit of 20 mph was imposed. Cyclists and motor cyclists had to paint their headlights black, leaving a narrow slit for the light to shine through.

THE CAR AT WAR
Home Front, 1939-45

Whereas there had been no petrol rationing during the First World War, and the only restriction on private motoring had been public opinion, the British Government reacted quickly in 1939. A rationing scheme was announced in August of that year and restrictions came into effect a month after war broke out. It allowed a basic ration for all cars and varied with the horsepower of the engine, giving an average mileage of 150 miles a month. On the day war was declared the Government also banned the import of cars, as well as textiles, clothes, glassware, clocks, watches, vacuum cleaners and toys.

Even all these restrictions were not enough to curtail people's pleasure during the months of the so–called phoney war. Although the horse had made a comeback in the country and there were bicycles in plenty to be seen in Whitehall, the RAC appealed to the Government for an extra petrol ration for the Easter weekend and even published a leaflet entitled "Why lay up your car?" on the somewhat tenuous grounds that the British motor industry needed encouragement. British motorists were by no means keen to forgo their motoring and the AA reported that holiday traffic over the Easter weekend of 1940 was at least 70 per cent of peacetime traffic.

But wartime motoring was a dangerous business. Blackout regulations made using the roads, whether as motorist, cyclist or pedestrian, extremely hazardous. The only lights allowed were the dim glow from masked traffic lights and the hooded torches of pedestrians. Road casualty figures rocketed. In the last five months of 1939, after blackout restrictions had come into force, more people were killed on the roads in Britain than were killed on active service. A night–time speed limit of 20 mph was introduced in February 1940, but did little to improve the situation. It was still more dangerous to be abroad in Britain at night than to face the enemy in Europe. The

casualty figures for the following year, 1941, were worse still.

More stringent petrol rationing improved the situation. Whereas horse racing had been a contentious issue during the First World War, interest during the Second World War was focused on dogs. A question was put to the Minister for Petroleum in the summer of 1940, asking what he proposed to do about the fact that several hundred cars had been observed at Catford Greyhound Stadium on the previous Saturday. Like his First World War predecessor, the Minister declined to take any action, declaring that he "deprecated the heresy–hunting of the motorist on every occasion". But there was plenty of Government advice for car owners. They were advised to remove the rotor arm as well as the ignition key when parking the car, and to ensure that their garage doors were securely locked, not so much to thwart the ordinary car thief as to baulk any enemy spies who might land in Britain.

There was also advice on what to do in the event of an invasion. This sombre advice came from the Minister of Transport and was to be found on a leaflet distributed with books of petrol coupons. To immobilise a car in the event of an invasion, the Ministry recommended smashing the magneto and the fuel pump with a hammer, and for those motorists who did not recognise either component the advice given was that they "should go to the nearest garage at once to find out".

Although the Government initially declined to ban pleasure motoring for what it called "social and political reasons", it was eventually forced to do so. Finally, in July 1942, the basic petrol ration was abolished, with fuel allowed only for essential business and for people living in the country, who were allowed sufficient for two shopping trips and one trip to church each week. The effect on the accident figures was dramatic, but the British motor industry was seriously worried. Although peace was nowhere in sight, the industry was beginning to plan its post–war future and petrol rationing on such a scale might continue well into peacetime.

Despite the scarcity of petrol, the British motorist was determined to keep on driving and the search for alternative fuel sources continued. There were experiments with gas–bags on the car roof, with a wood–burning stove towed behind the car, and even with rotting, gas–producing chicken manure, but none of these proved to be a long–term success and the British motorist resigned himself to a carless war.

Largely because the Second World War was a highly mechanised war, with both men and women driving all sorts of vehicles at home and abroad, it seemed likely that the demand for passenger cars would boom as soon as peace was declared. The motor car had ceased to be the sole prerogative of the moneyed classes and, furthermore, women had broken the male domination of the internal combustion engine. Princess Elizabeth had gone through a course of vehicle mechanics as part of her contribution to the war effort and her example encouraged women all over Britain to learn to drive. The fashion change which had taken place during the preceding war with the raising of women's hemlines was echoed during the second war with the acceptance of trousers for women.

It became apparent that post–war Europe would be geared increasingly to the use of the private car. In April 1944, the Standing Joint Committee put a strong argument to the Treasury that not only should taxation on motorists be reduced but that use of the car should be encouraged as it was crucial to Britain's post–war development. Part of the report stated that "the success of post–war plans for the distribution of population and industry, the creation of new towns and villages, better housing conditions, the revival of agriculture and the absorption of labour in new industries, is closely bound up with road transport, of which the private motor car and motor cycle form an integral part".

THE CAR AT WAR
On Active Service

If the First World War caught the European motor industry unprepared, the Second World War most certainly did not, and extensive use was made of derivatives of passenger cars. There were new types of vehicle as well. Only at the start of the war was an efficient cross–country, four–wheel–drive vehicle produced, and tracked vehicles, which laid their roads down in front of them and then picked them up behind, were in their infancy in 1939.

The first cross–country vehicle with four–wheel drive was the Volkswagen "Type 166", which went into service in 1942. It was an amphibious vehicle, designed by Dr Ferdinand Porsche, and used modified components of yet–to–be–produced passenger cars. In America, the army had been experimenting with four–wheel–drive prototypes for several years, but apart from the light "Quad" truck, built by Jeffery in 1910, had not produced anything significant. But on 27 June 1940, the American army announced the rules of a competition for the design and production of a light cross–country vehicle designated "Truck, $\frac{1}{4}$–Ton, 4 × 4". Although the military authorities invited 135 manufacturers to compete, only two replied: the American Bantam Company and Willys Overland Motors. The competition rules demanded seventy prototypes within seventy–five days – a virtually impossible task – and Willys asked for four months. The Defense Department refused their request and awarded the contract to Bantam, one of the smallest of all the American automobile manufacturers.

Although Bantam managed to produce the necessary prototypes within the time limit, Willys decided to produce a prototype at their own expense and submit it to the army even though it did not conform to the competition rules. The first Bantam prototypes underwent major testing in Louisiana

under the direction of Colonel Dwight D. Eisenhower. The Willys prototype was tested in November 1940 and was so successful that the Defense Department finally decided to give contracts to Bantam, Willys and to Ford, although the Willys "Jeep" was the basis of the vehicle which helped the allies to win the Second World War.

At the outbreak of war, all the participants had armoured vehicles at their disposal. The main ones were the two–seater Scout and the three–ton Daimler in Britain, an Italian "AB 41", which had wheels capable of pointing in different directions, and the German "Puma", which had 30 mm armourplate covering and needed eight wheels to carry its enormous weight. These vehicles looked more like wheeled tanks than any sort of car, as indeed did an armour–plated version of the Humber, known as the "Ironside", which was used by the Royal Family and Cabinet ministers in Britain. The royal version was based on the standard "Ironside", which had a Super Snipe chassis and had been produced for home defence after Dunkirk. The royal "Ironside", however, had hide upholstery and microphone communications between driver and passengers.

Humber cars were widely used by the Allied forces. The Pullman Limousine was used by senior officers in all three services as well as by the US Army, who acquired them under a reverse "Lease Lend" arrangement. But probably the most famous Humbers were the Super Snipe Tourers used by Field–Marshal Viscount Montgomery of Alamein. He had two favourite cars, one which he used in North Africa and Italy, called "Old Faithful", and the other, nicknamed the "Victory Car", which was used by the Field–Marshal in Western Europe in the closing stages of the war.

Of course Hitler and his officers chose their staff cars from the range of Mercedes available when war broke out. The picture of Hitler standing in the back of his open Cabriolet, giving the Nazi salute, is a familiar one. But the German Army was not too proud to use British vehicles too. Writing on 12 June 1945, Alan Moorehead, the famous war correspondent,

said, "It must have been pleasant for General Montgomery to see among our booty a number of British vehicles of the Morris make which the Germans apparently captured at Dunkirk and are still using."

There were plenty of experimental vehicles on the drawing boards, but few of them ever saw active service. One such was the Hillman Gnat, which looked not unlike an armoured motor bicycle. The engine was mounted at the rear and the driver sat at the front, with a single headlamp mounted in the middle of the front. Although another experimental vehicle did eventually reach the production line, it was only after the war ended. The Austin "Champ" began life as the Nuffield "Gutsy", a field–car project under the direction of Alec Issigonis. It had a stressed–skin welded body, four–wheel drive and independent suspension. Later it became the Mudlark, and finally, in a much modified form, the Champ.

Standard produced another interesting experiment known as the "Jungle Bug". This unlikely little machine was intended to be dropped from aeroplanes in the Far East and had the Standard Eight engine/gearbox unit. There was also an amphibious trailer into which the front end of the Jungle Bug was put for ferrying across rivers. Unfortunately, on the initial water tests the entire unit sank, and before the vehicle could be sufficiently improved, the war was over.

In addition to the specially built vehicles, ordinary passenger cars and light vans played a vital part in the war effort, both at home and abroad. Standard Flying Eights became tea cars; Ford 10 cwt vans became ambulances and personnel carriers, and one version of the Hillman Minx became a "ladder van", fitted out with equipment for airfield lighting maintenance.

Although the tank was unassailable during the Second World War, it was less important in terms of automotive development than some of its poorer relations. Nevertheless, the Churchill tank, with its air intake and exhaust pipes well clear of water levels, and the American Sherman tank, the last version of which weighed thirty–three tons, were a vital part of this highly mechanised war.

Hitler in a Mercedes *(top left)* receives a warm welcome from schoolchildren during a visit to Sudetenland in 1938.

Winston Churchill *(above)* thanks the Eighth Army in Tripoli in 1943. He is riding in "Old Faithful",

Field–Marshal Montgomery's Humber, accompanied by Monty himself and Lord Alexander of Tunis.

Troop train in Burma *(below)* carrying allied soldiers and drawn by an armoured car fitted with flanged railway wheels.

An Age of Elegance

Cars built after the First World War are generally known as Vintage – although to the Americans they are Classic. There were cars for the millions and cars for the millionaires – and in the latter category came some of the most prestigious vehicles ever offered in the super–luxury class. Postwar euphoria gave rise to such companies as Wills Sainte–Claire, which came and went in six years, and the more renowned Hispano Suiza, Isotta–Fraschini and Minerva. Also in the limelight were famous American names such as Cadillac and Lincoln, and naturally some of the most famous Rolls–Royces. Buyers for these cars were those who were fortunate enough to have made a great deal of money and were inclined to spend it before it was too late. Fortunately, there were enough people around who conformed to this description to keep most – but not all – of these prestigious marques alive.

It was a boom era for the affluent motorist. There was still plenty of space on the world's roads and cars were becoming ever more powerful, more elegant and increasingly safe to drive. These cars were definitely not family transport: they were designed without regard for cost or fuel economy. Their owners lived extravagantly, enjoying their wealth before the money and the champagne ran out. It is fortunate for us that they did, otherwise there would have been no demand for some of the most exciting cars in motoring history: cars which have a style and elegance very much their own, and whose like will probably never be seen again.

A Boost for Post-war Morale

"In the blue book of the automobile, the Hispano Suiza is Queen." This confident statement from a Hispano catalogue of the 1920s clearly reflects the image projected of these big, beautiful, luxury cars. Following the gloom of wartime, the wealthy car buyers of Europe wanted something to boost their morale – and Hispano Suiza were determined to provide it, building the cars in their Paris factory under the guiding hand of their Swiss design engineer Marc Birkigt. The company itself had originated in Spain, so it had an international flavour rare in the industry of the time.

Wartime mechanisation had bred a generation of men who no longer wanted the cumbersome, though superb, limousines of a class which before the war had been dominated by Rolls–Royce. They wanted speed and performance combined with elegance, and fortunately they had money to spend. Marc Birkigt, a brilliant man who had been with Hispano Suiza for many years, was experienced in aviation engineering as well as in the automobile world. In one of his rare recorded speeches he described himself as "only an engine designer", but his cars had more than just good engines. Cars like his first post–war design, which had a 6·5 litre light alloy, overhead camshaft engine, had a top speed of more than 90 mph, and cars which went as fast as that needed to be able to stop. The braking of the 1919 Hispano Suiza was quite unlike anything else on the road. The 6·5 litre car was followed by an 8 litre version capable of 125 mph, regarded by many as the finest car in the world. It may have been a little noisier than the Rolls–Royce,

La cigogne volante *(left)*, symbol of the marque, derived from that of a famous French squadron whose aircraft were powered by Hispano Suiza engines.

A 1926 Hispano Suiza *(below)* with a special coupé body designed by Weymann. The car had a 45 hp engine and a top speed of nearly 110 mph.

but it was modern, very fast, handled beautifully and was without doubt the fashionable car to own in the twenties. The long bonnet and distinctive radiator were embellished with a *cigogne volante* (flying stork) mascot, which reminded the public that the great flying ace Georges Guynemer had won his battles in the air powered by Hispano Suiza engines. On the ground, too, Hispano Suiza were equally determined to outclass all opposition.

And there was a good deal of opposition to eliminate. If the Hispano Suiza was Queen among cars, then the Belgian–built Minerva was Goddess. Though not as costly as the Hispano Suiza, the Minerva was *the* car for upper–class Belgians. It came in four–, six– and eight–cylinder versions, with elaborate bodywork and servo–assisted brakes. So successful was the six–cylinder, 6 litre model, that Minerva kept it in production for well over ten years, giving the Belgian motor industry a reputation which it would never have again.

Italy had its own competition for the Hispano Suiza and the Minerva – the Isotta–Fraschini. This company had grown up in the pre–war era making small cars not unlike the early Renaults, but by 1914 was building big, powerful, sporting cars which proved very popular with wealthy Americans. At the Paris Motor Show in 1919, where an impressive array of "anti–austerity" motor cars was to be seen, Isotta–Fraschini launched its most successful car, the Tipo 8. This car boasted the first straight–eight engine to be produced commercially, housed under a long, elegant bonnet. It was not a particularly refined car from the engineering point of view, having a three–speed gearbox and being very heavy to drive, but the standard of construction was very high indeed. Though it was extremely heavy on petrol, the Isotta–Fraschini proved immensely popular in America, particularly with the Hollywood set, where petrol and chauffeurs were in ample supply and stars had their public images to protect.

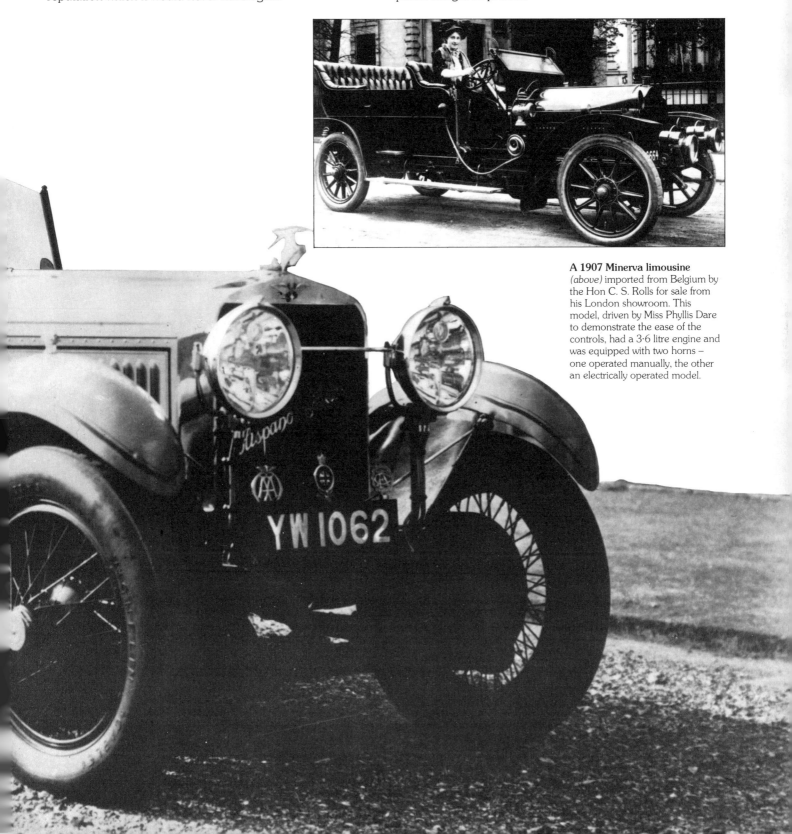

A 1907 Minerva limousine (*above*) imported from Belgium by the Hon C. S. Rolls for sale from his London showroom. This model, driven by Miss Phyllis Dare to demonstrate the ease of the controls, had a 3·6 litre engine and was equipped with two horns – one operated manually, the other an electrically operated model.

AN AGE OF ELEGANCE
A Pair of Thoroughbreds

Two famous names, those of Bentley and Lancia, stand out as being the makers of cars elegant not only in style but also in engineering terms, and both names live on today, although in the case of Bentley the company which bore his name was relatively, and sadly, short–lived. W. O. Bentley was born in 1888. As a child he had wanted to be an engineer, but not of cars. Railways were what really fascinated him and after leaving school he went to the Great Northern Works in Doncaster as an apprentice. After five years there, the cumbersome steam engines were beginning to lose their appeal for Bentley, who had become an ardent motor cyclist, and in 1912, together with his brother, he took over an agency for French cars, in a mews behind Baker Street in London.

His first successful design, however, was not a car at all, but a rotary aero engine which he produced in 1916 for the Admiralty. His first car, a 3·5 litre sports car, was first shown at the London Motor Show three years later, although in fact none was actually delivered until 1921. By then Bentley had moved to a small factory in Cricklewood and was proving the power of his products in motor sport. Bentley's confidence in his cars was such that they were sold with a five–year guarantee, and they sold to a very distinguished clientele: the first man to buy one was Noel van Raalte, a racing enthusiast and financier. The Bentley was particularly popular in the theatrical world – Tallulah Bankhead, Gertrude Lawrence and Jack Buchanan all owned one. However, the car's reputation for performance and advanced engineering was made on the race-track (especially Le Mans).

Almost all the finance for W. O. Bentley's small but sophisticated business came from Captain Woolf Barnato, a diamond magnate and a first–class racing driver with a great liking for bigger and more powerful cars than the original 3·5 litre Bentley, and it was perhaps this influence which ultimately led to the demise of Bentley as an independent manufacturer. To move up into the prestige market, Bentley needed to compete with Rolls–Royce, whose image as "the best car in the world" was virtually unassailable. It is said that in June 1924, a Rolls–Royce test driver, in France with a prototype Phantom 1 tourer, came up behind a heavily camouflaged car with British number plates, calling itself a "Sun". This vehicle was in fact an experimental 4·2 litre Bentley being driven by W. O. Bentley himself, and the two drivers became involved in

an impromptu road race which ended only when the Rolls–Royce driver lost his hat. Perhaps because of this episode, Bentley realised that his new car was not sufficiently powerful to compete with the opposition. He increased the capacity to 6·5 litres and launched the car in 1926. But although this car and its 8 litre successor were superbly successful on the race track, they tended to frighten off the customers, and more development was clearly needed to make them more suitable for society drivers on the road. At this point, in 1931, Woolf Barnato decided that, for economic reasons, he could no longer support Bentley financially, and there was nobody to replace him. To the dismay of the motoring world, the Bentley company was allowed to die. In a desperate attempt to retain his status as an independent designer, Bentley began negotiations with Napier, which had given up cars to concentrate on aero engines. Arrangements were well in hand when it was learned that Bentley Motors had been bought by a syndicate which, it was later revealed, was backed by Rolls–Royce, who had acquired at the same time a famous name and a potentially dangerous rival.

At the Paris Motor Show in 1922, the son of an Italian soup manufacturer launched a car which should have brought swift changes to automotive engineering, had the public not been slow to react to its advanced features. The manufacturer was Vincenzo Lancia and the car was the Lambda. Lancia had been a competition driver for Fiat, for whom he had won several major events, before he set up in business on his own. His name, Lancia, means "arrow" or "lance". Lancia was noted for his nonconformity. He was a very large man given to holding unusual views, notably that of preferring the operas of Wagner to the Italian composers. His first car was the Lancia Alfa, which was a conventional four–cylinder, 2·5 litre machine produced in 1904, and his most popular model up to 1922 was the 4·9 litre Theta, which featured electric lights and starting – the first time these had been available as standard fittings on a European car.

The Lambda, however, was years ahead of its time in several respects. Instead of a conventional chassis it had a monocoque hull built of hollow steel pressings, independent front suspension with sliding pillars and vertical coils, and four–wheel braking. Although the Lambda was intended as a touring car, its outstanding road–holding and handling made it ideal for competition driving, and in 1924 Lambdas were first, second and third in the "Bad Roads Race" held near Lille on appalling road surfaces. The Lambda was in production for nine years, during which 13,000 cars were built, and although the monocoque construction was eventually dropped be–cause of coachbuilding problems, the front suspension system was retained for many years.

Sopwith Camel *(top, far left).* W. O. Bentley designed one of the two original rotary aero engines which powered the Sopwith Triplane (the other was French). The engines were subsequently used to good effect in the Camel at the end of the First World War.

Veteran racing driver Sammy Davis *(top left).* Davis, who was one of the famous "Bentley Boys" of the twenties, is at the wheel of a 1927 Red Label 3 litre Bentley.

W. O. Bentley *(far left)* driving a 1930 Bentley Speed 6, considered by connoisseurs of the marque to be the best of the early Bentleys. The car won at Le Mans in 1929 and 1930, driven by Captain Woolf Barnato.

A new Lancia racing car *(left)* driven by Mr W. L. Stewart at the August Bank Holiday race meeting at Brooklands in 1909. This is the 20 hp model, the chassis for which even then cost £400.

AN AGE OF ELEGANCE
Inter-war Classics

The names of Packard, Lincoln and Cadillac are synonymous with the classic inter–war era of American motoring. Packard was no newcomer to the scene. The Packard brothers had started building cars in 1899 and one of their pre–war models – a 1911 six–cylinder luxury vehicle – was described by the manufacturers as "a car built for gentlemen by gentlemen", although a 1914 advertisement described the new 4–48 rather less elegantly as "boss of the road".

Packard Twin Sixes had been used extensively as transport for American army officers during the war – the open touring cars being ideal for the purpose as well as proving extremely reliable, but it was in the 1920s that Packard became strong contenders in the super luxury class. In 1923, the company launched a new prestige car to replace the Twin Six. Called the Straight Eight, it started life with a 5·9 litre engine but grew to 6·3 litres six years later. The Straight Eight featured such luxuries as automatic stop lights, windscreen wipers, and brakes on all four wheels, but bumpers were an optional extra until 1925. In 1931 the Straight Eight was somewhat overshadowed by the return to a V12 engine at the top of the Packard range. These big, elegant cars with 7·3 or 7·7 litre engines had the long, rakish lines which were much favoured by the coachbuilders of the period. Apart from their looks, the outstanding features of the big Packards were smoothness and quietness. Their owners were frequently film stars and wealthy industrialists, who enjoyed not only the cushioned luxury but also the privacy these cars afforded.

However, Packard did not have things all their own way. The luxury market was not overlooked by Henry Ford, who bought the two–year–old Lincoln company for $8 million from Henry and Wilfred Leland in 1922. It is alleged that Henry Leland had called his first car Lincoln after his preferred candidate when he had first voted in the 1864 Presidential election. Whatever the reason for his choice, the name was to endure as representing a very superior, aristocratic product. The original car was a 5·8 litre V8, but the Lelands were hit hard by the economic depression and lacked the finances to continue production. The pattern of the major companies buying out the smaller producers, and thereby subsidising the production of small–volume, expensive cars by the mass production of cheaper ones, proved to be generally successful. It gave companies of the scale of Ford and General Motors the resources to develop new technologies and engineering skills. Such was the case with the Lincoln, in particular the Lincoln Continental, which was conceived by Henry Ford's son Edsel for himself and his sons to drive. Only 5320 of these cars were ever built and today they are highly prized collectors' items. The first three examples were convertibles and Edsel Ford insisted that the spare wheel be carried on the outside of the boot, which was quite out of keeping with contemporary models. Amazingly, although the car was not originally intended for general sale, the Continental made an immediate impact on the public and it was put into production for the 1940 model year. Although it is unlikely that the car ever made money for Ford, it certainly made a reputation.

The trio of famous American marques is completed by Cadillac. This name was also no newcomer to the American scene, for the first vehicle to carry it was a 6½ hp single–cylinder light car which appeared in 1903 and was named after the French explorer Antoine de la Motte, founder of the city of Detroit. But the Cadillac company, which was another venture of the Leland brothers, was sold in 1909 to a recently formed consortium known as the General Motors Corporation, which produced, under the Cadillac banner, some very advanced

machines. The 1915 Cadillac was powered by an engine copied from the 1910 V8 de Dion unit and became the forerunner of the modern V8 engine. In 1912 Cadillac standardised coil ignition, electric starting and electric lights, while at the New York Motor Show of 1929 Cadillac put themselves into the upper echelons of the prestige car market with a car powered by a V16 engine. This new model had instant appeal for wealthy enthusiasts – it being generally considered that if twelve cylinders were good, then sixteen must undoubtedly be better. The car was a phenomenal success and more than 4500 were made during the ten years that it was in production, most with elegant bodywork by one of America's most famous stylists, the Fisher Closed Body Corporation.

1929 Packard roadster *(top)*, one of the Twin Six models. Its outstanding features were smoothness and quietness and it was fitted with adjustable rear seat windscreens and luxurious upholstery, designed to appeal to women in particular.

An earlier Packard *(above):* a 1916 Twin Six 6·9 litre tourer. This was the first of the Twin Sixes and cost, with electric lights, $2600.

The **1939 prototype** of the Lincoln Continental Cabriolet *(above left)*. Although the design concept was Edsel's, the car was designed by Bob Gregorie. When the prototype was driven on the road in Florida it created such public interest that the car went into production in 1940.

A 1912 4-cylinder 30 hp Cadillac *(above):* a demonstration model advertising the fact that for the first time electric lighting and starting systems were standard on Cadillacs.

A seven-seater sedan version of the 1930 Cadillac *(above)* with a 12 feet 4 inch wheelbase, a V16 engine and a synchromesh gearbox. With chromium–plated trim and safety glass, this elegant machine cost a little over $7000.

A 1940 Cadillac 60 Special *(below)* with more than a hint of trends to come. The "snarl" was to become a familiar feature of American automobile styling during the fifties and sixties.

The Opulent Auburn

Of all the famous American cars, the Auburn was the one in which trendy Americans of the 1900s could cut a dash. They loved the rich leather upholstery, the nickel trim, the spacious luggage compartment and, most of all, the sleek elegant lines of these hand–built cars from Auburn, Indiana.

However, the real motoring buffs loved the marque for its advanced engineering. By 1912, Auburn owners could boast that their six–cylinder cars had electric lights as a standard fitting and almost every year brought some new technical innovation. In 1919 a new, more streamlined body was introduced; in 1921, cycle–type mudguards, disc wheels and step plates instead of running–boards; in 1924, low–pressure balloon tyres and stylish new two–tone colour schemes.

Alas, the days of these splendid cars were numbered. Despite a take–over by the American Cord company in 1924, the Auburn failed to make money. By the end of 1936 the picnic was over and the Auburn was no more.

Incomparable Cord

Of all the American cars, the Cord is the one which has the greatest charisma. Although the cars themselves and the man who gave his name to them still fascinate enthusiasts, why it should be so is a mystery. The Cord was the epitome of affluent 1930s America – being forward–looking, if not entirely successful. The first Cord was the L29, the third in the trio of Auburn, Duesenberg and Cord to make up the empire of Erret Lobban Cord.

Cord was a romantic figure. He began his professional life by respraying secondhand Model T Fords (the ones you could have from the manufacturer in any colour as long as it was black) and selling them at a considerable profit. He then went on to become a salesman for the Moon Motor Car Company of St Louis. Then, in 1924, Cord was introduced to the Auburn Automobile Company – a firm which made magni–ficent vehicles, but which was having considerable difficulty in selling them. Cord took over the company, and shortly afterwards sold the existing stock of seven hundred cars (which he privately considered to be ugly and expensive) by some clever advertising. He then had the entire Auburn range redesigned and exhibited at the New York Motor Show. To Auburn, Cord added Duesenberg, Lycoming, American Airways, the Checker Cab Company, New York Shipbuilding and a host of smaller companies, which combined to make him a multi–millionaire. By 1929 he was ready to launch his own car. His L29 had a 5 litre straight–eight engine, made by Lycoming, and, more important, front–wheel drive; it was also much lower and more elegant than other machines of the period, and had a top speed of 80 mph.

The year of the Wall Street Crash was not a good time to launch a new high–quality car, particularly one which featured technical innovations, and although 4500 cars were sold it seems that every one of them lost money. The price of $3000 was high, even in boom years: it proved too much for Depression–hit Americans and the Cord went out of production in 1932. Three years later, however, the name re–emerged. Cord hired Gordon Buehrig, one of the most prominent designers of the thirties and the man who had been responsible for the four–seater open Duesenberg, to style a new Cord. This machine was to appear at the New York Motor Show on 1 November 1935. However, there were problems. In the tradition of wealthy car–manufacturers Cord was unable to make up his mind about the exact specification of the new car, but in order to exhibit it at the New York Show he had to produce at least a hundred cars. Just in time the required hundred cars were completed – by hand. All were without gearboxes – or rather without gears inside the gearboxes – and the cars were pushed onto the show stands (a practice which is by no means unknown today). The new Cord Model 810 was also front–wheel driven and had headlights which could be wound in and out of the wings by hand. The fascia panel had aircraft–type instruments with indirect green lighting – a feature that appeared to be highly advanced but was, in fact, derived from a job lot of aircraft instruments which Buehrig had bought in an attempt to keep down the price of the car. The new Cord was a huge success at the New York Motor Show, but although enthusiastic salesmen were promising delivery by Christmas 1935, all the customers actually received in time for the festivities were toy replicas of the car mounted on scraps of marble. One modification made on the 810 has been much lamented by John Bolster, an expert on elegant motoring, in his book *The Upper Crust:* the car lacked running–boards.

"A gentleman's car needs running–boards so that his friends have somewhere flat to stand their glasses when spectating at sporting events. The stylists were evidently teetotallers, for they threw away the running–boards and wings too, replacing those with little mudguards more suitable for a bicycle. This fashion did not appeal for long simply because the cars became so plastered in mud that even the windscreen and windows were covered and the door handles were too dirty to touch. It was then realised that running–boards were necessary, but they were not reinstated. Instead, the front wings were continued in a sweeping curve. The mud was kept down all right but these pseudo running–boards gave poor crash protection and were expensive to replace. Above all, they were entirely useless for their main purpose of supporting glasses."

A **1964 Cord Sportsman** *(top)* with bodywork moulds in the background of the picture.

A **1929 Cord L29** *(above left)* on display, with a notice reading "Stop, look and drool, but please, pretty please, do not touch".

The **L29 Cord Phaeton** *(above)* was made in open and closed versions and cost up to $3000, which was far too expensive for most Depression–hit Americans to contemplate. The car was in production for only three years.

1925 Model A Dusenberg *(left)*, the first production car of the marque and forerunner of the Cord. Though beautifully made, it was not a great seller.

The Model 812 *(above)*, successor to the 810.

Model 810 Cord *(right)*, designed by Gordon Buehrig and featuring retractable headlamps operated by hand. The car was launched at the New York Motor Show in November 1953 with salesmen promising delivery by Christmas, but problems with the gearboxes meant that the only car the customers received by Christmas was a tiny model of the 810 – mounted on marble.

The Hollywood Image

Not surprisingly, the cinema and the motor car grew up together. Both reflected the way in which people lived, or would like to live; both were a reflection of incomes, life–styles, dreams and fantasies. The cinema and the motor car both had their roots in the latter years of the nineteenth century, and during the first thirty years of the twentieth century both managed to achieve a remarkable degree of sophistication.

The cinema was curiously dependent on the motor car, and all manner of vehicles appeared in films long before the noises they made could be heard in the cinema. They provided then, as they still do today, comedy, drama, tension and excitement. One of the most durable and popular elements in action films has been the chase, from the very earliest westerns to films like *The Italian Job*, in which the plot is little more than a scene–setter for one of the most imaginative stunt–driving sequences ever filmed. Other films, like *Bonnie and Clyde* and *American Graffiti*, owe much of their pace and atmosphere to the cars which feature in them.

Off the screen, the luxury car became a tangible symbol of the film star's success. The bigger the star, the bigger the car. Leading ladies had the most stylish limousines and liveried chauffeurs, while the screen images of the leading men were reflected in their sports cars and tourers.

It was only a matter of time before cars became stars in their own right, and so they did: cars such as Genevieve, Herbie, Chitty–Chitty–Bang–Bang and the Yellow Rolls–Royce are perhaps better remembered than their human co–stars – and even Sean Connery, in *Goldfinger*, was hard stretched to hold his own against that scene–stealing Aston Martin.

THE HOLLYWOOD IMAGE
The Chase

It was inevitable that the combination of movies and motor cars would produce The Chase. And it did – right from the start. The early Mack Sennett/Keystone Kops comedies positively revelled not only in the chase but in the crash which invariably followed it. Laurel and Hardy, predictably, never won a chase and Charlie Chaplin's attempt to elope was foiled by one (in a film called *A Jitney Elopement*, in which Edna Purviance played the girlfriend).

As the motor car became more sophisticated, so did the cinema, and the chase. The advent of the talkies made chases very much more realistic, but the motor car was no longer quite such a novelty and it was not until the thrillers of the forties and fifties that the motor car came back into its own. James Cagney and Humphrey Bogart, the great movie tough guys of the period, were involved in the chase as both cops and robbers, but at this stage of the cinema's development, the car was only another prop in the film–maker's repertoire.

The really exciting chases emerged in the films of the late sixties and seventies, some of the most outstanding examples being those which appeared in the James Bond series. The chase through Tokyo in *You Only Live Twice* was typical. The car, specially designed by Toyota, was driven in the chase by Bond's assistant, played by the Japanese actress Akiko Wakabayashi. A six–cylinder GT2000 with a highly tuned engine and a top speed of over 140 mph, the car featured closed–circuit television as well as a video recorder fitted in the glove–box.

In another Bond film, *Diamonds Are Forever*, the getaway vehicle was a "moon buggy". In the twelve–minute chase sequence James Bond, who has "borrowed" the buggy from an experimental space laboratory, drives it at great speed across the rugged desert terrain outside Las Vegas, chased by

Three Minis *(above)* hurtle down the staircase into a Turin arcade during *The Italian Job*. Constantly pursued by the police in an Alfa Romeo, the Minis proved impossible to catch up with, and the film, inadvertently or otherwise, provided marvellous sales propaganda for the Mini.

"Follow that man!" *(left)* – a scene from an early Keystone Kops comedy. Films like this, which made extensive use of specially constructed vehicles, showed the motor car in a new light.

"baddies" in 1971 saloon cars. The latter, needless to say, are considerably the worse for wear at the end of the sequence. The buggy was built for the film by a Hollywood designer, Dean Jeffries, and although it looks not unlike the authentic version which made the moon landing in 1969, the Bond machine was capable of 90 mph by comparison with the original's top speed of 12 mph.

A more conventional car chase featured in *Cleopatra Jones*, a story about a girl government agent who drives a Chevrolet Corvette. The script included a car chase through a dried–up river bed, but heavy rains fell during the filming in Southern California and the Corvette had to be extensively modified in order to stop the engine flooding.

Perhaps the most endearing chase scene was the one in *The Italian Job*, in which a trio of Minis drove through the porticos of Turin, leaped off buildings, dived down sewers and apparently vanished into thin air in front of the Italian police.

Another classic chase occurred in the drug–smuggling thriller *The French Connection*, in which a Pontiac is chased by police around the massive concrete supports of the "El" (elevated railway) in Chicago. The Pontiac was driven in the film by one of Hollywood's top stuntmen, Bill Hickman, who also took part in what is probably the most famous of all film chases – the one in *Bullitt*. The *Bullitt* chase lasted ten minutes, during which Steve McQueen, playing a tough detective, drove a high–performance 1968 390GT Ford Mustang in pursuit of a 1968 440 Magnum Dodge Charger up and down the steep hills of San Francisco. The scenes of the cars hurtling over the brows of the San Francisco hills were authentic, with both cars frequently becoming airborne at speeds of over 100 mph. In view of the considerable dangers involved, McQueen, though an experienced driver and motor–racing devotee, reluctantly let stuntmen drive some of the more hair–raising sequences. Some of the latter were stunted for him by his friend Bud Ekins, who is reported to have earned $1000 a day for the work. Dangerous it may have been – but it did look tremendous fun!

Peter Cook helping to fit his car with skis *(above)* in *Monte Carlo or Bust.* One of many films based on the famous rally, this one was set in the 1920s and made in 1969.

The most celebrated chase of all *(right). Bullitt*, released in 1968, starred Steve McQueen, who is seen here getting airborne in a 390GT Ford Mustang.

Celluloid Stardom

By the 1950s, cars were beginning to assume a new role in film–making – that of stars in their own right. Until that time the car had been purely an addition to the basic plot – albeit an important one – and the vehicles themselves were usually production models or special–effects cars which were designed to come apart in the right places at the right times like those used by Laurel and Hardy in their early comedies.

One of the earliest "car stars" was Genevieve, which appeared in a film of the same name in 1953. The plot was constructed around the London–to–Brighton Veteran Run. Genevieve, a 1905 Darracq, co–starred with Kenneth More, Dinah Sheridan, John Gregson, Kay Kendall and a 1905 four–cylinder Spyker. The motor car had joined children and animals in the categories of co–stars with which actors find it very hard to compete.

Equally successful in its own right was *Chitty–Chitty–Bang–Bang*, a film starring Dick Van Dyke as an inventor who makes his car fly and float. The history of the original car, Chitty–Bang–Bang, goes further back than 1968 when the film was made. The three original cars had been built between 1921 and 1924 by Count Louis Zborowski and all three raced at Brooklands. The most successful one was powered by a 23 litre Maybach airship engine. The cars got their name from the noise they used to make.

Walt Disney's film *The Gnome–Mobile* was based on the Upton Sinclair novel in which the central car star was a small sports car. The Disney studios, feeling that a small car would not be suitable as the central character for a major feature film, decided instead to use a 1930 Rolls–Royce as the vehicle in which two homeless gnomes find their lost colony in the Californian Redwoods. But the size of this car did not deter Disney from using a Volkswagen Beetle as the main character in a series of films about Herbie. In a series of four films – *The Love Bug*, *Herbie*, *Herbie Rides Again* and *Herbie goes to Monte Carlo* – the little car accomplished some amazing feats, many of them accomplished by using top stunt drivers, others being filmed with the help of small–scale models.

The Pink Panther, star of television as well as the cinema screen, is one of a group of custom–built cars which have become enormously popular in the last fifteen years. The Panther is twenty–six feet long and is by no means a cardboard cutout. Built by George Barris, it has a 500 hp engine behind the driver's seat and a lounge compartment equipped with telephone, television set and drinks cupboard. The doors open like wings and the controls are similar to those found in aircraft cockpits.

The Batmobile is even more bizarre. It was built in the mid–1960s, also by George Barris, for a television series of *Batman and Robin*. The glass–fibre body is based on a Ford chassis, and the machine is powered by a V8 engine. The twenty–six–foot body is covered with black flocking and outlined in shocking–pink fluorescent paint. Again the car really works and is fitted with two braking parachutes. The original Batmobile cost $75,000 to build, and as with Chitty–Chitty–Bang–Bang and the Pink Panther, was in such demand for

Tinkering with Genevieve *(above left)*. Alan (John Gregson) works on Genevieve's engine while Wendy (Dinah Sheridan) feeds him on chicken legs. The film *Genevieve (left)* was made in 1953 and directed by Henry Cornelius. As well as Kay Kendall and Kenneth More, the film also starred a 1905 Darracq as Genevieve and a 1905 Spyker as her opposition. At the time the film was made, both cars were believed to be 1904 models and therefore eligible for the London–to–Brighton Veteran Run, around which most of the action is centred. After the film's release, the Veteran Car Club re–dated both cars as 1905 models and so neither has been able to take part in the run again. (31 December 1904 is the latest date of eligibility for the Run.) The Spyker has gone home to Holland, its country of origin, and Genevieve is now in Australia, privately owned.

DINAH **SHERIDAN** JOHN **GREGSON** KAY **KENDALL** KENNETH **MORE**

Genevieve

Colour by TECHNICOLOR

Story and Screenplay by WILLIAM ROSE
Produced and Directed by HENRY CORNELIUS

motor shows and publicity appearances that several replicas had to be made. Amongst the Batmobile accessories are a "detect–a–scope", special fire extinguishers, a revolving closed–circuit television camera and a bullet–proof body.

Elaborate though the Batmobile is, the ultimate in car stars was the Aston Martin used by James Bond in the film of Ian Fleming's epic, *Goldfinger*. Unlike the Pink Panther and the Batmobile, the car was a real production model – but with several differences. There are few Aston Martins on the market which feature an ejector seat, machine–guns, oil sprays, homing devices, wheel–slashing knives which extend from the hub caps and revolving number plates with which to confuse pursuers! The car captured the imagination of the public to such an extent that thousands flocked to see it when it was put on display and the model car which copied it proved to be one of the best–selling toys in history.

The Gnome–Mobile *(left)*: a scene from the Walt Disney film of Upton Sinclair's novel.

Chitty-Chitty-Bang-Bang *(below)*, a fantastic flying car which took its name from three famous racing cars of the 1920s.

Herbie *(above)*, an amazing little Volkswagen Beetle with a mind of its own. The series of enormously popular films in which Herbie starred were very much part of the Volkswagen cult in America, and formed the basis for Herbie fan clubs all over the world.

"Chitty Chitty Bang Bang"
the most fantasmagorical
musical entertainment in the history of everything!

Albert R. Broccoli
Dick Van Dyke
Sally Ann Howes
Lionel Jeffries
in Ian Fleming's
"Chitty Chitty Bang Bang"

with Gert Frobe
Anna Quayle · Benny Hill
and James Robertson Justice · Robert Helpmann

Producer ALBERT R. BROCCOLI · Director KEN HUGHES · Musical Numbers Staged by MARC BREAUX and DEE DEE WOOD
Music and Lyrics by RICHARD M. SHERMAN and ROBERT B. SHERMAN · Music Supervised and Conducted by IRWIN KOSTAL
Screenplay by ROALD DAHL and KEN HUGHES · Production Designer KEN ADAM · Filmed in SUPER-PANAVISION · TECHNICOLOR · **United Artists**

The original soundtrack album including 12 exciting new songs is now available on United Artists Records.

Dramatic Vehicles

It was Mack Sennett who first realised the potential value of the car on film, and it is said that his inspiration came from the Bible: Ezekiel, Chapter 10, v. 10 – "As if a wheel had been in the midst of a wheel." Whatever the source of his inspiration, the film debut of the motor car with the Keystone Kops added a new dimension to film–making. The potential of the motor car for comedy was endless and the Kops were followed by Charlie Chaplin, Harold Lloyd, Laurel and Hardy and W. C. Fields, who, in a film called *The 300 Yard Drive*, attempted to play a round of golf in one. In 1921, Broadway saw the first full–length comedy play based on the motor car. Called *Six–Cylinder Love*, it went on to become a film two years later.

The car was not only used for comedy. It provided the ideal medium for every type of drama from romances to thrillers –

being more manageable than a train and more versatile than a horse or a bicycle. Jean Harlow seduced in cars, and Garbo smouldered in them. *A Woman of Affairs*, made in 1928 starring Greto Garbo and directed by Clarence Brown, features Garbo and her leading man John Gilbert getting away from it all in a motor car – not so surprising in view of the fact that Brown had started his career working as a mechanic for the Duryea company.

The classic screen villains needed cars for a very different sort of getaway. Humphrey Bogart, James Cagney and Edward G. Robinson frequently came to a sticky end at the wheel with the police in hot pursuit. The majority of war films would have been impossible without vehicles of all shapes sizes and nationalities.

The car also took on a new significance in the film of John Steinbeck's classic novel *The Grapes of Wrath*, in which the Joad family fled the dustbowl of Oklahoma in a battered pick–up truck, hoping to make a new home in California. The film

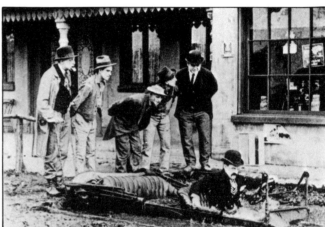

Automobile in trouble *(above right* and *left)*: shots from a typical two–reel silent comedy of the 1920s, starring the Australian comedian Snub Pollard (1886–1962).

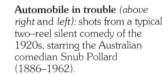

Harold Lloyd *(left)* in one of his early silent films, co–starring with an unlikely–looking vehicle named "Butterfly Six".

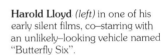

Graham Hill *(above right)* talks to director John Frankenheimer during the making of the film *Grand Prix*, released in 1966. Part of the car has been cut away to allow the camera to be bolted onto the front.

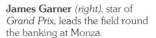

James Garner *(right)*, star of *Grand Prix*, leads the field round the banking at Monza.

vividly illustrated how the car had given mobility even to those who had suffered during the Depression.

From the earliest days of silent films, motor racing has attracted film–makers and film stars alike. *Burn 'em Up Barnes* – a twelve–episode serial shot in 1934 – contains some of the most entertaining racing sequences of the pre–war era as well as a shot of a car being driven down the Capitol steps. It is a far cry from that to the modern motor–racing epics starring Paul Newman *(Winning)* and Steve McQueen *(Le Mans)*, both avid motor–racing enthusiasts. Perhaps the ultimate motor–racing film is John Frankenheimer's *Grand Prix*, which made extensive use of actual motor–racing footage as well as of the racing drivers themselves.

The car was of very little use in front of the cameras in the great Hollywood epics such as *The Ten Commandments* and *Ben–Hur*, but none of them could have been made without the help of the motor car behind the scenes. In *The Last of the Mohicans*, made by Clarence Brown in 1920, Brown improvised a camera trolley, which he called a perambulator, from a Ford axle and wheels, with a handle to pull it down the road. An early type of camera–car kept pace with the chariots in the 1925 version of *Ben–Hur*, on a day when forty–two cameramen shot 53,000 feet of film for a sequence which eventually only used 750.

The move towards realism in films brought about the demise of the back–projection technique for high–speed action sequences. Today's chases, whether on horseback or in cars, are shot "live" on location with cameramen operating from the backs of specially modified cars or pick–up trucks. These work–horse vehicles of the film–maker also carry powerful winches, batteries of lights, generators, control equipment and countless other accessories required by the special–effects technicians – including huge fans for the creation of wind and sand– and dust–storms. In film–making, as in many other industries, the car has a multitude of roles to fill from the most glamorous to the most mundane.

"Positions, please"

see illustration overleaf

The early days of the cinema mirrored to a surprising extent the early days of the motor industry. There was no established ladder up which the protagonists of either could climb with any guarantee of success. By the 1920s, the car was playing an important role in the film world. Apart from making the sheer logistics of filming easier, it was also beginning to emerge as a personality in its own right. Directors looking for an atmosphere of intimacy, nostalgia, danger – or humour – often found it in the inanimate motor car.

THE HOLLYWOOD IMAGE
Struggling through the Lean Years

Makers of luxury motor cars had cause to be extremely grateful to Hollywood in the twenties and thirties. While America was in the grip of the Depression, stars of the silver screen were among the very few who could still afford extravagant motor cars. The list of famous names with famous cars is seemingly endless, because a glamorous car was as much a part of the film star's stock in trade as a stylish partner and a luxury home. Whether it was the studio or the star that actually paid for these accoutrements was largely irrelevant: the resultant publicity was of value to the star and the studio alike – to say nothing of the manufacturer of the car.

Hollywood's favourite type of car was, of course, the convertible. Put a convertible on a studio lot, set up a wind machine behind it and there, on the screen, will be an image of freedom, speed and excitement. As a prop, it was versatile, too. Actors could stand up in it, jump out of it, play a love scene in it – yet, even sitting down, remain visible to their audience. Off–screen, the convertible was a mobile platform from which celebrities could acknowledge their admiring public.

Hollywood's location in the sunny climes of the USA's West Coast also contributed to the convertible's popularity: had Jean Harlow appeared in her giant Packard soaked to the skin, her glamour would undoubtedly have been subdued.

Meanwhile, as Hollywood basked in sunshine and luxury, the rest of America struggled to make ends meet. Not for the ordinary people the flashy convertible with the plush leather interior: if they could afford any car at all, it was a broken–down truck. The ideal car for the times – small, enclosed and economical – had yet to be invented.

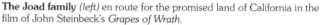

The Joad family *(left)* en route for the promised land of California in the film of John Steinbeck's *Grapes of Wrath*.

Al Jolson *(left)* taking delivery of a 1936 Buick.

Errol Flynn *(below left)* sitting at the wheel of a 1935 supercharged Auburn.

James Cagney *(right)* at the studio with a 1932 Auburn 12.

Gary Cooper *(below right)* in his original 1930 Derham Tourster Duesenberg "in Goldenrod Yellow with pale green fenders". Later he had a special boat–tail back built to replace the car's separate boot.

Jean Harlow *(bottom right)* stepping into her 1932 Packard.

The Racers

A great racing driver is one who takes to the race–track with a combination of skill, courage, sensitivity and obsession. For motor racing is the most demanding and dangerous sport there is – as well as one of the most glamorous. It has been so ever since the first motor–sport event, the Paris–Rouen Reliability Trial of 1894.

Motor sport breeds personalities. In the early days drivers were recognisable by their driving styles as well as by the cars they drove. Today, the arms and elbows have given way to helmet decorations and sponsors' decals as means of recognition. Radio and television now bring the drivers out of their cars and into people's homes, giving the public a chance to judge whether the heroes of the track are as articulate off the race circuit as they are on it.

Circuits too have changed – the dirt–tracks and straw bales of yesterday have been transformed into a network of steel barriers and catch–fencing, and if they so desire spectators can relax over a three–course meal in the comfort of the track restaurant.

Aldous Huxley once claimed that speed is the only genuinely modern pleasure: perhaps that is one reason why, year after year, motor racing continues to draw the crowds. The demands it makes of men and machines are huge – at times even intolerable. Nevertheless, its importance – to those who take part in it, to those who watch it and, in contemporary motor sport, to those who sponsor it – makes this worth while. It may have the added advantages of providing mobile test–beds and public showcases for the cars themselves, but these are very much a spin–off rather than a *raison d'être* for the sport. Essentially, it is man's love of speed that keeps motor racing alive.

THE RACERS
First in the Field

Almost as soon as there were motor cars, there was motor sport. And almost as soon as there was motor sport, there had to be race–tracks. The world's first real race–track was opened on 6 July 1907 at Weybridge in Surrey; it was called Brooklands. The land on which it was built formed part of an estate belonging to Hugh Locke–King, a keen motor sport enthusiast, and to build Brooklands, 2000 men cleared thirty acres of woodland, diverted the River Wey and used 200,000 tons of cement. They created a pear–shaped track, a hundred feet wide, with steeply banked curves at each end.

Originally, Brooklands was intended as a test track for car manufacturers, but soon after the official opening, its future was assured by an attempt by Selwyn Edge on the American–held world twenty–four–hour record. Driving a 60 hp Napier, Edge covered 1581 miles at an average speed of 65·905 mph, stopping only for fuel and tyre changes. His record stood for seventeen years.

The first race meeting to be held at Brooklands took place on the opening day and consisted of several short races in which the drivers were identified by the colours of their shirts, following standard horse–racing practice.

Members of the Brooklands Automobile Racing Club had their own enclosure and a clubhouse for which they paid an annual subscription of five guineas. There were 30,000 seats for the public and on days when there was no racing, anyone could drive around the track, the fee being ten shillings for cars and five shillings for motor cycles.

Unlike race–tracks on the Continent, Brooklands was a very carefully run circuit. It had to be, for it was built in a residential area and local inhabitants with gardens bordering the race–track complained not only about the noise but also about

the fumes, which, they alleged, damaged their raspberries.

By 1912 Brooklands was booming and continued to do so until after the First World War. All the great British names in motor sport were to be seen there regularly – Malcolm Campbell, Kaye Don, W. O. Bentley and Henry Seagrave among many others. Brooklands was also the home of internationally famous races – Empire Trophies, the 200s, the Double Twelves, a 1000–mile event and the first British Grand Prix, sponsored by the RAC, held in 1926.

The first lap record at Brooklands was set up in June 1908 by Felice Nazzaro driving a Fiat Mephistopheles. Although his time was never officially recognised, it was accepted as 89·5 mph. The last record was set by John Cobb on 7 October 1935 in a Napier–Railton at a speed of 143·44 mph.

Motor racing at Brooklands was quite unlike anything to be found at other tracks. Drivers "stabled their mounts", meetings had their selling plates and handicaps and until 1908 the starter was provided by the Jockey Club. When the track reopened after the First World War, the clubhouse was still serving an excellent Sunday lunch and tennis courts were provided for the additional entertainment of the members and their guests. Bookies had their stands in the paddock and the atmosphere was very much that of the socially more acceptable horse–race meeting.

An enthusiastic amateur driver could have an entertaining season's racing for an outlay of about £200. His car would probably cost £180; garaging at Brooklands cost nothing, and fuel, oil and plugs came free from the manufacturers.

Finally the Second World War called a halt to the activities at Brooklands. The last race to be run there was held on August Bank Holiday 1939, although a last–ditch attempt to break the lap record was made on the eve of the declaration of war. By the time the war was over, the track was unrecognis-able. There were buildings on parts of the circuit, the banking was overgrown and even young trees had broken through the concrete surface of the track.

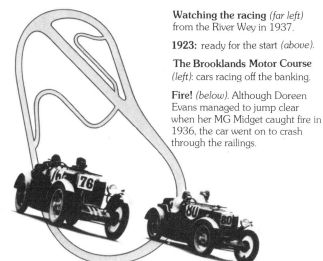

Watching the racing *(far left)* from the River Wey in 1937.

1923: ready for the start *(above)*.

The Brooklands Motor Course *(left)*: cars racing off the banking.

Fire! *(below)*. Although Doreen Evans managed to jump clear when her MG Midget caught fire in 1936, the car went on to crash through the railings.

The driver of a Type 13 Bugatti *(above)* encounters a problem on a 1920 hill climb in front of an enthusiastic crowd.

J. Lemon Burton *(left)* racing his T59 Bugatti up the Prescott hill climb in 1939. The event was won by the Bugatti works driver Jean Pierre Wimille in a similar car.

THE RACERS
The Race-track King

To many motoring enthusiasts the name of Bugatti epitomises some of the most important developments in the history of the motor car. Certainly Ettore Bugatti was a complex figure – a brilliant inventor, unorthodox engineer, artist and cult figure. His greatest achievements were in the realms of motor sport, where he reigned supreme for more than a decade, and those same cars are still winning races today.

Ettore Bugatti was born in Milan in 1881 but lived for most of his life in France. His family was artistic and Ettore found art in the engines he designed. As a young man he built and raced motor cycles and tricycles and his talent was immediately recognised by motor car manufacturers. He designed and engineered vehicles for de Dietrich, Mathis, Isotta–Fraschini and Deutz, but in 1909 resigned from that firm and moved to Molsheim in Alsace to set up his own business. With his friend and business associate Ernest Friedrich, and financial help from the Darmstadt Bank, Bugatti produced his own first car, usually referred to as Type 13, which had an 8–valve, four-cylinder engine. (The Bugatti type numbers are somewhat confusing, although several attempts have been made to put them into chronological order.)

The Type 13 was immediately successful in local motor sporting events and the Bugatti factory, housed in an old dye–works, expanded rapidly. Bugatti and Friedrich went on to complete a new 7 hp prototype known as the Bébé Bugatti, the licence for which they sold to Peugeot, where it became known as the first Bébé Peugeot.

At Molsheim, Bugatti continued to improve the Type 13, producing power and handling which amazed the motoring world. The sporting successes of the Bugattis on both sides of the Atlantic established Bugatti as a serious manufacturer, and his next car – with a new sixteen–valve engine – confirmed the fact. The First World War interrupted the flow of Bugatti models, while the man himself concentrated on aero engines. However, once the war was over, Bugatti re–emerged as almost unbeatable.

It was not only the cars which captured the imagination of the public. Ettore Bugatti was a man of considerable charm and style. He was fanatical about the cleanliness of his factory, which he frequently toured on a bicycle of his own design, dressed in riding breeches, boots, a red waistcoat and a yellow

The Schlumpf Story

One of the strangest stories in the annals of motoring is that of the Schlumpf brothers of Mulhouse, Strasbourg. Hans and Fritz Schlumpf made their fortunes in the textile industry, but shared an interest in cars that amounted to obsession. Over a thirty-year period, they built up a collection of beautiful and expensive cars, which no one other than themselves, their personal visitors and the mechanics employed to keep the cars in mint condition was allowed to see.

Eventually, in March 1977, the workers of their own textile factory revolted, by occupying the museum and declaring the collection open to the world. Inside, they found nearly 500 superb and costly cars, including the world's biggest collection of Bugattis. The latter, comprising over 130 cars, includes two of the only six Royales ever made. As well as the museum, the building houses three banqueting rooms complete with chandeliers, gilt mirrors, period furniture and the Schlumpfs' specially bottled champagne.

Before the revolt, the brothers had promised on several occasions that they would open the museum to the public, but never took steps to carry this out. Had the workers not taken matters into their own hands, this Aladdin's cave might still be unopened.

coat. He was passionate about horses and it was from his love of thoroughbred animals that he drew the concept of "pur sang" (thoroughbred) – a phrase which he applied to his cars. Apart from his factory and stables, Bugatti also owned a distillery which produced liqueurs, a generator for electricity, and a hotel called "L'Hostellerie du Pur Sang", where the size of the bill depended on the popularity of the guest with the owner. In an era of colourful characters, Ettore Bugatti shone. He was also a keen inventor and accumulated more than 500 patents for such diverse and unlikely devices as venetian blinds and fishing rod reels.

But Bugatti was not prepared to adopt technical innovation solely for reasons of fashion: he stuck resolutely to his own principles. His domination of motor sport culminated with the Type 35, which made its debut at the 1924 French Grand Prix. Many people still consider the Type 35 to be the most aesthetically satisfying racing car ever produced. After its appearance at the French Grand Prix, *Autocar* reported: "When it appeared for the race, the little horizon–blue car captured the imagination immediately. It was so well finished with its nickelled axles and controls, its almost show–polished engine and its shapely radiator, that it was the kind of toy which enthusiasts had only to see to desire."

Despite its appearance, the first Type 35 was not a success, but subsequent versions redeemed the Bugatti reputation and it was on the Type 35 and its derivatives that the Bugatti cult was founded. The cars were small, light, easy to handle and good–looking. They had straight–8, 2 litre engines and cast aluminium wheels with integral brake drums. By 1927 Bugatti was claiming more than 2000 motor sport successes and in 1926 his cars had won no less than twelve major Grands Prix. But it was not only on the track that his cars were successful: they were also in great demand as road cars, although a contemporary writer, Mr E. N. Duffield, writing in *Automotor Journal* in March 1925, described driving a Type 30 Bugatti on the road as "using a Grand National winner to haul a cart full of mangolds".

Bugatti's most remarkable road car was undoubtedly the Royale – a product of Ettore Bugatti's ambition to build the biggest, best and most beautiful car ever seen. Only six of these huge cars were ever built, and despite the name no member of any royal family ever owned one. The original car had a 15 litre engine, although the remaining five had 12·5 litre units, and cost £6500 – more than twice as much as an equivalent Rolls–Royce. All six are still in existence today – a permanent tribute to one of the most remarkable men in automotive history.

A Winning Combination

The name Auto–Union, and its famous four–ringed badge, epitomises the German supremacy in motor sport in the years immediately before the Second World War. Auto–Union – an amalgam of Audi, DKW, Horch and Wanderer – had been formed so that the four companies might survive the German economic depression which followed the First World War. The new composite company was heavily subsidised by the Hitler regime, which hoped to disseminate propaganda through motor sport. The Auto–Union Grand Prix car, designed by Dr Ferdinand Porsche, had a 4·4 litre, V16 engine mounted behind the driver, and was very fast indeed. Despite an unsuccessful debut at Arvus, it went on to win the 1934 German Grand Prix – the first rear–engined car to win a Grand Prix formula race.

The Supreme Test

Of all motor sport events, the one which captures the imagination of enthusiasts the world over is the Le Mans 24–hour race. The event was born out of an extremely lively motor club, the Automobile Club de l'Ouest, and the existence of a circuit which had first been used for racing in 1906 and which had hosted the first French Grand Prix to be held after the First World War. At a meeting at the Paris Motor Show in October 1922 three men, Charles Faroux, Georges Durand and Emile Coquille, discussed the idea of running a new sort of motor race based on endurance rather than speed. Faroux suggested that the cars should be exactly as they were advertised in the manufacturers' catalogues and Durand, an energetic motor sport organiser, proposed that it should last for twenty–four hours. He also managed, somehow, to obtain the necessary permissions for the race to take place – for the Le Mans circuit is partly on public roads.

The first race took place in 1923. The rules were simple and required, amongst other things, that cars with open bodywork should have a protective hood which must stay in place for at least twenty laps and that, in the event of a breakdown, the driver had to repair the car himself without help. The race was a gruelling test for production cars, which were not renowned for their reliability, but the first, held in June 1923, was won by Lagache and Leonard in a 3 litre Chenard et Walcker at an average speed of 57·21 mph. The race immediately became an established date in the motor sport calendar and, apart from a gap during the Second World War, has taken place annually ever since.

Today the race at Le Mans has become a legend. Every year about half a million spectators arrive at the circuit, many of them with tents and sleeping bags, prepared to spend the best part of a week there. The circuit becomes a giant village with fairgrounds, churches, restaurants, dance halls and shops. Even agriculture in the area is geared to Le Mans week.

Le Mans by night (above). All the fun of the fair as the cars roar on through the night.

Spectators overlooking the pit counter (below) during practice for the 1977 24–hour race. The boxes behind the pits are reserved for timekeepers and mechanics, but the stands above the pits, which are highly priced, are coveted for the first–class view they provide of the action. In the centre is the British driver–turned–team–manager Vic Elford.

The strong arm of the law (right). All police leave is cancelled during race week. Gendarmes drafted in to control the crowd sleep under canvas.

An enthusiastic crowd invades the track after the 1978 race (far right above).

A closer view of the cars (far right below) after the race.

Fast through the Esses (above): Lang and Riess in the 300 SL Mercedes in which they won the Le Mans 24–hour race in 1952.

Farmers plant acres of lettuces ready for the demand and even the chickens are programmed to be at their tasty best at the beginning of June. The race is reported by more than 450 journalists and in 1970 the organisers estimated that more than twenty miles of film were exposed on the race. There are special trains which remain in sidings so that passengers can use them as hotels, and every bed in every private house for miles around is fully occupied.

The race has not been without its problems. In 1955 it was the scene of the biggest motor racing disaster in history when, during the third hour of the race, a Mercedes–Benz 300 SLR, driven by Pierre Levegh, catapulted over the bank and landed in an enclosure opposite the pits killing the driver and eighty–five spectators. The organisers decided not to stop the race, believing that to do so would hinder the complex emergency rescue operation, but two days later the French Government banned motor sport in France for an indefinite period, as had been done in 1903 after the disastrous Paris–Madrid Race.

During the early years of the race, the British were very much in command – Bentleys winning it in the four years from 1927 to 1930. The legendary "Bentley Boys", led by Captain Woolf Barnato, seemed unbeatable in their big green cars and had a tremendous following. It is interesting that race wins have frequently fallen in sequences – the Bentley wins being followed by four years of Alfa Romeo success. In the fifties Jaguar reigned supreme for five years and in the sixties Ferraris clocked up six consecutive wins. Then it was the turn of Ford for four years before the French Matra team pulled off three wins in the seventies to bring the trophies back to France.

It is undeniable that Le Mans is the most strenuous race in the calendar, for both men and machines – not only for the drivers (there must be two to each car, sharing the driving) but also for the mechanics and pit crews, who are alert throughout the night to service, repair and refuel the cars. Although some professional drivers dislike the race because it mixes small and large cars with inexperienced and professional drivers, the event is still enormously popular with the crowds – and more importantly with manufacturers, for whom a Le Mans win is the ultimate accolade. There is no other race quite like it.

THE RACERS
Racing in the Park

In 1935 a motor race called the Donington Grand Prix, held at a relatively unknown circuit in the English Midlands, marked the emergence of Britain as a major motor–racing force. Donington Park stands on the site of an ancient manor near the River Trent, which for generations had belonged to the Marquises of Hastings, the last of whom died in 1868. Following his death the estate passed through several hands, and was finally bought in 1928 by Mr J. Gillies Shields, who had been agent to the estate for nearly fifty years.

In the meantime, the Derby and District Motor Club had been formed and its energetic secretary, Fred Cramer, was hunting for a suitable venue for motor–cycle races. Mr Shields was sufficiently enthusiastic about motor sport to allow races to take place on some of the drives and paths in the Park. He then agreed to lay down a permanent circuit and in 1933 cars raced there for the first time. The circuit was then 2·19 miles long and lay through one of the estate farms. The track was narrow and winding, but meetings were popular with drivers and spectators alike, particularly those for whom the southern home of motor sport, Brooklands, was too far away.

The golden years of Donington were 1937 and 1938, when the initiative of Fred Cramer persuaded the Mercedes and Auto–Union teams to race on the recently enlarged circuit. Grand Prix motor racing was totally dominated by these two teams, both heavily backed by government money in order that they might prove their supremacy over other countries. In 1937 they came to Donington at the end of a hectic season in which Mercedes seemed unbeatable, but in the Donington Grand Prix it was the turn of Auto–Union to take the chequered flag, with the brilliant Bernd Rosemeyer just beating Caracciola's Mercedes. The two teams shared the lap record at 85·62 mph. The following year the Donington Grand Prix was overshadowed by the threat of war. There were rumours of general mobilisation in Germany, slit trenches were being dug in Hyde Park, and air raid shelters were sprouting like mushrooms all over the country. The race was scheduled for 8 October and a huge crowd was anticipated, for the two German teams with their fleets of vehicles and armies of mechanics had become a motor–racing legend. As it happened, before the race took place the Germans were twice ordered to pack up and leave Germany and twice they were halted by signals from Berlin.

The race itself was a sensational success. The huge crowd saw many of the cars eliminated by oil on the track, and witnessed the great Tazio Nuvolari bring his 3 litre Auto–Union home two minutes ahead of Herman Lang's Mercedes. It was a fitting end to pre–war Donington, for shortly after the outbreak of war the Park was requisitioned by the Government and no motor racing was seen there for many years. But in 1971 a local entrepreneur, Tom Wheatcroft, bought the circuit and rebuilt the track and facilities, enabling international motor racing to return to Donington in 1976.

After the war, it became obvious that although the greater

Alberto Ascari (above right) leading Luigi Villoresi around the straw bales on the first lap of the 1948 British Grand Prix, the first International Grand Prix to be held in Britain since 1927 and the first major event at Britain's newest motor–racing circuit, Silverstone. The race was won by Villoresi driving a Maserati. Villoresi set a lap record for the new circuit of 76·82 mph. Second was Ascari in another Maserati and third was Bob Gerard of Britain, who drove an ERA.

Donington 1938 (right): despite oil on the track, Tazio Nuvolari wins the Grand Prix in an Auto–Union at an average speed of 80·49 mph.

Troops (centre right) lining the track at the start of the 1938 British Empire Trophy Race, held at Donington.

Froilan Gonzales (far right), ace Argentinian driver and close friend of Fangio, wins the 1954 British Grand Prix at Silverstone.

part of the European motor industry was in disarray, enthusiasm for motor sport had not diminished. Apart from general interest in the sport, motor racing is an important shop window for car–makers and has played a vital part in the development of the passenger car, being a mobile test–bed for some of the most advanced engineering techniques. It was clearly important that motor racing should restart as soon as it was practical. The French held their first race meeting in record time, in the Bois de Boulogne in September 1945, and were the guiding force behind a new controlling body for motor sport, called the FIA (Fédération Internationale Automobile), which had its headquarters in Paris. The FIA devised a new Grand Prix formula for cars of not over 1·5 litres supercharged, and not over 4·5 litres unsupercharged.

The French having set the pace, the Italians were eager to join in with their highly competitive Alfa Romeos. The Germans were in no state to indulge in motor sport, but the British were anxiously searching for new venues – both Brooklands and Donington having been effectively destroyed by their wartime tenants. By the autumn of 1948, two new British circuits had been established. One was Goodwood, home of the Duke of Richmond and Gordon, at the foot of the Sussex Downs, and the other was a disused airfield near Towcester, called Silverstone. It was here, on 2 October 1948, that the circuit was inaugurated with the first post–war RAC British Grand Prix, won by Luigi Villoresi driving a Maserati. Now the home of the venerable British Racing Drivers Club, Silverstone holds the longest unbroken record of any British racing circuit and enormous expenditure has made it one of

the best–equipped circuits in the world. It is also one of the fastest – and probably the wettest; several historic races have been curtailed by torrential rain, which gives the spectators excitement and the competitors headaches.

For the first seven years of its existence, Silverstone hosted the British Grand Prix, which it now shares with Brands Hatch. It also introduced a race of its own to the international calendar, the International Trophy – the longest–established non–championship Formula 1 race – giving the crowds a chance to see the Grand Prix protagonists at the beginning of the motor–racing season.

The first post–war British Grand Prix having been won by Villoresi, it was ten years before a British driver was to win the event at Silverstone. Then it was Peter Collins, driving a Ferrari, who delighted the home crowd, but the intervening years had not been without excitement. Ferrari had dominated the Silverstone scene with epic drives by Froilan Gonzales in 1951 and 1954, Alberto Ascari in 1952 and 1953, and the master, Juan Manuel Fangio, in 1956.

However, it was the British Grand Prix of 1975 which proved Silverstone to be safe as well as fast, when one of the biggest accidents in Grand Prix history happened at the end of the first lap. Jody Scheckter, lying fourth, lost control coming out of the fast Woodcote corner, bounced off the pit wall and brought the rest of the field to a virtual standstill. Miraculously there were no serious injuries. The race was restarted and was to prove equally sensational – Peter Revson winning it from Peterson, Hulme and Hunt with only 3·4 seconds covering the four of them as they crossed the finishing line.

Opening ceremony at the Nurburgring circuit *(above)* in 1927, before the start of the first race ever held there. This was a sports–car race with three Mercedes in the front row – car no. 1 driven by Carraciola in pole position, car no. 2 driven by Rosenberger, and car no. 3 driven by von Mosch. The cars finished in the same order.

Paul Pietsch *(below)* attempts to explain to the Alfa Romeo mechanics how his car came to be on a road outside the Nurburgring circuit during the 1951 German Grand Prix. In fact, Pietsch had lost control on the North Curve, and the car had flown over the banking and landed on a road below. The car was a write–off, but Pietsch was unhurt.

Dicing with Death

The Nurburgring, forty miles south of Cologne in Germany, is the longest and probably the most dangerous motor–racing circuit in the world. Built during the economic depression following the First World War, in order to provide work for the unemployed, the circuit is 14·19 miles long and rises to 1250 feet. It has 172 corners, many of them bordered by steep drops to the valley below, and few drivers have completely conquered it, although many have crashed there.

A crowd of more than half a million watched "Rudi" Caracciola in the latest Mercedes–Benz "S" model win the opening race at the Nurburgring in 1927. For the sheer number of victories, Caracciola rates as one of the greatest drivers of all time. A German, despite his name, he won amongst other races every Continental Grand Prix at least once, and the German Grand Prix six times. In a career which lasted from 1922 to 1952, he drove exclusively for Daimler–Benz, apart from a brief time with Alfa Romeo in 1932, and his prowess at the Nurburgring earned him the nickname of "Der Regenmeister" (the Ringmaster).

As with Ferrari at Monza, the Nurburgring was the home track for Mercedes–Benz cars, and the five years from 1934 to 1939 stand out in motor–racing history. Spurred on by the formation of the Auto–Union company and "encouraged" by the German Government, Daimler–Benz went Grand Prix racing despite the worsening economic situation. The organisation behind their efforts has become a motor sport legend, displaying unbelievable Teutonic thoroughness. Each season the team took part in at least ten major events and before each of them the racing department at Stuttgart analysed the track to ensure that the cars were correctly prepared in every detail.

Under the famous team manager Alfred Neubauer, the Mercedes–Benz circus itself was as stunning to see as the cars on the track. The team consisted of eight large diesel trucks, which carried racing cars, practice cars and spare engines, as well as tons of spare parts. There were two crews of racing mechanics with twenty–five men in each and a vast mobile workshop, as well as a high–speed truck standing by to make urgent deliveries of last–minute requirements. After each event the cars went back to the factory and were completely overhauled before the next event. The German Government subsidised the operation heavily in the expectation that the silver cars with the three–pointed star would demonstrate German supremacy all over Europe – and in general the Government was not disappointed.

Caracciola was not the only driver to make history at the Nurburgring. A bow–legged Argentinian, who burst upon the European racing scene in 1949, drove the best race of a very great career at the Nurburgring when, despite a pit stop during the 1957 German Grand Prix, he caught and passed the Ferraris of Mike Hawthorn and Peter Collins, breaking the lap record ten times in the process. Juan Manuel Fangio was the greatest driver the sport has ever known – World Champion five times and winner of twenty–four major Grands Prix. Unlike Caracciola, he drove several makes of car, winning the world championships in Alfa Romeo, Mercedes–Benz, Ferrari and Maserati machines before he finally retired in 1958.

Today, the Nurburgring is another circuit under threat of closure. Its sheer length makes it impossible to make every foot of the track secure, and the Grand Prix drivers now question whether it is safe enough for today's extremely high–powered Formula 1 cars. But its superb facilities and unique atmosphere make it inconceivable that the Nurburgring will go for good.

A Lola follows a Ford Capri
(above) at the Nurburgring.

James Hunt *(left)* waits for
something to happen in the pits
during practice for the 1000–
kilometre race at Nurburgring in
1973. This annual classic was won
by Ickx and Redman driving a
Ferrari, while Hunt, in a Gulf
Mirage, was unplaced. This was
the first year that James Hunt had
been seriously considered as a
world–class driver. A year earlier
he had been rescued from
obscurity by Lord Hesketh and
given a Formula 1 drive. Three
years later he was World
Champion.

A novel vantage point *(below)*.

The Spa Circuit

The Spa–Francorchamps came into being on public
roads in 1924, and in the following year hosted the
first Belgian Grand Prix, which was won by Ascari in
an Alfa Romeo at an average speed of 74·56 mph,
his last race before being killed at the French Grand
Prix in a similar car. The original Spa track was
narrow and winding, but by the 1950s the circuit had
been transformed into one of Europe's fastest tracks
with wide, sweeping bends and very fast straights. In
1970, after a series of accidents on this very long and
dangerous circuit, the Grand Prix drivers vetoed it.
Despite public protest, the Belgian Grand Prix was
moved, and Spa is now used only for saloon and
sports–car races.

THE RACERS
Two Faces of Motor Racing

The face of Juan Manuel Fangio tells its own story, as he mourns, with Froilan Gonzales, the death of their compatriot Marimon during practice at the Nurburgring in 1954. Motor racing is dangerous, frightening and often infinitely sad. Moments of glory – like that below in which John Surtees celebrates his victory at the 1964 German Grand Prix – are less frequent, and are short–lived. But if motor racing is so dangerous, why do people go on

doing it, particularly after seeing friends lose their lives in the pursuit of speed? No one can really answer the question. Perhaps it takes more courage to retire than to continue. Fangio had that courage. He retired in 1958 because he recognised that he no longer wished to drive himself to the brink of death.

The glamour of motor racing comes not so much from the driving as from the world around it. To lie behind a steering wheel, cocooned in fuel tanks, at speeds of up to 150 mph is in no way glamorous. The glamour described by the media – the yachts in the harbour at Monaco, the victory champagne, the private jets of the world champions, the blondes and the swimming pools – is the public face of motor racing, the face which it turns to the world for adulation. The private face – the sweat, agony and heartbreak – it keeps to itself.

Stirling Moss once said: "It is hard to be a racing driver – very hard." Only the drivers know just how hard.

THE RACERS
Monaco-Monza Magic

If Nurburgring is the most daunting race circuit, Monaco is certainly the most picturesque – twisting round the harbour and houses of Monte Carlo to provide a perfect setting for the most socially acceptable event in the motor–racing calendar. First used in 1929, the circuit remained unchanged until 1973, when the harbour section was slightly extended to give a circuit length of 2·06 miles. For drivers it is a difficult track – there are no escape roads and few convenient passing places – but for the spectators, particularly those fortunate enough to be watching from the deck of a yacht or the terrace of a luxury hotel, the Monaco Grand Prix has unparalleled charm.

The winner of the first Monaco Grand Prix was a Mr W. Williams driving a Type 35B Bugatti. He was an Englishman living in France and won the race at an average speed of 50·23 mph with the fastest lap of 52·7 mph. In fact the Monaco circuit has always been a lucky one for British drivers – more than half the post–war races having been won by British or Commonwealth drivers. A particular favourite with the crowds was Stirling Moss, who before his retirement after a near–fatal accident, won the Monaco Grand Prix three times, once in a Maserati and twice in a Lotus. For sheer versatility Moss was hard to beat; it is most unfortunate that in a brilliant fourteen-year career the World Championship always eluded him.

Graham Hill, on the other hand, not only secured two World Championships, in 1962 with a BRM and in 1968 with a Lotus, but also won the Monaco Grand Prix five times – a record in itself. Graham Hill was a driver characterised by sheer determination. From his first race, when he spun his Austin Seven on every lap (which must also be something of a record) he fought his way into the top league of drivers by hard work and persistence. Driving a Lola he won the Indianapolis 500 at his first attempt in 1966, but broke both legs in a bad crash at the US Grand Prix in 1969. The story of his return to racing echoes the same determination shown in his driving, but he finally decided to retire and become a constructor. His last drive was at the International Trophy Race at Silverstone in 1975, only a few months before he was killed in a flying accident, but it is as the master at Monaco that the crowds will remember him best.

In Italy, motor sport has always had a following unrivalled by any other country in the world, save possibly Argentina. So it was scarcely surprising that after the end of the First World War it was Italy which took the lead in the revival of the sport. The first major post–war race was the Targa Florio, which was held in November 1919. The first car away was an Alfa Romeo driven by a rather mediocre driver called Enzo Ferrari, and the race was won by a Frenchman, André Boillot, in a Peugeot. Boillot made motor–racing history by crossing the finishing line backwards, having spun to avoid spectators on the road.

It took rather longer for Grand Prix racing to get its breath back after the war, but by 1921 it had regained its former status, with Italy demonstrating its enthusiasm by completing, in record time, a magnificent circuit called the Monza Autodrome. The first post–war European Grand Prix was held there in 1922 in front of a record crowd of 150,000, all of whom had to pay an admission fee. This practice, hitherto unheard of in Italy, where most racing was on public roads, was not received with any great enthusiasm by the spectators, but it enabled the organisers to offer £6000 in prize money.

The Monza circuit, ten miles north–east of Milan, was then 3·6 miles long with high–speed banking making it almost excessively fast. The first race on the circuit, however, appears

The 1933 Monaco Grand Prix *(above)*. Achille Varzi, who won the race in a Bugatti, leads the Alfa Romeo of Nuvolari at the station.

Graham Hill *(below)*, five times winner of the Monaco Grand Prix, three times in a BRM and twice driving a Lotus.

to have been a somewhat tedious affair, held in the rain and with only eight starters. But with the gradual return of the great teams to motor racing, Monza became the scene of some historic races.

The 1923 Grand Prix saw two famous prototypes make their sole appearances. One, the P1, was withdrawn after one of the drivers, Sivocci, was killed in practice. The other was a revolutionary mid–engined Mercedes with a cigar–shaped body, known as the "Tropfenwagen" (drop–shaped car), which had been refused an entry at the French Grand Prix. But despite its unusual shape, the car was not successful.

The design of the Monza circuit enabled the new Grand Prix cars to attain very high speeds. Louis Chiron, driving a Bugatti, won the 1928 European Grand Prix at Monza at a speed of just under 100 mph. In the same race Emilio Materassi, driving a Talbot, crashed into the crowd, killing twenty–three people – the first ever Grand Prix accident involving a large number of spectators. Gradually the circuit was modified and chicanes were introduced to make the track safer.

Even more famous than the circuit itself is the team which has virtually made Monza its own – Ferrari – now the team with the longest unbroken record of any in motor racing. Enzo Ferrari, who was born in 1898, came into motor racing as a

The harbour at Monte Carlo
(above), setting for the Monaco
Grand Prix. The only two drivers
to have crashed into the water
since the race started in 1929 have

been Alberto Ascari in 1955 and
Paul Hawkins in 1965. Both drivers
escaped unhurt.

Niki Lauda's fans at Monza *(below)*.

driver for Alfa Romeo, taking over responsibility for the Alfa
racing team in 1929 for ten triumphant years.

After the Second World War, Enzo Ferrari set up as a car–
constructor in his own right. His main rival in the early post–
war days was his old team of Alfa Romeo. The combination of
Ferrari, Alberto Ascari and the Monza circuit seemed almost
unbeatable. It won the Italian Grand Prix in 1949, 1951 and
1952, by which time Ferrari had also scored the first of nine Le
Mans wins. Ascari went on to become World Champion in
1952 and 1953, but the Ferrari–Ascari–Monza combination
proved tragically fatal in 1955 when Ascari was killed while
practising privately at Monza only four days after he had
crashed into the harbour during the Monaco Grand Prix.

Ferrari, however, continued to thrill the Monza crowds, who
saw the marque win six more Italian Grands Prix, although, it
must be admitted, not always with Italian drivers. The scene of
the spectators invading the track, swamping the successful
drivers and engaging Italian policemen in close fighting has
become a familiar sight and when Niki Lauda took the
chequered flag at the 1975 Grand Prix to win for Ferrari both
the World Drivers' and Constructors' Championships, it
seemed as though Monza would explode. National fervour is
never greater than when Ferrari wins at Monza.

THE RACERS
"Gentlemen, start your engines"

When the first Indianapolis 500 race was run in 1911, the organisers provided space for 3000 horses, and seats cost 50 cents, $1 and $1·50. Today, about half a million people pay up to $50 for a seat to watch the oldest closed–circuit race in the world. The exact number is uncertain because the organisers keep it secret, but what is certain is that the Indianapolis 500 is the richest race in the world – the prize money paid out in 1975 being $839,500.

Promoters and advertisers alike claim that the Indianapolis 500 is the world's greatest motor race, and today it is preceded by at least a month of promotional parties, parades and a host of other festivities.

"Indy" was the brainchild of one Carl Fisher, a motoring enthusiast with an eye for making money. He had seen many European motor races and was convinced that the only way to make racing pay in America was to build an enclosed circuit

and charge an admission fee. With three friends, Fisher bought 320 acres of land near Indiana and started work. It took 450 men, 300 mules, 150 road–scrapers and several tons of equipment less than a year to build the two–and–a–half–mile oval, surfacing it with gravel, crushed limestone, stone dust and thousands of gallons of liquid tar. In August 1909, the first cars ran at "Indy". It was an unqualified disaster. In front of a crowd of more than 15,000 spectators, the surface of the track disintegrated under the heavy cars: one car left the track killing the co–driver and two spectators. The race was stopped and the organisers went back to the drawing board. Despite the enormous cost, Carl Fisher decided to pave the entire track – with bricks.

It took 63 days and 3,200,000 paving bricks to resurface the track, which has been known ever since as "The Brickyard". After some trial race meetings, one of which had forty–two races, Carl Fisher decided that it was possible to have too much racing. He announced that there would only be one race a year at Indianapolis; that it would take place on Memorial Day (30 May) and that it would last for as long as the public could sit still – 500 miles. And so it has been ever since.

Apart from resurfacing, the track is unchanged since Carl Fisher made his epic decision. It is still a flattened oval giving all

Aerial view *(top)* of the Indianapolis Speedway during practice for the Indianapolis 500. The crowds can be seen already gathering.

A course car *(above)* leads the field into a rolling start for the 1965 Indianapolis 500. In the front row are A. J. Foyt and Jim Clark. Driving a Lotus–powered–by–Ford, Clark became the first European to win the race for forty–five years, and the first Briton ever to do so. The race was won at an average speed of 150·686 mph, breaking the 150 mph barrier for the first time. Second was Parnelli Jones driving an Agajanian Hurst Special. The course car is given to the winning driver as part of his prize.

Pit stop during the 1967 race *(right)*. A. J. Foyt, three times winner of the race, stops for a swift tyre check and refuel.

the spectators a good view of the racing. The long straights are five-eighths of a mile long and the corners are banked at nine degrees. For a long time it was fashionable to dismiss the Indianapolis circuit as one which required very little skill. Indeed an American, Bill Vukovich, who won the 500 in 1953 and 1954 and was killed during the race in 1955, said: "All you have to do is stand on the gas and turn left." It would appear that he was wrong, although it is true that for many years after the First World War European cars and drivers made very little impression on the Indianapolis winners' board.

During the years between the wars emerged many of the great "Indy" names – Fred and Augie Duesenberg, Jimmy Murphy, Harry Miller and Frank Lockhart. These Americans were unbeatable. They had developed a car which, even if it was good for nothing else, could lap the Brickyard at 120 mph – that being Lockhart's qualifying time for the 1927 race, driving a Miller.

Indianapolis was closed during the Second World War and was reopened for the 1946 race. American drivers still dominated and many Europeans hoping for a share of the substantial prize money went home disappointed. Caracciola crashed in practice for the 1946 race; Ascari retired his Ferrari

after forty laps in 1952, and the great Fangio declined to race because he had no car capable of beating the traditional Indianapolis winners – the so-called "roadsters" often powered by the four-cylinder Offenhauser engine. So drivers like A. J. Foyt, a three-times Indianapolis winner, and Parnelli Jones had it all their own way.

Then came 1961 and Golden Jubilee Year in which Jack Brabham, the reigning World Champion Grand Prix driver, brought to Indianapolis a Cooper Grand Prix car powered by a rear-mounted Coventry Climax engine. During the qualifying laps he ran at a steady 145 mph, and although in the race he finished ninth it was clear that although the "roadsters" were faster on the straights, the Cooper was considerably faster through the corners. The chase was on. In 1963 Jim Clark in a Ford-powered Lotus finished second to Parnelli Jones and in 1965 won outright at an average speed of 150·69 mph. As if to prove that the Europeans now had the measure of the Brickyard, Graham Hill won the 1966 race from Jim Clark. But the American drivers and manufacturers were equal to the challenge and have won every race since. And every year, on Memorial Day, half a million spectators pack the Indianapolis Speedway to hear the starter give the traditional command: "Gentlemen, start your engines."

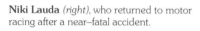
Jim Clark at the wheel of a Lotus 49 *(above)* winning the British Grand Prix in 1967. This was one of the first appearances of the Ford Cosworth DFV V8 engine, which was to dominate Grand Prix racing for a period lasting more than ten years.

Niki Lauda *(right)*, who returned to motor racing after a near–fatal accident.

THE RACERS

The Rise of the Superstars

During the early sixties a fundamental change overcame motor sport. From being a sport which largely attracted the wealthy amateur who had both time and money to spend, it gradually became a highly professional branch of the entertainment business with huge sums of money at stake. Competition was fiercer than it had ever been: the camaraderie of the circuits began to fade, and the advertising and promotion men moved in. In a way the change was inevitable. If the racing car was to be developed technically, and men were to drive it to the limit, then the costs would have to be borne by somebody. Sponsors from outside the motor industry considered motor racing a good medium for promotion – the ever-present possibility of a dramatic accident being good for crowd appeal – and so cigarette companies, banks, finance houses, cosmetic manufacturers and even a contraceptive manufacturer were persuaded to pour money into the outstretched palms of the world's motor-racing fraternity.

In this commercial environment drivers became particularly valuable properties. When Phil Hill won the World Championship in 1961, few people had ever heard of him. We would have to be blind and deaf not to have heard of today's motor-racing superstars – Niki Lauda, Emerson Fittipaldi and James Hunt. It is doubtful whether they drive any better than Ascari, Fangio, Nuvolari or Caracciola, but it is certain that many more people have heard of them.

The change began with the phenomenal success of Jim Clark, a quiet, charming sheep farmer from Scotland, who, driving a Lotus, won his first World Championship in 1963, took the championship again in 1965 and also won four consecutive British Grands Prix – one of them the first to be held on the newly opened Grand Prix circuit at Brands Hatch in Kent. If motor racing was to become a branch of the entertainment business, then it was important that the public should be able to see it. There was a great need for a major circuit within easy distance of London, and Brands Hatch filled that need. At 2·6 miles long, it not only had excellent viewing over a large part of the circuit, but it was sufficiently close to London to attract huge crowds.

Jim Clark was a great favourite with the crowds at Brands Hatch. His long partnership with Lotus and Colin Chapman, the constructor of his cars, produced some highly sophisticated and technically advanced cars. It also led to a new driving style. The old "arms and elbows" style of the earlier drivers disappeared and was replaced by smooth, controlled and almost invisible driving effort, with the driver himself encapsulated in his car. Clark was one of the steadiest of all racing drivers, capable of placing a wheel in precisely the same spot, lap after lap. He was also one of the fastest drivers and, when he and his car were on form, was considered to be unbeatable. Inexplicably, Jim Clark was killed at a Formula 2 race at Hochenheim in Germany in 1968, but he was to be replaced in the firmament of motor-racing stars by another Scotsman, Jackie Stewart.

In many ways Stewart mirrored Clark's career. He formed a successful partnership with constructor Ken Tyrell, which provided him with the cars he needed to win three World Championships before he retired at the end of the 1973 season. But he exploited his success in a way in which his predecessors had not. Articulate and informed, he was a friend of the media, appearing regularly on television to plead the cause of motoring in general and motoring safety in particular, but at the same time giving his sponsors great value for money.

As World Champion, Stewart set a new standard of behaviour to which his successors to the title, Fittipaldi, Lauda and Hunt easily aspired. To watch this new breed of motor-racing millionaires ease their way through a variety of social engagements one can easily forget that these are the same men who earn their money in racing cars at high speeds on inadequate circuits, pushing their skills – and their luck – to the limit. It is only the sight of the terrible burns Lauda received in his near-fatal crash at the Nurburgring which brings reality back to the fore.

Perhaps the most surprising change in motor racing is in the crowd. Whereas private motoring has been subjected to all kinds of repressive measures, the enthusiasm for motor sport has blossomed. Even during the 1974 fuel crisis, when petrol for private motoring was restricted, motor sport flourished. Today, despite speed limits and other restrictive legislation, dearer fuel, economic depressions and anti-motorist lobbies, the following for the sport increases. If this is a product of the publicity machines, the ad-men should be well pleased. But it is more likely to be a reflection of everyman's attitude to motoring, and the vicarious pleasure he gets from the sport.

For the drivers, however, the world of motor racing can be surprisingly fickle. The world loves a winner but has little time for an also-ran. In 1973, the wealthy young English Lord Alexander Hesketh rescued James Hunt from obscurity, where he had acquired the nickname "Hunt the Shunt", and put him into a Formula 1 car. The Hesketh team was flamboyant, extravagant and extremely successful. Hunt, young and good-looking, took only three years to become World Champion, having taken over Emerson Fittipaldi's drive in the McLaren team. After that, he seemed to lose the magic touch and although he is still a driver of world-championship class, the eyes of the motor racing world, and of the crowd, have shifted to new faces.

Colin Chapman with **Mario Andretti** *(below)* during practice for the 1978 British Grand Prix at Brands Hatch, which Andretti won in a Lotus.

Jackie Stewart with his wife Helen *(far left)* before his retirement in 1973.

Emerson Fittipaldi *(centre left)* relaxes at Brands Hatch.

James Hunt *(left)* during the 1978 season.

THE RACERS
Land Speed Battles

Just as in the era of the horse the question on everyone's lips was "How fast does it go?", the horseless carriage had hardly turned a wheel before its top speed became a matter of burning importance.

The first vehicle to set an official record was an electric car driven by Comte Gaston de Chasseloup–Laubat, who, on 18 December 1898, achieved a speed of 39·24 mph. This record stood for a month before being broken by Camille Jenatzy in another electric car, *La Jamais Contente*, with a speed of 41·42 mph. This determined pair battled it out until finally Jenatzy reached 65·79 mph, in April 1899. This record stood for three years and remains to this day the official record for an electric car.

Steam took over from battery power in the record–breaking business in 1902, when Leon Serpollet, driving one of his own cars, set a record of 75·06 mph. In its turn, steam gave way to petrol and attempting to break the land speed record became a millionaires' pastime as one after another tried to prove that their car was faster than the others.

Medical experts of the early 1900s predicted that these intrepid drivers, whose cars had no windscreens to protect them, would surely suffer heart attacks or, at the least, would be unable to breathe at speeds approaching 100 mph. Others thought the vehicles themselves would disintegrate.

Even Henry Ford got into the record–breaking act – in 1904, driving his 16·7 litre *Arrow* on the frozen Lake St Clair near Detroit at a speed of 91·37 mph. L. G. Hornsted, driving a Benz, pushed the record up to 124·1 mph at Brooklands in 1914. In 1922 the first vehicle powered by an aero engine made its appearance, driven by Lee Kenelm Guinness, and set a new record of 133·75 mph. Malcolm Campbell, an ex–Royal Flying Corps officer, steadily improved on this record and in 1931 was knighted for his achievements in his famous car *Bluebird*. When Campbell retired in 1935, his record stood at 301·129 mph. This, like most subsequent attempts on the land speed record, took place at Bonneville Salt Flats, Utah, although in 1963 Sir Malcolm's son Donald, driving a new *Bluebird*, set a new record on the dried–up bed of Australia's Lake Eyre. His achievement, 403·1 mph, was rather overshadowed by the 407·45 mph of Craig Breedlove's *Spirit of America*, set up three weeks later at Bonneville. However, Campbell's victory was conceded because *Spirit of America* was powered by a jet engine which did not drive the wheels and was therefore not recognised by European officials.

Whatever the official attitude, jet–powered vehicles were undoubtedly faster – and besides, European recognition was not of prime importance to the Americans. Art Arfons in *Green Monster* pushed the record up to 576·553 mph and Bob Summer's *Goldenrod* broke 600 mph before Gary Gabelich, driving the first rocket–powered vehicle, *Blue Flame*, set his record of 630·388 mph. *Blue Flame* looks more like *Concorde* than a motor car: next stop the sound barrier?

La Jamais Contente *(far right above)*, driven by Camille Jenatzy at a speed of 65·79 mph in 1899. The car, powered by 6 cwt of batteries, is now in the Musée de la Voiture at the Château de Compiègne, France.

Sir Malcolm Campbell *(above centre)*, pictured with *Bluebird* at Daytona Beach, Florida, prior to a record attempt in March 1935. Campbell is second from right.

Gary Gabelich and *Blue Flame* *(right)* on the Bonneville Salt Flats in Utah, September 1970, before the attempt which resulted in a land speed record of 630·388 mph. The first rocket–powered car to set a record, *Blue Flame* is 38 feet long, with four wheels (earlier jet–powered record cars had only three). During training for the attempt, Gabelich made tests in zero–gravity capsules as well as long parachute jumps.

Motoring for the Masses

Motoring grew quickly from being a pastime for the elite to being an almost essential part of everyday life. Despite the excitement of motor sport, the drama of the adventurers and the thrill of the death–defying land speed record attempts, motoring has always been destined to be a popular pursuit. For the car–makers to stay in business, the motor car had to be accessible not only to the wealthy but also to the masses. During the First World War, motorised vehicles were accessible to many people who would never have encountered them under normal circumstances and who, as a result, became hungry for the freedom private transport could provide.

Mass production began to satisfy that hunger, spurred on by those who saw the motor car as an investment. Henry Ford's Model T, retailing at $260, became a legend in its own time and was succeeded by many other relatively cheap cars on both sides of the Atlantic. The Second World War stimulated the demand for private cars still further and in the post–war years the world's motor industry expanded to meet that demand, with the inevitable result that the industry itself became one of the great employers of labour and the motor car one of the greatest providers of revenue. The motorist himself has become an important element in present–day society. Not only do governments rely on him for economic stability but he has also become a political pawn both socially and environmentally. Yet only eighty years ago the motor car itself scarcely existed and its driver was a very exclusive creature indeed.

MOTORING FOR THE MASSES
Early Production Lines

If there was one single development which established the motor industry as a major economic force on both sides of the Atlantic, it was mass production. It is widely supposed that mass production was the invention of Henry Ford. Certainly his Model T was the first motor car to be made for very large-scale production, and in order to make it in sufficient numbers Henry Ford developed mass production into a science, but the actual processes go much further back in history. In 1798, for example, a musket-maker called Eli Whitney was given a rush order by the American Army for 10,000 muskets. Instead of building each musket by hand, Whitney invented machines which would produce the ten component parts of the muskets, which could then be assembled by hand with astonishing speed.

The basic principle of moving the work and not the worker was not new. The techniques of mass production were recorded by Vannoccio Biringuccio, an Italian metallurgist who died in 1539. The Venetians used an assembly line to build their famous Mediterranean galleys in the sixteenth century, and one Oliver Evans used power conveyors in an automatic grain mill which he designed and built. This simple idea was taken one step further in Chicago during the 1860s when meat packers hung carcasses from a moving overhead rail. As the carcasses moved along, each worker removed a portion of the beast until, at the end of the line, "there was nothing left except the squeak".

The production of interchangeable parts in large quantities having been established by Eli Whitney, and automatic conveyance of work by Oliver Evans, it was left to Elihu Root to develop the principle of dividing the work into small simple tasks to make it more easily manageable. Root, who worked for Samuel Colt in the 1850s, speeded up the manufacture of Colt six-shooters considerably by increasing the number of operations which could be performed more quickly and with less chance of mistakes.

The motor car was an obvious candidate for mass production, many of the components being suitable for sub-assembly before being combined to make the complete car.

Dis-assembly line (right) at the Swift and Co. meat-packing house in Chicago in 1902. Pigs were brought into the factory on a rail and progressively dismembered. Here, hams and shoulders are being removed and the ribs split.

Mass production of Smith and Wesson revolvers in 1880 (far right). In sixteenth-century Italy, similar though less elaborate processes were used in a Milanese brass foundry to produce brass candlesticks and thimbles.

Cars in Quantity

Although Henry Ford is regarded by many as being the father of mass production, in the motor industry de Dion, Renault, Rambler and Oldsmobile all anticipated his techniques to some extent. Ransom Olds, who was also responsible for establishing Detroit as the motor-industry centre of America, built a plant in 1900 which was the first factory specifically designed for making cars. Unfortunately, while he was away visiting his parents, the factory was totally destroyed by fire, together with all but one of the cars. The sole survivor was the little runabout which became known as "The Curved Dash" because of its scroll front. As it was the only car Olds had left, it had to be made in large quantities. This he achieved by standardising the components. Henry Leland, creator of the Cadillac, supplied him with engines, and transmission assemblies were bought from the Dodge brothers. By 1905 the Curved Dash was being manufactured at the rate of 5000 a year, and cost less than $700.

Mass production as we know it today is largely the result of Henry Ford's combining the experience of his predecessors with his own imaginative ideas. His first experiment was a production line for magnetos. It was so successful that he went on to design a prototype final assembly line for complete cars, which was pulled along the floor by a system of ropes and pulleys. For the first appearance of this bizarre invention, Henry Ford himself and some influential business associates turned out to do the pulling. Encouraged by the success of the prototype, Ford installed power-driven moving conveyors and gradually he established sub-assembly lines for each section until, as he put it, "everything in the plant moved".

The first complete moving final assembly line was installed at the Ford factory at Highland Park in 1913. There had been enormous expenditure on the specially built machinery, but despite this the price of a Model T Ford dropped from $850 in 1909 to $440 in 1915, and Henry Ford was also able to double the minimum daily wage for his workers to $5. By 1920 the Model T was being produced at the rate of a car every ten seconds, and the basic retail price had fallen to $260.

Farmers out for a spin (above) in a Model T Ford in 1919. The Model T is the car most associated with Henry Ford's development of assembly-line techniques. More than 15 million were made in the sixteen years of its production life.

Joining the bodies to the chassis (right) at Highland Park, Detroit, in 1914. This Ford plant was built in 1911 for assembly-line production.

Henry Ford (below) on his 1896 quadricycle.

MOTORING FOR THE MASSES
Britain Hesitates

Unfortunately the traditional British resistance to change meant that mass production was slow to develop in the British motor industry, allowing the Americans to gain a substantial lead in the passenger car market. Even a remarkable demonstration which took place at Brooklands in February 1908 failed to convince the British that mass production was here to stay. Three identical Cadillacs were dismantled, their components jumbled up and certain parts removed and replaced by others from stock. The parts were then re-assembled into three complete cars, which completed a demonstration 500-mile run around the Brooklands circuit. But impressive though the demonstration undoubtedly was, and although standardised components and interchangeable parts were already features of the bicycle and sewing-machine industries in Britain, the industry still believed that motor cars were best built one at a time like houses.

Ford cars had been sold in Britain since 1903, when they were imported complete. Then, in 1909, the Model T was assembled in Britain. These early cars were built individually by four men, who assembled each chassis with its wheels, lifted the whole unit onto trestles and completed the car with a body brought on a handcart from Scott Brothers, a body-building firm which Ford eventually bought.

In 1911, Ford opened a Model T assembly plant at Trafford Park in Manchester, thus giving the British industry an opportunity to observe his techniques at first hand. Annual sales rose dramatically from 1485 in 1911 to over 40,000 by 1924. But despite the Ford success there was still a reluctance to accept that what was right for an American company could be right for a British one. The makers of British cars in small factories felt that volume production was too great a risk to take in a country where the average level of income was much lower than in the USA and where the subsequent demand for passenger cars was small. It was not until the mid-1920s, when the economic outlook began to appear a little brighter, that the British motor industry began to take itself seriously.

Between 1919 and 1922 thirty-eight new makes of car appeared on the British market, but few of them were to survive the Second World War. Only Austin and Morris had applied mass-production techniques with any degree of success. Those who profited most from the growth of the motor industry were the manufacturers of components.

The first Ford specifically designed for Europe, the 8 hp Model Y (left), launched in 1932. This one was photographed outside Hollingsworth's, a Ford retailer in Hastings, during a 72-hour endurance run.

The 1904 Model A (below left) cost £230 inclusive of "tonneau, double-tube tyres and brass rails".

Model T production line *(right)* at Trafford Park. Ford chose the factory because of its proximity to the Manchester Ship Canal.

An early Model T *(below),* preserved in mint condition.

Down on the farm: a 1921 Model T in Michigan *(right).* Ford vehicles, being rugged and reliable, were commonly used for various agricultural purposes.

Forerunner of the modern caravan *(below right):* a house built on a Model T. The "Tin Lizzie" also formed the basis for tractors and delivery vans.

MOTORING FOR THE MASSES
The Crumbling of the Class Barrier

Mass production of the motor car (seen below at the Ford Factory at Highland Park in 1913) brought employment to those who made it and those who sold it. The social implications were even further–reaching. Freedom of movement, which motoring gave to the middle classes, meant that people could choose where they wanted to live, where to pass their leisure time and where to spend their comparative wealth. The suburb grew up as a direct result of increased mobility, provided by both the private car and improved public transport systems. It was no longer necessary for man to live either "over the shop" or within walking distance of his place of employment. He could now, if he chose, live farther away from polluted city centres; instead, he and his motor vehicle would be taking a degree of pollution to the countryside. In evenings and at weekends, he could go farther afield. The "seaside" was no longer the exclusive playground of the moneyed classes – who, indeed, were soon to start travelling still greater distances for their pleasures.

As more and more people flocked to enjoy the delights of the beach, the beaches in high season became as crowded as the cities. (Shown on the right: Nantasket Beach, Massachusetts, on Independence Day in the early 1920s.) While this development was to make environmentalists shudder, it also brought to seaside townships, rural beauty spots, historical sites – and the roads that led to them – important economic benefits.

The growth of tourism created new demands – demands for roads, petrol stations, hotels, restaurants, car parks and facilities for a range of leisure activities. It was the era of the picnic hamper, the rowing boat and the fair, the holiday in the country and the day–trip to the sea; it was also a time when many middle–class misconceptions of how the other half lived were broken down. Cynics argue that the mobility provided by motoring merely gave people the freedom to follow the herd and render one place after another uninhabitable, and that the suburb and the dormitory town are no more socially desirable than the overcrowded city. Nonetheless, the motor car fulfilled a need at a time when technology was beginning to bring leisure to vast numbers of people to whom the very concept had previously been unknown – perhaps even undreamed of.

Inter-war Activity

The years between the two world wars were years of opposites. Economically there was a brief euphoric boom followed by a prolonged slump and in the automotive world the big luxury limousines contrasted with the mass–produced, middle–class cars. These same years saw the beginnings of hire–purchase, compulsory insurance and legislation governing levels of traffic noise. The motorist became an important element in the economy, paying road taxes, petrol taxes and even fines for dangerous driving. However, as if to emphasise the prevailing ambivalent attitude towards the motor car, the speed limit of 20 mph was abolished in 1929, only six years before a 30 mph limit was introduced for built–up areas.

One manufacturer who attempted to make the most of the social climate in Britain was Herbert Austin. Immediately after the First World War, during the boom and in an attempt to provide employment, Austin produced an Austin 20 – a four–cylinder, 20 hp car which retailed at £695. But Austin had read the signs wrongly. Admirable though the 20 was, it was much too expensive to provide motoring for the millions and its production very nearly brought the downfall of the company. Just in time, Sir Herbert Austin had a second thought – this time a winner. He produced the Austin Seven, first seen in 1922, and a very unusual vehicle for the period. It was powered by a 747 cc engine, had a wheelbase of six and a half feet and, a very advanced feature, four–wheel brakes.

Although there had been dark mutterings about the sanity of Sir Herbert Austin in undertaking such a venture, the Seven was an enormous success and, because of its price, gave many people their first opportunity of buying a real motor car. To add to its appeal, the Seven had various sporting successes and set up some impressive records at Brooklands. Three hundred thousand Austin Sevens were made between 1923 and 1939, making it one of the most successful cars of the era.

Not all manufacturers were as fortunate as Austin. The inter–war years saw a rapid decline in the number of makes available. In America 200 were listed in 1922, but by 1939 the figure was down to seventeen. Another major change was in the type of car demanded by the private motorist. Here Britain led a move towards the saloon car body in preference to the open tourer, very probably because of the inclement British weather. Less than half the cars sold in Britain in 1927 were saloons, but by 1931 this figure had risen to 92 per cent.

The same period also saw the growth of the car accessory market. In 1928 Sunbeam offered "Triplex" safety glass windscreens as optional extras on their limousines and landaulettes. Car radios were available, as were up–and–over garage doors and mechanical windscreen wipers. By 1937 one person in twenty in Britain owned a car and in the United States one person in ten owed his living to it. The move towards the car brought with it the first supermarkets, motels, motorways, multi–storey car parks and even parking meters, the first of which was installed in Oklahoma City in July 1935.

Another important development of the inter–war years was that of the agricultural vehicle. Although the tractor is a familiar sight almost everywhere in the world, it only became widely used in the 1920s. The Charter Gas Engine Company of Chicago experimented with a single–cylinder–engined tractor in 1889 and by 1900 there were several basic but useful machines in use in America. But, as with the passenger car, Britain was slow to relinquish the horse and allowed Ford and the International Harvester Company to establish themselves as leaders in the field of agricultural vehicles.

"AS DEPENDABLE AS AN AUSTIN"

Think it out.. and you'll buy an Austin Seven... the only small car that has proved itself for seven years

Before you decide on a small car, remember . . .
There is only one which has been thoroughly tried and exhaustively proved for seven years.
There is only one which has behind it a seven year record of spectacular success on road and racing track, in every part of the world.
There is only one which has, in indisputable evidence of its outstanding dependability, over 100,000 enthusiastic owners.
That car was the first—the pioneer—small car . . . The Austin Seven.
Think it out. Then examine this car at your nearest Austin dealer's showrooms. Drive it yourself, without any obligation whatever. Literature free on request.

£140
Coupe, Coachbuilt or Fabric Saloon
Two Seater or Tourer £130
Sunshine Roof £5 extra, Triplex Glass, Chromium Plating, Wire Wheels, Dunlop Tyres.

Austin 7

The Austin Motor Company Limited, Longbridge, Birmingham. Showrooms, also Service Station for the Austin Seven: 479-483 Oxford Street, W.1. Showrooms and Service Station: Holland Park Hall, W.11.

Newspaper advertisement *(far left)* for the Austin Seven. The first Seven had appeared in 1922, replacing the cycle car. It had a 747 cc engine and was available as a coupé, tourer, saloon with a fabric roof and as a coachbuilt saloon. When this advertisement appeared late in 1929, the car had become popular among the young and had also had considerable success on the race–track. In 1930 it was to win the 500–mile race at Brooklands, despite the fact that its top speed was only 55 mph.

A Dixi *(centre left)* driving through the Black Forest town of Freiburg in Germany in 1937. The Dixi was an Austin Seven built under licence in Eisenach as a two–seater roadster. In 1928 the company was taken over by BMW, who continued to make the model. Other Austin Sevens were made under licence in Japan by Datsun, in France by Rosengart and in the USA by the American Austin Company, who retailed the car with disc wheels and detachable rims for $445.

A lino-cut of the 1920s *(above)*. It was designed by C. A. Angrave and published in *Commercial Art*.

Madam about to embark in her Fiat Tourer *(left)* of about 1922, while her chauffeur awaits instructions. Once on the road, the chauffeur would receive his orders through a speaking tube conveniently placed close to his right ear. He was however denied the convenience of windows to protect him from the elements.

The Bullnose Breed

The Bullnose Morris was to William Morris what the Model T was to Henry Ford. It brought prosperity to Oxford, where it was built, and success to the British motor industry, even though the components of the car were predominantly American. It also made its maker a household name.

The predecessor of the Bullnose Morris Cowley was the Oxford, built on the one–at–a–time assembly principle and with only two seats. For this reason it could never become a volume seller, so Morris decided to produce a four–seater version of the car. In order to keep the cost as low as possible he bought American components.

The prototype was shown to an enthusiastic press in April 1915 and production started the following autumn. The car was easy to drive and had such innovations as a dipstick and a twin–plate cork–lined clutch. But the first budget of the war imposed a 33 per cent import duty on cars and accessories, which increased the price of the Bullnose to 185 guineas. Production plans received a further severe setback with the loss of 1500 engines at sea.

After the war, the Bullnose became available in greater numbers and became correspondingly better value. To keep the price down, the Bullnose underwent only minor changes during its lifetime of eleven years, and its rounded bonnet became one of the most common sights on British roads.

MOTORING FOR THE MASSES
The People's Car

The first Volkswagen Beetle rolled off the production line in the factory at Wolfsburg, Germany, in June 1945. The last one came down the line at Emden, on the north German coast, in January 1978, thirty–three years later. In that time, more than nineteen million Beetles were built – even more than the legendary Model T Ford. The little rear–engined, air–cooled car, with its rounded body and characteristic engine note, hardly seems to have changed since its inception.

The VW Beetle was intended to be "a car of the people" right from the moment when the newly elected Chancellor of Germany, Adolf Hitler, announced plans for it at the opening of the Berlin Automobile Exhibition in 1935. For Hitler the project was a political manoeuvre. He wanted to bring the German people a means of personal transport, "a car which is low priced and cheap in operation, similar to those the American people have enjoyed for a long time".

Adolf Hitler, however, knew nothing about car production and had no idea how his dream would be achieved. Nor indeed did Dr Ferdinand Porsche, the sports–car designer chosen by Hitler to make his dream come true. Dr Porsche faced the impossible task of producing a car which would sell for less than 1000 marks (then approximately £50) at a time when most small cars were selling for 2800 marks.

We shall never know whether Dr Porsche would have succeeded in reaching his goal. After prototypes had been built and tested, and the foundations laid for the brand new factory, the black shadow of war fell across Europe. Dr Porsche turned his talents from sports cars and land speed record cars to tractors and military vehicles. The building of the plant at Wolfsburg went on at top speed, but the first car it produced, early in 1940, was a military version of the people's car for use by the German army.

It was not until 1946, when the Volkswagen plant was under the control of the British Occupation forces, that the miracle started to happen. Although experts from the British motor industry had written off the Volkswagen "Beetle" as a commercial proposition, it was necessary to operate the Wolfsburg factory to provide employment. Under the direct control of the British authorities production expanded from nothing to 46,500 vehicles a year in 1949, and the company was handed back to Germany. The people's car had arrived.

The man almost wholly responsible for the Beetle's post–war success was Heinz Nordhoff, whose greatest attributes were an ability to inspire those working with him and a unique understanding of mass–production techniques. When he

joined the company in January 1948, production stood at 8989 vehicles a year: when he retired ten years later, he had brought the Beetle to 13·5 million people throughout the world – more than any other European car.

Since then, the Beetle has become many things to many men. Beetles have crossed the Sahara countless times; an amphibious Beetle crossed the Strait of Messina in two minutes less than the ferry takes. Graz University students crammed fifty–seven people into a Beetle and in America there is a "Born in a Beetle Club" – a select association with about fifty proud members.

The Beetle became a cult. Suggestions that it was outmoded were met with howls of protest from owners all over the world. At the height of its success, Volkswagen were

Series 30 prototype Beetles *(above)*, characterised by the absence of a rear window, pictured in a Stuttgart street. These prototypes were built with government sponsorship during the first four months of 1937 and, unlike previous prototypes, were made by Daimler–Benz.

Adolf Hitler *(above)* laying the foundation stone for the new Volkswagen factory at Wolfsburg in March 1938. In front of him stand three prototype Volkswagen cars.

The Schwimmwagen *(left)* – a wartime version of the Beetle with retractable propeller, waterproofed engine and four–wheel drive.

VW assembly line *(right)* at the point where the body joins the chassis. The techniques used in the plant were based on those of Ford and General Motors and made Volkswagen one of the world's most productive car plants.

A GT Special *(above)*, based on the Beetle chassis and engine unit, but with a stylish glass–fibre body. The "Nova", built in Devon by Richard Oakes and Phil Sayers, had a forward–opening flap–door.

The VW Polo *(below)*, baby of the new generation of Volkswagens, designed, with the Golf and the *Scirocco*, to carry on the traditions of the Beetle while updating it technologically.

producing more than 5000 Beetles a day, and exporting them to 140 countries.

Inevitably its days were numbered. Although the original design had endured for forty years, it could not go on for ever. A sleek new generation of Volkswagens has appeared to carry on the Beetle tradition and devotees must now turn to Brazil, Mexico, Nigeria and South Africa to indulge their passion.

Producing this new family nearly finished Volkswagen. The company had been too dependent on the Beetle for too many years. Plans for a successor had been delayed and while to design and produce one new car was expensive, to produce a complete range was almost prohibitive. Volkswagen suc–ceeded – but for many people the new models will never quite replace the remarkable Beetle.

MOTORING FOR THE MASSES
Post-war Trends

Following another determined post–war effort to revive the world's motor industry, in the 1950s the private motor car proliferated almost embarrassingly in the Western world. Now that motoring was available to the masses, it was becoming apparent that there would have to be some form of restraint – the sheer volume of traffic was too much for the available fuel resources, the existing roads and for the non–motorists to tolerate. The 1950s saw the beginning of the era of road safety. "Keep Death off the Roads" was one of the most famous British campaigns and there were threats of petrol rationing and road taxes, seat belts, vehicle testing and the breathalyser. Governments were faced with the almost insuperable dilemma of how to retain a balance between restraining car ownership, preserving the natural environment, the cost of providing new roads, and the need to support the motor industry as a major provider of employment and producer of revenue.

While attitudes began to change, cars did not. Most post–war models were hangovers from pre–war ancestors and it took some time for new trends to emerge. When they did, they were almost all on the "small outside, large inside" basis, giving maximum space for the occupants while using a minimum of

1953 Standard Eight (above) designed for the family motorist with economy in mind. The 803 cc engine had a top speed of 62 mph and averaged 50 mpg. The car cost £481, of which £142 was purchase tax, but it proved too sluggish even for the family motorist. As an alternative, a 948 cc version was produced, costing £100 more, but with a far superior performance.

Traffic jams (right) were becoming a familiar sight on British roads as more and more people took to wheels in the 1950s. This tail–back, in a heatwave during the summer of 1957, was caused by cars trying to cross the bridge onto the Isle of Sheppey. The RAC recorded that cars were making for the coast at the rate of 20,000 an hour, and some motorists had not reached their destination before it was time to turn back for home. Traffic jams continued to increase in intensity: the longest ever recorded by the motoring organisations in Britain was in the summer of 1964, when motorists trying to reach Torquay found themselves in a queue stretching 25 miles.

Citroën Berline 11 Légère *(top)*, a model still in production after the Second World War. The original car was launched in 1935, with front–wheel drive and a choice of engines. Production restarted after the war, but the cars were only made in black.

Cheap and cheerful *(above centre)* – the popular 2CV Citroën.

Nicknamed "the flying lawn–mower", the 2CV was Citroën's answer to the demand for a car which would provide economic transport for all and sundry. The car first appeared in 1949, powered by a 375 cc engine, and sold well not just in France but abroad as well.

1953 Chevrolet Corvette *(above)*.

materials. In addition, large numbers of people wanted their personal transport, no matter how small and uncomfortable it was. Germany was the birthplace of the bubble–car, which satisfied all the demands as well as being extremely small and uncomfortable. The Goggomobile was also a big seller – an ugly little utility car with an air–cooled engine and a top speed of not more than 60 mph. The French best–seller was the rear–engined Renault Dauphine, which was powered by an 845 cc engine, had independent suspension, a three–speed gear box and a nasty tendency to roll over.

Although the Dauphine was produced in millions – indeed it holds the record for the quickest first million of an individual model – the French hit of the 1950s was undoubtedly the Citroën DS 19, a car way ahead of its time both in styling and in engineering. Although the engine was an old favourite, the car had an advanced streamlined shape which made it extremely stable and which endured with only minor modifications for nearly twenty years. The DS also had a hydraulic control centre, which operated the brakes, steering, clutch and suspension. It is probably true to say that the production of a car as advanced in 1955 could only have happened in France, where styling has always been unusual if not bizarre. But while the British would never have counten–anced the Citroën DS, the French would have poured scorn on the Morris Minor, an Issigonis forerunner of the Mini and a classic car of its very British type. A solid, sensible–looking car, the Minor was the first British car to sell over one million units and the convertible version is regarded today as a highly prized collectors' item.

In Italy, Fiat was producing its own best–seller – equally small and economical – the 600. The pre–war Topolino had made Fiat famous in the mass–production market, but it was the 600 which put much of post–war Italy on wheels, more than two and a half million of them being made before the car was finally replaced in 1970.

In America too the accent was on smaller cars, although by European standards they still appeared to be vast. The imported car market had reached such proportions by the mid–fifties that American manufacturers counterattacked with

the so-called "compact". The Ford Falcon, the Plymouth Valiant and the Chevrolet Corvair (America's first mass-produced rear-engined car, later to be made infamous by Ralph Nader) were instant successes. But while there was no threat of an oil shortage in the United States, American cars were still, by European standards, bulky, cumbersome, thirsty and extravagant in their styling.

Although the general trend was towards economy motoring, luxury cars were still to be found. One of the famous cars of the period was the Mercedes Benz 300 SL coupe, which had gull-wing doors extending into the roof. Another beauty was the first post-war Lancia, the Aurelia, first seen in 1950. Britain boasted one of the most beautiful cars ever to come from Bentley, the Continental Coupé, a superbly gracious machine of which only about two hundred were ever made. But despite these mouth-watering exceptions, the rule for the average motorist was that although big was beautiful, little was undeniably lovelier – and much cheaper.

A 1956 advertisement for a de Soto convertible *(top)*, a strong seller in the USA in the 1950s. De Soto became a division of Chrysler in 1928 and was intended to compete with Oldsmobile, Pontiac and Nash.

A 1956 Fiat 600 Multipla *(above right)*, a taxi-cum-estate car variation of the current 600. In 1936 Fiat produced the famous "Topolino", a two-seater convertible with a 570 cc engine. The 600, which appeared in 1955, was a replacement for the Topolino and had a rear engine, independent suspension and a 633 cc power unit. By today's standards the baby Fiats were unsophisticated, but very popular with the Italians.

Under the bonnet *(right)* of the rear-engined Fiat 600.

MOTORING FOR THE MASSES
Little but Lovely

In July 1959 important twins were born to the British Motor Corporation. They were a new generation of baby cars – one called the Morris Mini–Minor, the other the Austin Seven – and were identical apart from their radiator grilles and badges. The car, brainchild of designer Alec Issigonis, was revolutionary in engineering and styling and set a new standard in economical motoring. The Mini – as both cars soon became known – had one immediately important feature. It provided space for four adults and a small amount of luggage in a car which measured only ten feet in length and weighed less than 1300 lb. The space was achieved by mounting the 850 cc engine, which drove the front wheels, transversely, thus allowing the maximum interior space for the occupants. The suspension was based on rubber units and the remarkable machine was capable, in its basic form, of 70 mph, and at a steady 50 mph had a fuel consumption of about 50 miles per gallon. As a concept, the Mini was way ahead of its time and it took the public a while to get used to it.

The creator of the Mini, Alec Issigonis, was a designer of the old school, and was more artist than engineer. Indeed he admitted that mathematics were not his strong point. The original Mini designs were drawn freehand on a layout pad to be translated later into engineering realities. There had been older cars with front–wheel drive and with transverse engines, and even some with rubber suspensions, but the overwhelming success of the Mini was the concern Issigonis had for the people who would use the car. The Mini was often

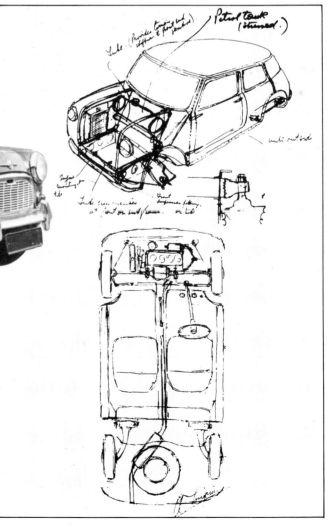

"Yumping" a Mini (top). Timo Makinen on a special stage during the 1966 RAC Rally. The Mini had a phenomenal success in motor sport, particularly rallying, during the sixties. The first big success was in 1962 when Bengt Soderstrom won the Swedish Rally. Minis also won the Monte Carlo Rally in 1964, driven by Paddy Hopkirk, 1965, driven by Timo Makinen, and 1966, also driven by Makinen. But in 1966 the first three cars, all Minis, were disqualified in the biggest scandal in rallying history on the tenuous grounds that their headlights did not conform to international regulations.

Sir Alec Issigonis (above) with the first Morris Mini–Minor on the day the new cars were announced, in 1959. The cars came as a big surprise to the motoring public, most of whom had no idea that a revolution was in the air. Apart from the package, the cars also had rubber cone suspension. In 1970 the Mini was granted its status as an individual make, and the complete range included a basic 848 cc car and a 1275 cc GT Mini. Although Issigonis is usually thought to have invented the front–wheel–drive/transverse engine combination, it had appeared on a DKW in 1931.

described as looking like a box with a wheel at each corner. Certainly it was an unusual shape, but the car was extremely stable and this, combined with the front–wheel drive, led the Mini to instant competition success.

Strangely the Mini got off to a somewhat shaky start. Even at an artificially low price, the public was not immediately seduced by this unorthodox little vehicle and it took some time to become acceptable. It also had teething troubles – the body leaked like a sieve and the brakes were decidedly inadequate. But scarcely a year after its introduction the Mini was transformed into a 90 mph saloon with the help of an engine developed by John Cooper, and as the Mini–Cooper became one of the world's most successful rally cars.

It was only one of dozens of Mini variations. There were vans, pick–ups, estate cars, and even Mini beach buggys, which had open sides and basket–work seats. There was a push–pull Mini with an engine at both ends, and an Ogle GT Mini with a sleek Italian–style body. One of the most popular derivatives was the Mini Moke which, although originally intended for farmers and foresters, became a very fashionable form of transport with the jet set. The most expensive Mini on record was a Mini–Cooper S costing £5300 in 1970. This Mini had electric windows, an opening tailgate, and a luxury interior which took 2300 manhours to convert.

It took five and a half years to produce a million Minis – a meagre performance by the standards of Ford and General Motors, but highly commendable for a company the size of BMC. The two–millionth Mini was made in June 1969, and the car is still in production and likely to remain so. The Mini has had many critics and many imitators but remains nevertheless one of the greatest and most enduring achievements of the motor industry.

Original sketches *(far left)* of the Mini, by Sir Alec Issigonis. In the early stages, he sketched on envelopes and menu cards. The result is history: a saloon car which virtually dominated the 1960s.

Low-flying Mini *(above)*. A 1275 GT driven by Malcolm Leggat gets it all wrong at Castle Combe in the 1977 Mini Championship.

Push-me-pull-you Mini *(left)*, an experimental vehicle with an engine at both ends. A two–engined racing car also got as far as the prototype stage, but without great success.

MOTORING FOR THE MASSES
Eastern Competition

The success of the Japanese passenger car industry has caused many knowledgeable observers of the motor industry to eat their words. Whereas twenty–five years ago Japanese cars were pale imitations of American and European mass–production models, today they figure amongst some of the most technically advanced cars on the world market. The Japanese industry has its roots in the 1930s, when Kiichiro Toyoda, son of a textile machinery manufacturer, decided that the company should diversify into automobile engineering. The Austin Seven was already manufactured under licence by Nissan, and General Motors and Ford were both assembling imported cars in Japan, so the chances of a domestic industry being successful seemed good. To make sure, Kiichiro consulted a numerologist – a traditional Japanese procedure – who recommended that the name be changed to Toyota, which in Japanese can be written with eight strokes, and is therefore lucky, unlike Toyoda, which is written with ten, and is apparently not.

The first Toyota prototypes were seen in 1935 and the plant went into production two years later. Before embarking on the construction of the factory, Toyota unashamedly copied what they believed to be the world's most advanced factory – the Packard plant at Detroit. A Toyota engineer went on several conducted tours of the Detroit works, returning to his hotel room each evening to make plans and notes. Toyota was not the only company making original cars before the Second World War. As well as Nissan, who marketed their cars under the Datsun label, there was a third company, the Toyo Cork Kogyo Company Ltd.

Toyo Kogyo already produced a motor cycle and in 1930 had gone into production with a three–wheeler, a version of which was being produced in 1937 at the rate of over 300 units a month. In the same year, the company had imported machinery to make a conventional four–wheeled car, but the outbreak of war put a stop to all passenger–car development and it was only in the 1950s that the Japanese industry was able to return to the automobile fray. Two important factors helped the growth of the industry. Firstly, the success of the other Japanese industries – shipbuilding, steel and textiles – meant that there were literally millions of potential car–buyers in Japan, able to afford a car or motor cycle for the first time. The second factor was the almost total dominance, in the world's motor–cycle industry, of the Japanese manufacturers, whose technology and engineering were almost unbeatable. The Japanese Government also assisted its fledgling passenger–car industry by applying economic restrictions to imports, thus allowing the domestic manufacturers to make the most of the potentially huge domestic market.

It still took some time, however, for the cars to achieve the excellence of the Japanese motor cycles. In 1962 Toyo Kogyo produced a two–door, four–seater car called the Carol, which owed a great deal to the Ford Anglia, even to the extent of the inward–sloping rear window. Four years later Toyota launched the Publica, a vehicle similar in conception to the Citroën 2CV, which sold in vast quantities to the new Japanese motorists. But it was not for long that the Japanese manufacturers needed to copy their foreign competitors. By 1967 the Nissan R–380 prototype racing car was breaking international speed records, the Toyota Land Cruiser was enjoying a runaway success in export markets and John Surtees won the Italian Grand Prix in a Honda Formula 1 car.

With the same determination that had characterised the growth of the industry at home, the Japanese now attacked export markets. By carefully planned marketing strategy, Toyota overtook all other importers in the United States except Volkswagen, and other Japanese manufacturers followed. Today the Toyota Corolla has become the world's single best–selling model, with the Datsun Sunny not far behind. But there are signs that it is not only with conventional saloons that Japan intends to dominate the world market. The Honda CVCC "stratified–charge" engine has made great strides in the control of exhaust emission and Mazda has developed the rotary engine to a greater extent than its competitors. The Datsun 240/260 Z has had phenomenal success in international rallies and Subaru has produced a four–wheel–drive estate car destined for success in those countries where the going, even on the roads, is tough. In just fifty years, Japan has become a major contributor to the international motoring scene.

The first Datsuns *(top and above)*. The 1932 Phaeton on the left was based on the Austin Seven and was also built in saloon, coupé and roadster versions.

A 1936 Toyota *(above)* Type AA, powered by a six–cylinder engine. The chequerboard radiator was a feature of the model, which was also made as a four–door saloon.

Cars as far as the eye can see *(below left)* on Honmoku Pier, Yokohama, in 1974, awaiting shipment to the USA.

A 1970 prototype Nissan electric car *(right)*.

The Young Idea

There is something about the sports car which keeps people young, but exactly what it is cannot easily be defined. Perhaps it is the idea of speed rather than speed itself; perhaps it is the "hair–in–the–wind" image – the feeling of freedom and exhilaration that can never quite be equalled in a family saloon. The media have for decades used the sports car as a symbol of the trendy, stylish way of life, and as shorthand for an unfettered existence it has long proved acceptable to the public. In films and magazine fiction, the image is still exploited.

Psychologists have suggested that it is the desire for something which is different, albeit slightly uncomfortable but certainly exciting, that has drawn motorists to some of the more unusual cars of the past eighty years. Whatever the explanation, there has always been a demand for such cars. Even the advent of speed restrictions, fuel economies, production difficulties and ever–increasing costs has not deterred the real enthusiasts from acquiring Astons, Rileys, Morgans, Bearcats and Thunderbirds.

In the early days of the motor car it was difficult to find different images, but rallies and hill climbs established the "boy racer", with his leather–covered steering wheel, driving gloves and woolly hat. Local motor clubs sprouted and the country "pub" became the accepted venue for the young–at–heart whose cars were their hobby, if not their life. Today there are few open sports cars. Those that are to be seen are well–preserved relics of a recently bygone age, when suspensions were stiff, steering was heavy, engine notes were a burbling, throaty roar – and motoring was fun.

The Sporting Life

The question "What is a sports car?" has been asked regularly since the earliest days of the automobile. Strictly speaking it should be a car which is used for sport, but in general terms the sports car has become synonymous with the sheer pleasure of driving – and with a car which reflects the personality of the owner. One could argue that the very earliest cars were all sports cars and certainly the Bugattis and the first Mercedes were. So too were the Vauxhall Prince Henry models, although the term "sports car" did not come into general use until after the First World War.

The period between the wars was the golden age of sports cars. One of the earliest and most famous models was the Stutz Bearcat, which first appeared in 1914 and continued in production until well into the prohibition era in America. The Stutz had a reputation for being well and solidly built, so much so that when one dissatisfied customer returned his car because he believed the engine to be faulty, Harry Stutz, founder of the company, took the engine from the car and subjected it to a transcontinental run. The run lasted nearly twelve days, during which the allegedly faulty engine never missed a beat.

British enthusiasts believe that Bentleys were the first true sports cars, although W. O. Bentley never applied the name to them. But with the Le Mans successes behind them, the name of Bentley spelt social success for those motorists in the 1930s wealthy enough to own one. Italians on the other hand would insist that the early Alfa Romeos were the supreme sports cars of the inter–war years and certainly the image of the Italian sports car lives on. Even Henry Ford is reported to have said, "I lift my hat when I see an Alfa Romeo go by." Perhaps the star of the Alfa Romeo firmament before the Second World War was the 8C 2900 sports car, which marked the end of the classic sports car era.

By the end of the war, when the motor industry was starting to get back into its stride, the term "sports car" was beginning to mean "convertible" – a term which struck horror into the hearts of the purists, although some post–war models showed enormous technical advances over the pre–war cars. This was largely due to the use, during the war, of advanced

Stutz Bearcat *(left)*, one of the best known of the American sports cars of the 1920s and extremely popular despite being highly priced. One of its innovations was a three–speed gearbox integral with the rear axle. The car had a low–slung chassis and a variety of engines, the largest being a 6·2 litre, and the fuel tank was mounted behind the seats.

1952 Jaguar XK 120 *(below).* The original XK 120 was introduced at the 1948 London Motor Show and the model was subsequently a great success in motor sport. By 1954 the XK 120 range included two–seater, hard–top and convertible models, and a 178 mph streamlined version.

technologies as well as to the training of many people in engineering who had never previously had the opportunity to develop these skills.

One of the most famous sports cars of the post-war years was the Aston Martin DB1. Before the war, Aston Martin had a small but distinguished reputation as a small-volume manufacturer, but in 1947 David Brown, of tractor fame, bought the company and with it the designs for an Aston Martin "Atom" which raced successfully at Spa in 1948. At the London Motor Show that year, Aston Martin announced the first of a famous series of sports cars – the DB1. The car was powered by a 2·6 litre engine originally built by W. O. Bentley for Lagonda, which had also become part of the David Brown empire, and the DB1 continued in production until 1950 when the DB2 took over.

Other famous names of the forties included Frazer-Nash, Morgan (founded in 1910 and still going strong), Jowett Javelin, MG and Standard-Triumph. In all these marques, performance, road-holding and panache came before comfort, but with relatively uncrowded roads, cheap petrol and a huge band of new and enthusiastic drivers, comfort was largely irrelevant.

While this generalisation was true for Europe, the very opposite was the case in America, where the post-war years produced glitter, chrome, air-conditioned comfort, power steering, automatic transmissions and very little in the way of road-holding or handling in the European sense. Along with spiky fins and snarling radiators came the first power-driven hood, which folded away at the touch of a button and hid itself in a vast boot. The 1957 Ford Skyliner, which caused a good deal of mirth at the time of its introduction, was the forerunner of a generation of convertibles (or rag-tops as they were popularly known) which were anything but sports cars. The real American motoring enthusiasts had to turn to Europe for motoring excitement. There, at the London Motor Show in 1948, appeared a car which was the ultimate in sports cars and which set the scene for the next decade – the Jaguar XK 120. The pre-war company SS Cars Ltd had been re-formed in 1945 as Jaguar Cars Ltd and concentrated initially on saloon models. But the XK 120 reversed that trend. It was an elegant two-seater coupé powered by a brand-new six-cylinder 3442 cc engine which was officially timed at 132 mph. The XK 120 put Jaguar in the forefront of serious sports-car manufacturers, a position it was to hold for more than twenty years.

1937 Frazer Nash "Shelsley" *(left)*, a 1·5 litre supercharged, chain-driven two-seater. Although the Frazer Nash was conceptually very simple (the principle of chain drive had been abandoned by other manufacturers much earlier), it provided real competition for imported sports cars, particularly on race tracks and hill climbs.

Aston Martin DB2 convertible, 1951 *(below)*. The DB2 series replaced the DB1 models in 1951. The engine was a six-cylinder, 2·5 litre unit which Aston Martin made themselves, a contributory factor to the relatively high price of the car. The reputation of Aston Martin was based mainly on the motor-racing successes of the marque.

A Bachelor's Delight

The Healey 3000 went into production in July 1959 at BMC's Abingdon factory, and since its launch later that year dozens of enthusiasts' clubs have sprung up all over the world. Though the 3000 was scarcely a new model, being almost identical in styling to the earlier big Healeys (the 100 series), it had a larger, more powerful engine. The Healey already had a reputation for being a "man's car", with its hard ride and positive steering, and had also enjoyed considerable competition success. Certainly the 3000 discouraged family motoring: the original version was a two–seater coupé, the second a very occasional four–seater, with a back seat that provided cramped quarters for two small children or one concertina'd adult.

Much of the Healey's popularity stemmed from its achievements in international endurance events, such as Le Mans and Sebring, and from record–breaking attempts at Bonneville Salt Flats. American safety regulations finally made production of the 3000 unviable, but its memory lingers on.

THE YOUNG IDEA

The End of the Sports-car Era

Although many great sports–car marques have survived throughout the 1960s and 1970s, these decades have proved to be the graveyard of the convertible, as the term "sports car" gradually came to be associated with sporty saloon cars rather than the open–topped dream cars of earlier years. In March 1961, the motoring world saw the launch of one of the greatest sports cars the industry has ever produced, either before or since: the E–type Jaguar. From every point of view the new car made its predecessor, the Jaguar XK 150, appear un–believably dated, even though the XK's engine and front suspension were carried over to the new model. The body styling, constructed on the monocoque principle, with elegantly rounded lines, was a show–stopper. The car was powered by a 3·8 litre engine and featured all–round disc brakes and independent suspension all for a cost of £2100. Fuelled and ready for the road it weighed only 23 cwt, had a top speed of 148 mph, and from a standing start took only 16 seconds to reach 100 mph. From the start the E–type was recognised universally as an outstanding car on both the road and the race–track and was to continue in production in various forms for more than a decade.

An outstanding sports car of the late fifties, still in production at the time of the E–type announcement, was the Lotus Elite. The genius behind Lotus was Colin Chapman, who has probably had more influence on modern sports–car design than any other individual car–maker and is considered by many to be the greatest technical innovator of the contemporary motor industry.

Chapman's first car, built in a garden shed in Wood Green, London, in 1948, was a trials special based on an Austin Seven, but there were several further models, of increasing sophistication, before the Elite was announced at the 1957 London Motor Show. This Lotus was the first to be designed for road use and intended for volume production. Its engine was a 1216 cc unit originally designed for use in a portable fire pump and was therefore both light and reliable.

When the Elite was first announced, there was a good deal of scepticism about Chapman's use of reinforced glass–fibre as a major part of the structure: it was the first car ever to have this feature. It was also the only small British sports car to have an overhead camshaft engine, four disc brakes and inde–pendent suspension. The success of the Elite on the road and on the race–track effectively silenced Chapman's critics and this car, followed by the Elan two years later, played an important part in changing the face of sports cars. Lotus had always received a great deal of support for competition ventures from the Ford Motor Company and in 1963 the two companies launched the 125E "Cortina–developed–by–Lotus" – a high–performance version of the standard car which had been co–developed by both companies. It had a top speed of 108 mph and extremely impressive acceleration. This model signalled the gradual demise of the genuine sports cars, which were no longer in sufficient demand for the volume manufacturers to produce them economically, and which were too expensive for most of the smaller manu–facturers to contemplate.

Only in the United States was there still a big enough market to support such genuine sports cars as MGs, Triumphs and Jaguars, and even there the dark clouds of legislation were gathering. One reason for the continued survival of European sports cars in the USA was the ugliness and inferior performance of the domestic product in the late fifties and

sixties. A marvellous example was the 1959 Cadillac convertible, which set new standards in horrific design. The car was 23 feet long and its fins, which appeared to have been styled expressly for impaling passing pedestrians, gleamed with chrome and coachwork lines. It is small wonder that the American cognoscenti preferred the E–type Jaguar.

By the mid–sixties, American manufacturers had under–gone a change of heart and were producing the "compact" saloons that were to become part of the American way of motoring life, led by the Ford Falcons and Mustangs and the Corvair Monza Spyder. It was the latter model that became the target of the campaign "Unsafe at any speed" instigated by the consumer protectionist Ralph Nader, who described the car as a "lethal rattletrap". Whether or not Nader was right is still hotly debated. What is certain is that Nader put one more nail into the coffin of the sports car by drawing the attention of politicians to the issues of speed, pollution and safety, which were soon to become subjects of debate and subsequently of legislation.

Although it is fashionable to blame emission controls, speed limits and other safety legislation for the disappearance of the sports car, it is also true that car owners preferred hard–topped cars, which thieves could not break into so easily, which did not leak and which were quiet enough, in motion, to allow the occupant to listen to his stereo tapes in comfort. The last real convertible from an American manufacturer was the 1976 Bicentennial Fleetwood Eldorado, which carried a plaque proclaiming: "This 1976 Fleetwood Eldorado is one of the last 200 identical US production convertibles."

Of course, sports cars are still made today, though not by the mass–production companies. You can still buy a Morgan or a targa–topped Porsche, and Panther will gladly sell you a Lima. Let us hope that legislation and economics allow them to survive.

The E type Jaguar *(above)*, a classic sports car of the 1960s. Powered by a 3·8 litre engine, with disc brakes all round, the car cost £2100 when it was launched in March 1961.

The tail-fins and lights *(top)* of a 1959 Cadillac. The whole car was 23 feet long and the body extended 8 feet beyond the wheelbase. This car revealed the ultimate horror of the styling trend towards fins and spikes, and was in production for only two years. Despite the vulgarity of this particular model, to own a Cadillac was, and still is, an international status symbol.

Colin Chapman *(left)* with the Lotus Elite, the car that created a sensation when it first appeared at the London Motor Show in 1957. It was the first production car to use a glass–fibre structure.

The contemporary successor to the traditional sports car was the sporting saloon Ford Lotus Cortina *(above)*. The car first appeared in 1963. Built at the Lotus factory, it was a two–door, four–seater saloon to which Chapman had fitted a twin–cam version of the 1·5 litre Lotus engine. The car also had coil–spring rear suspension, disc brakes on the front wheels and wide wheels and tyres. It had a top speed of 106 mph and a 0–60 mph time of 9 seconds. In 1966 production was transferred to a Ford factory and the car was slightly modified to increase its appeal to family motorists.

The Exhibitionist on Wheels

Over the years, production cars have tended to become more and more alike in their styling and performance, and at the same time road conditions have become increasingly restrictive. As a result, a trend has developed among enthusiast owners to develop the individuality of their vehicles, to the extent that the finished creation will not only be guaranteed to draw the attention of every other road–user but, for the driver, will be a passport to a world of fantasy. "Personalising" in this way usually encompasses both the mechanics and the aesthetics of the car: bizarre colour schemes, exotic interior fittings and technical modifications that will make it go faster.

The individuality cult began, as might be expected, on the West Coast of the USA, where hot–rodding (a term derived from "hot roadster"), high–riding, customising and the use of dragsters and buggies all reflect a desire to create something different – and where young people have enough money to transform their dreams into reality. Yet the desire to be different existed long before the age of mass production; even in the earliest days of motoring, customising was by no means unknown and some weird vehicles resulted. Today, anything goes – from expressionist abstracts in fluorescent paint adorning elderly Ford Populars to satin drapes lining the interiors of Transit vans. The humble VW Beetle, the Morris Minor – even buses and lorries – have regularly been subjected to similar treatment.

For some, appearance is only the beginning: the car has appeared in a wide range of attention–seeking guises around the world and been the victim of some hair–raising experiments. Can dune–buggies and dragsters really be relatives of the Rolls–Royce? Can driving a car on two wheels or turning it full–circle in mid–air really be what Daimler and Benz had in mind? And as for the "demolition derbys" that attract vast, cheering hordes – what more can the car be asked to endure in the name of entertainment?

THE EXHIBITIONIST ON WHEELS
Personality Cars

The desire to be different is not a modern trait. As far back as 1909, when every car was different by virtue of the fact that relatively few were being built, a car was built in the shape of a swan. It featured a horn with organ pipes, a beak which opened and shut with a hiss, and nostrils that squirted water. This incredible vehicle was designed by R. N. Mathewson, an Englishman living in India; it was built in Britain and shipped back to India, where, it is safe to say, there was nothing like it. Mr Mathewson was at the forefront of a new cult – that of customising cars to suit the personality of the owner. In later years, this cult has become a very profitable business, particularly in the United States, where customising first put down its roots. The essential point about customised cars is that no two are alike. Some are customised as advertising gimmicks, such as the Mini glass–fibre oranges built for Outspan, and some commissioned by wealthy individuals.

Inevitably, Hollywood was the breeding ground for customised cars. One of the principal protagonists was George Barris, who customised his first car when he was thirteen and went on to become the trendsetter in custom–built cars on the West Coast of the USA. He was immortalised in Tom Wolfe's book *The Kandy Kolored Tangerine Flaked, Streamlined Baby* – an apt description of his creations.

Funny Ford (far left above) prepared for the drag strip with the wings cut away to accommodate the enormous engine.

A customised rear end (above left) chromed and polished for public exhibition.

"The Sheik" (far left below), a customised Ford Transit van commissioned by the Ford Motor Company from a British customising expert, Steve Stringer, at a cost of £10,000. The artwork was inspired by Rudolph Valentino's movie escapades in the desert and the interior has red plush upholstery in the style of a Bedouin tent. However, the Sheik was a motor–show special, and as such rather an outsider in a field where catching the eye of other road–users is all–important.

Mister 7 (above), a dragster loosely based on a Model T. Although hot–rods and dragsters can be built using genuine chassis and body shells, a thriving industry in the USA produces components for replica Model Ts so that those who wish can build their own cars.

An Austin (left), lovingly restored but with strictly non–original paintwork. Multiple layers of paint and lacquer produce a perfect looking–glass finish.

THE EXHIBITIONIST ON WHEELS
Airbrush Artistry

Custom paint–specialists sometimes receive peculiar requests. Naked ladies on the bonnet are by no means unusual, but the fellow who drove away in a Cadillac painted nail–varnish pink and emblazoned with Elvis Presley's face must surely have felt he had got something unique.

A custom paint job can take from one week to six to do, and can cost anything from £300 upwards. First of all, the old paint is stripped off and any defects in the bodywork repaired, then three or four coats of primer are applied. The surface is hand–smoothed, then three to four coats of base colour are applied and the surface hand–smoothed again. The design is drawn on, then air–brushed with acrylic paint. Once the painting is finished, about ten coats of lacquer are applied to produce a mirror–deep shine.

The car being given the treatment in the sequence above was a dragster called Minor Might, and it took about a day to airbrush on the car–within–a–car design. Shown on the right are a Ford Popular and a Mustang together with a close–up of a decorative side–panel. After spending a small fortune on such a flight of fancy, a car owner could be forgiven for keeping the car permanently in its garage.

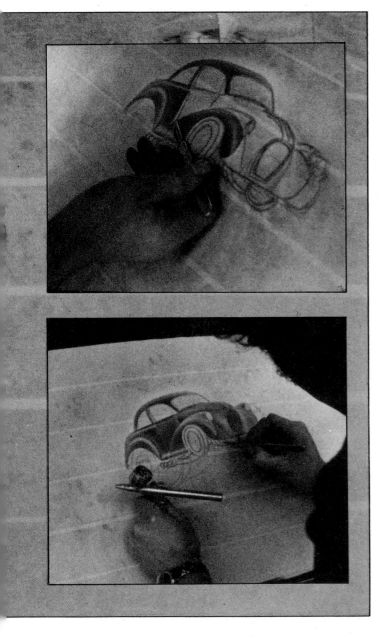

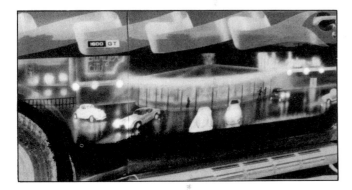

Queen of the Night

See illustration overleaf

This amazing vision in black, white and flaming orange started life as a 1948 Oldsmobile four–door coupé. Inspired by the pictures in some elderly American hot–rod magazines, two Belgian enthusiasts, Chris Seynaeve and Patrice Debruyne, decided to effect some radical changes. The body was reshaped and the chassis rails cut to accommodate the result – a two–door car some four feet shorter than it had been when it left the factory. A 1970 Plymouth was plundered for parts, among them the 5 litre engine, front suspension, power brakes and steering system – even the rear bench seat, which was reupholstered in red velour. The rear bumper was one that had started life behind another elderly American car, but even Seynaeve and Debruyne have no idea what it was. Finally, chrome parts were sent off for rechroming and the painting of the bodywork was done. The creators of this butch and bulbous beauty estimate that the job took about 700 man–hours and cost 400,000 Belgian francs. Now their sights are set on a 1945 Cadillac hearse.

The Oldsmobile's fame has spread through its guest appearances at race circuits (it was pace car at the 1978 Belgian Grand Prix) and in films, so it is possible that it could one day be as famous as Elvis Presley's customised Cadillac. On this car, valued at more than $100,000, almost everything except the engine is gold. There are gold–plated wheel hubs and badges and the passenger compartment, decorated with gold buttons, features a telephone, television set and refrigerator – all made of gold. There is even a gold shoe–polisher. The outside of the car is painted in gold murano pearl with a matching top and all the windows have gold lamé curtains. The roof of the car is lined with copies of Presley's most popular recordings on gold discs.

However, customising does not have to be quite as extreme as these two examples suggest. It can simply mean adding gadgets and accessories to ordinary mass–produced cars. Trendy Mini–owners of the sixties customised their cars by fitting darkened glass in the windows – a relatively inexpensive modification. The American actor Gene Barry, on the other hand, had his 1966 Rolls–Royce painted "crème de cocoa" and pin–striped in white. Nonetheless in the Rolls–Royce customising stakes he was an also–ran compared with V. I. Lenin, who is said to have equipped himself for the Russian winter by fitting skis to the front of his.

How different from the early days of motoring, when every buyer could choose what bodywork to buy for his chosen chassis. Had that situation continued, customising as we know it today need never have come about. The spur to innovative "personalising" has been discontent with the products of mass production, which has tended to standardise the sizes, shapes, colours and interiors available. As the cult of the younger generation gained a foothold in the late fifties, bringing with it revolutions in popular music, clothes and life–styles, the cult of the custom car would seem to have been a logical development.

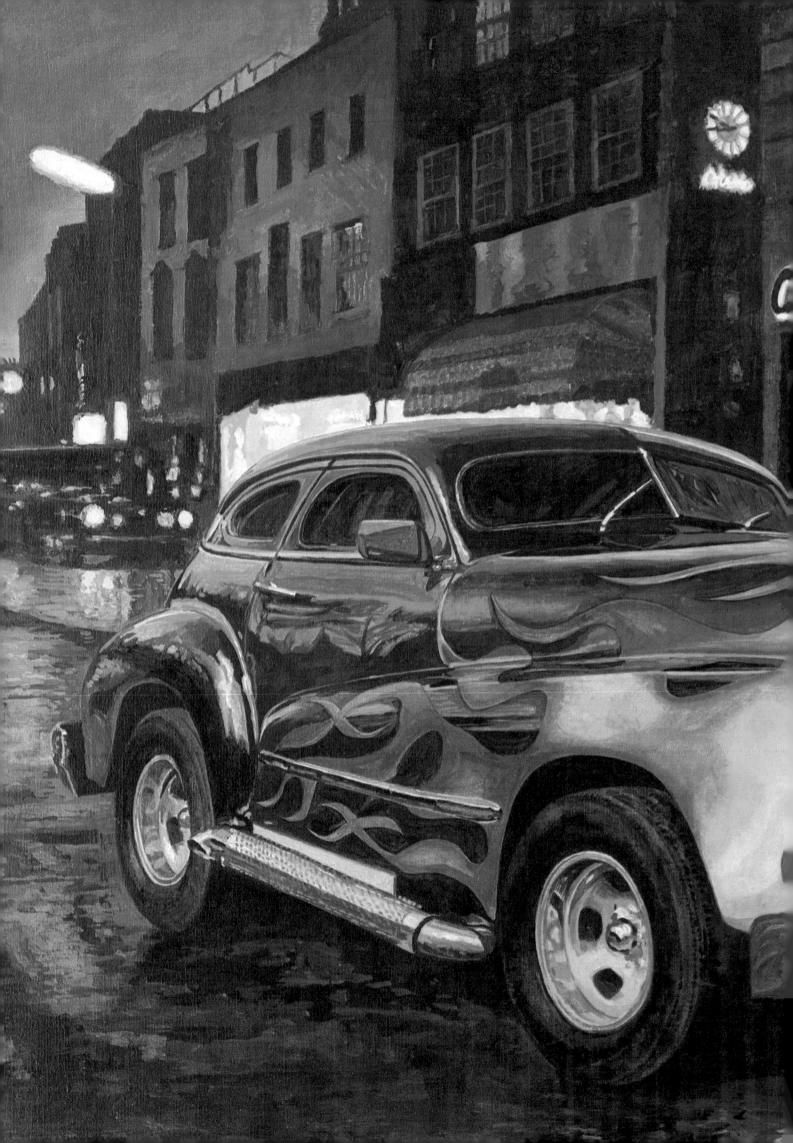

THE EXHIBITIONIST ON WHEELS
The Stunt Merchants

No matter what the invention, man has always wanted to push it to the limit. The car is no exception, and today stunts and car acrobatics are a lucrative feature of the acceptable face of show–business. The first stunts, and still some of the most amazing, were those devised by the film companies in the early days of Hollywood. The Keystone Kops were among the earliest screen characters to exploit the discovery that cars could be made to fall apart at will, survive fire and water – and make people laugh. Modern stunts are usually designed not for laughs but to make audiences catch their breath in tense anticipation of disaster.

At the 1935 Chicago Fair, an American racing driver called Barney Oldfield organised a display which set the scene for car stunters around the USA for years to come. Basing his performance on the animal routines long familiar to fairground audiences, Oldfield put his cars through blazing hoops, jumped them off ramps and made them do somersaults in the air. Oldfield was a great success and suddenly the motor car was big news on the fairground circuits.

The number of people trying to make cars do things they were never intended to do seemed to increase substantially after the Second World War. Again, most of them were film–makers – but not all. In the 1960s a Frenchman known to his English colleagues as Sunny Jim devised a way of driving his car on only two wheels. He would drive up a ramp which tipped the car, usually a Simca, onto the two nearside wheels, and, by careful balancing, prevent it from toppling back onto all four wheels. In this curious, crab–like fashion, Sunny Jim (actually Jean Sunny) managed to complete a lap of the circuit at Silverstone. On another occasion, he set out to drive from Paris to Le Mans, but was defeated by tyre wear.

His idea was however copied by an American team, the Hell Drivers, who extended the range of accomplishments. As a team, they toured Europe and North America driving cars on two wheels, but with the addition of two men balanced on the top. Like others before them, they crashed cars through blazing obstacles, but with a man lying on the bonnet. They were also adept at jumping cars over cars.

While the Hell Drivers attempted to keep their cars and drivers intact, a British team sought to do the opposite. Called the Destruction Squad, this team toured Britain demonstrating to enthusiastic crowds just how many cars they could destroy in one evening. This type of "entertainment" had in fact become hugely popular in Britain and America during the 1970s. At a very amateur level there were the demolition derbys, held on dirt tracks and featuring vehicles which were no longer roadworthy. These spectacles always drew large crowds, eager to watch the motor car treated with as little respect as a tin can.

To date, the ultimate stunt must surely be the "Astro Spiral", the technique for which was worked out on a computer by scientists of the Calspan Corporation in Buffalo, New York. It consisted of a launching ramp so designed that if a car hit it at 40 mph, it would turn 360 degrees and land on its wheels on a second ramp. The driver of the car in the first instance was a stuntman called Chick Galiano, whose responsibility it was to ensure that the car took off at the right speed (the computer could not do that for him): too slow, and the car would come down before it reached the second ramp; too fast, and it would overshoot. Not surprisingly, Chick Galiano rarely made a mistake when attempting this remarkable stunt.

Astro Spiral *(below)*: completing a lateral roll from one ramp to another. Scientists of the Calspan Corporation designed the ramps with the aid of computers. The car was an American Motors Javelin.

Stunt driver Mick Stirrups attempting to leap over 24 cars to equal a world record at the Thanet Raceway in Kent. Unfortunately, the car took a nose–dive, but the driver emerged unhurt.

THE EXHIBITIONIST ON WHEELS
Ego-builders

Revenge *(right)*, a custom–built dragster with modern mechanics and old–style lamps. Fortunately for the paintwork on the glass–fibre canopy, accidents in drag racing are infrequent.

Wall-to-wall carpet *(far right above)* in the driver's cab of a Ford Transit van.

The executive suite *(far right below)*: inside a transformed van. Customising vans was an important part of the pop culture of the 1960s, vans being cheap to buy secondhand and also big enough to accommodate a bed in the back – hence their nickname "passion–wagons". Extravagant interiors were very much a part of the customising process.

THE EXHIBITIONIST ON WHEELS
Rough Riders

As the motor car became available to more and more people whose leisure time and personal affluence were steadily increasing, it was natural that the possibilities of motoring as a leisure pursuit should be more freely exploited. Although it may have been the dream of many young motorists to become Grand Prix drivers, most of them had neither the dedication nor the finance for this dream to become a reality. Despite this, it was perfectly possible to use the newly liberated car for other, less ambitious sporting pursuits whereby the car that was used for some weekend motor–sporting activity would also be fit to get the owner to work on Monday morning.

Motor sport on the open road had been subject to severe restrictions since as long ago as 1925, when sprint racing in Britain on public roads was banned after a spectator and a marshal were injured. Nonetheless, this did not prevent sprints and hill–climbs taking place on closed and private roads, both forms of sport being extremely popular weekend entertainment for drivers and public alike. One form of hill–climbing, particularly known as mud–plugging, involved climbing steep hills over rough terrain. It inspired several enthusiasts to construct their own special cars for the sport, which required the passenger to throw himself from one part of the car to another in order to provide traction for the driving wheels. Colin Chapman's earliest Lotuses were particularly successful in this spectacular sport.

In the USA, where there is an abundance of open space, much of it in the form of deserts, sand dunes and beaches, a new breed of vehicle was developed specifically for driving on these rough and undeveloped terrains. The "buggy", as it is now known, first appeared in California in the 1950s. It was usually based on a VW Beetle chassis, that being the most rugged as well as the most suitable, having the engine and transmission at the rear and being within the financial reach of many people. For the buggy, the standard VW bodywork was replaced by a variety of glass–fibre shells, often with no roof, and with two or four seats. The buggy first appeared as a beach vehicle, but it was followed by more sophisticated versions,

Competition across the sand dunes *(above* and *right)* in buggies. This form of motor sport grew up in the sand dunes on the West Coast of the USA and was popularised by Steve McQueen. Most of the vehicles are based on Volkswagen Beetle chassis and engines, which are rugged in construction and usually easy to buy secondhand.

including the dune buggies, which, fitted with highly tuned engines, competed in such classic off–the–road races as the Baja 1000. The Baja Bug was a particularly popular derivative of the buggy, for with a change of wheels and tyres it could be used on the road as well as off it.

Hot–rodding sprang up, also in the United States, in the 1920s. It began as a method of obtaining increased performance on the road, but spread rapidly to off–road races and desert speed–trials. The 1950s saw a craze for trans–forming old Fords to hot–rods, notably the models T, A and B. Today, "T–rods" are built almost entirely by en–thusiasts, and the vast majority bear only a passing re–semblance to their distinguished ancestors.

Off–the–road motor sport in Europe is less spectacular but equally popular. Autocross and its younger sister rallycross have proved very successful as television sports, which has widened the audience of enthusiasts. Rallycross was born in Britain in 1967 when an outbreak of foot–and–mouth disease caused the international RAC Rally to be cancelled at the last minute, leaving many top–ranking cars and drivers with nothing to do. The result was an impromptu event on some open ground behind the Grand Prix circuit at Brands Hatch, where a "special stage" (timed section) was set up on which the world's top rally–drivers battled through the mud to achieve the fastest time. Through the media, autocross and rallycross attracted many young enthusiasts by virtue of the fact that they were easy to organise and comparatively inexpensive for the competitor, as well as providing a great deal of harmless fun for the spectators. Such has become their popularity that manufacturers, notably Citroën, have promoted similar events around Europe, tempting those who can afford only a modest car to get the maximum pleasure from it.

"Mud-plugging" in the Surrey woods *(bottom left)*.

Autocross *(bottom right)*, with one wheel of a sedate Morris 1000 well off the ground.

THE EXHIBITIONIST ON WHEELS

The Showmen of the Circuits

Motor racing has produced some unusual offshoots. Traditional circuit racing has its roots firmly in the good old days when the drivers were wealthy amateurs – and needed to be, for it costs a surprising amount to finance a race car. Today, there are various different sorts of track racing which, although they cost much less and have no traditions, are nonetheless colourful and exciting.

Karting, or go–karting as it is sometimes known, is one of the most popular. It began in 1956 when an American racing mechanic fitted a lawnmower engine to a simple tube chassis and used it for getting around the paddock at race meetings. The kart's potential as a racing machine was soon recognised. Karting spread to Britain via the American Air Force in 1958, and although the karts were initially despised by supporters of motor racing proper, the sport appealed so strongly to young people that it soon spread all over Europe, in particular to France and Italy. Modern karts are capable of 130 mph and several of today's top–class racing drivers got their first experience of high speed on four wheels at kart tracks.

Drag racing is another form of motor sport frowned on by traditionalists, but with a huge following among the young.

A masked driver *(above)* in the cockpit of a dragster. Drivers wear special clothing and breathing aids as protection against fuel fumes and the constant fire–risk.

A Pro-stock *(below)*. These cars resemble ordinary saloon models but are fitted with very powerful engines and glass–fibre bodies to reduce their weight.

Like karting, it started in the USA in the early 1950s. The idea was very simple: two vehicles at a time compete in a timed speed trial over a quarter–mile strip. In the early days, any car would do, but today the vehicles come in a bewildering variety of specialised shapes and sizes.

Most familiar are the long, slim cars with huge wheels at the back and narrow wheels and tyres – similar to a bicycle's – at the front. Obviously, these machines are not designed to go round corners and would find it very difficult to avoid obstacles, but such problems are rare in drag racing. A real problem with these cars, which can reach speeds of 300 mph, is getting them to stop when they have completed the quarter–mile. Parachute brakes are obligatory on dragsters that have a top speed of more than 150 mph. The cars usually run on methanol or nitro–methane – extremely volatile and expensive fuels – and a single run in a very powerful car can cost up to £300.

Less expensive but just as much fun are the cars known in drag–racing jargon as "Street". These are ordinary road cars with highly modified engines. These cars can cover the quarter–mile in about twelve seconds. Pro–stocks, however, are considerably faster. They have glass–fibre panels on the body and very powerful engines and can achieve times of seven or eight seconds. The "Funny" class of dragsters is probably the fastest of all, and the most entertaining for the crowd. These look not unlike a standard saloon car but have a body made entirely of glass–fibre and are without doors; the driver climbs in through the window. The engine is usually so large that it is sitting in the passenger seat and the wheels and tyres are huge. Funny cars regularly break six seconds for the quarter–mile.

Although drag racing began in the USA, like so many of the most bizarre offshoots of motor racing, Britain has proved a fertile ground for the sport, with a permanent drag strip, Santa Pod, in Bedfordshire. There are also countless little dirt–tracks around the country, where virtually anyone who wants to can try his hand at stock–car racing, or at an even cheaper version, banger racing. Certainly the tracks are small – and the facilities few – but they provide drivers and spectators alike with superb entertainment.

American drag racer Bill Maropulos *(above)* on the track. A time of six seconds for a standing quarter–mile is commonplace for dragsters, which can reach speeds of over 300 mph, yet drag racing accidents are rare.

Stock-car racing *(below)* on an American quarter–mile oval track. The cars are reinforced with steel cages to protect the drivers.

An airborne competitor *(bottom)* during a stock–car race.

Playboy Specials

Ever since the motor car was first thought of, there seems to have been no shortage of people wealthy enough to regard it simply as an expensive toy, and – fortunately for the development of the car itself – designers and engineers prepared to indulge this privileged minority. Were it not for the fortunate few, there could never have been a Bugatti Royale, a Lamborghini Miura, a Porsche 928 or a Rolls–Royce Camargue. Initially, it was mainly heads of state who were in a position to commission the ultimate in luxury motor cars, but gradually, as social developments produced a new breed of rich people, the style of elitist motoring changed from the dignified and stately to the powerful, flamboyant, occasionally vulgar – but always costly – vehicles that are made for this market today – albeit in small numbers.

The playboys of the early days of motoring were able to order, from a host of specialist coach–builders, any body they chose to fit a particular chassis. Those days passed, and after the Second World War there emerged a handful of car–makers whose ambition it was simply to build the ideal car – usually for buyers to whom money would be no object. In this way such eminent names as Ferrari, Maserati, de Tomaso and Monteverdi found their way onto the motor–show stands. While such cars may be only the gilt on the gingerbread of mass production, they play an important role in bringing glamour to an otherwise mundane industry. Of such things dreams are made. . . .

"Never mind what it costs, build it"

Was the Duesenberg the perfect car? Almost certainly, the answer to this frequently asked question is "no", but the Duesenberg *was* one of the most memorable cars of the elegant twenties – one of the fastest and one of the most luxurious. Frederick and August Duesenberg had been brought to America from Germany by their parents when they were very young – Frederick being eight years old. Although largely self–taught, he became an automotive engineer, working first for a garage in Des Moines and later, with his brother, for the Rambler company in Wisconsin. In 1898 he set a world record for cycling two miles and in 1904, again with his brother, built the first Duesenberg racing car.

Although Duesenberg high–performance engines in cars and boats were very successful in competition, they were less successful in financial terms, and eventually the Duesenberg brothers sold their factory and moved to Indianapolis, where they concentrated on building racing cars. In 1920 Duesenbergs were almost unbeatable. They finished third,

fourth and sixth in the Indianapolis 500, and Tommy Milton established a new land speed record of 156 mph at Daytona in a car which was powered by two Duesenberg engines mounted side by side. Their competition success enabled the brothers to start work on the car of their dreams. The first Duesenberg passenger car, the Model A, appeared in 1926. It was extremely expensive and moderately successful, but went no way towards solving the Duesenberg financial problems. That solution lay with Erret Lobban Cord, who, although he was not an engineer, knew a great deal about sales promotion.

"Never mind what it costs, build it," is what Cord is alleged to have told the Duesenberg brothers when he took over their ailing business. They did. In 1929 the Model J appeared with bodies built by the most illustrious coachbuilders. The Model J was followed by the Model SJ, capable of 130 mph, powered by a supercharged 6·9 litre engine and with a price to match. Only 490 Duesenbergs were ever built and they were cars of the most superior quality. The buyer of a Duesenberg could choose any sort of upholstery and the driver of such a car was the best informed on the road. The car was not only fitted with a speedometer and tachometer but it also had an altimeter which doubled as a barometer, a compass, warning light for battery acid level and a split–second stop–watch. Often the instruments were duplicated so that they could be seen by the

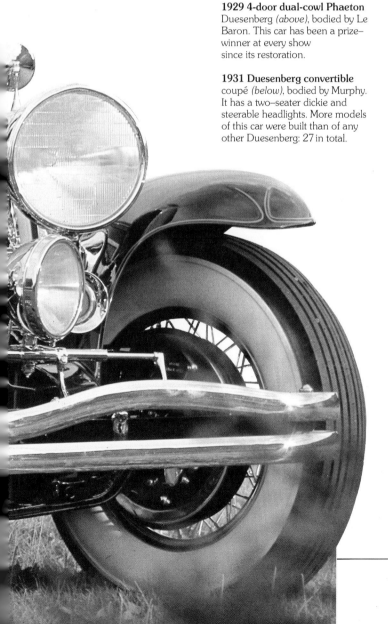

1929 4-door dual-cowl Phaeton
Duesenberg *(above)*, bodied by Le Baron. This car has been a prize–winner at every show since its restoration.

1931 Duesenberg convertible
coupé *(below)*, bodied by Murphy. It has a two–seater dickie and steerable headlights. More models of this car were built than of any other Duesenberg: 27 in total.

rear–seat passengers, who were also provided with cocktail cabinets and perfume sprays. The owners of Duesenbergs were the top socialites of the era and it was *de rigueur* for a film star to have access to one at least.

Messrs Duesenberg and Cord were clearly in no doubt as to the quality of their products. In the introduction to their 1929 catalogue they said: "The superlatively fine has no need to be boastful. So confident is Duesenberg of the unquestioned supreme position its product occupies, that a name plate is considered superfluous. Nowhere on the car do you find the name Duesenberg. . . . Necessarily its appeal is to only a very few. Any masterpiece can only be appreciated by those who understand the principles on which its greatness is based. Therefore the ownership of a Duesenberg reflects discern–ment far above the ordinary."

Those discerning customers included several European heads of state. Prince Nicholas of Rumania put a special body on his, and raced it. King Alfonso of Spain, who had a fleet of more than thirty cars, took only the Duesenberg into exile with him, and Queen Marie of Yugoslavia extolled the virtues of her Duesenberg in a letter to the makers. Events of the future were foreshadowed by Duesenberg when they sold one of the last Model Js to the President of the Republic of Syria.

In Hollywood a Duesenberg was the hallmark of success. Mae West had a Phaeton and Clark Gable drove a convertible coupé. Both Gary Cooper and Clark Gable had SJ roadsters, and Cooper also had a 1930 model, which was painted yellow, with a special boat–shaped back.

However, although the rich and famous loved the car, politics and the Depression combined to ensure that there were not enough of them about to secure the future of the marque, and production ceased altogether when the Cord Corporation was wound up in 1937. There followed one or two unsuccessful attempts to resuscitate the name, but finally, in 1966, the "Duesie" was laid to rest.

Fanfare for the Depression

29 October 1929 was "Black Thursday". In one fell swoop the New York stock market collapsed, taking with it businesses and bank accounts all over the USA. The collapse followed a period of vast expansion and speculation. The "Roaring Twenties" had been particularly fruitful for the automobile industry, and the USA was turning out about 90 per cent of the world's production. One in five Americans were car–owners. A crop of new manufacturers had mushroomed, most of them making luxury cars to satisfy a growing market of affluent people. The Wall Street Crash changed all that. The weaker companies were wiped out and the number of manufacturers decimated.

It was by no means an auspicious time in which to launch a new car, particularly one costing $3000, but Erret Lobban Cord was committed to producing what was to be the first car to bear his name, the L29 Cord. At first, ironically enough, the Depression actually helped the makers of luxury cars, because the fortunate few who had survived the Crash with money to spend were eager to demonstrate the fact: what better way than to buy an expensive automobile? But it was only a matter of time before the Crash was to take its toll of the world's motor industry.

The decline of the US economy had far–reaching effects. Those European countries that depended on long–term loans from American banks for the purchase of American raw materials and manufactured goods suffered in their turn. Of the car–producing countries, only Great Britain managed to keep her automobile industry on a relatively even keel. The Cord's days had been numbered from the start. The car went out of production in 1932, and things were never quite the same again for the makers of the playboy specials.

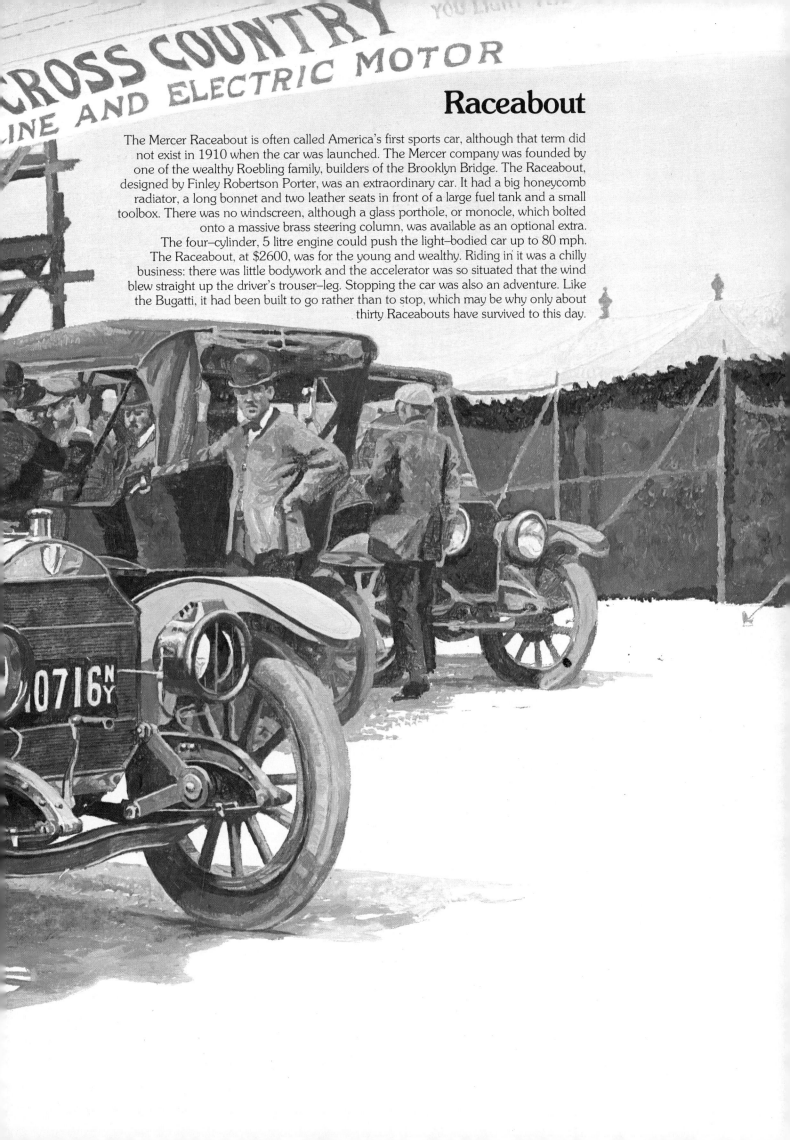

Raceabout

The Mercer Raceabout is often called America's first sports car, although that term did not exist in 1910 when the car was launched. The Mercer company was founded by one of the wealthy Roebling family, builders of the Brooklyn Bridge. The Raceabout, designed by Finley Robertson Porter, was an extraordinary car. It had a big honeycomb radiator, a long bonnet and two leather seats in front of a large fuel tank and a small toolbox. There was no windscreen, although a glass porthole, or monocle, which bolted onto a massive brass steering column, was available as an optional extra. The four–cylinder, 5 litre engine could push the light–bodied car up to 80 mph. The Raceabout, at $2600, was for the young and wealthy. Riding in it was a chilly business: there was little bodywork and the accelerator was so situated that the wind blew straight up the driver's trouser–leg. Stopping the car was also an adventure. Like the Bugatti, it had been built to go rather than to stop, which may be why only about thirty Raceabouts have survived to this day.

Masterpieces of Exotica

Those fabulous, glittering machines that attract the greatest crowds at the motor shows, despite the fact that few of the admirers could ever hope to buy one, are living testimony to the fascination of automotive exotica. When the motor car was in its infancy, everything was exciting, expensive and modern, but with the development of mass–production techniques, and the growing tendency for cars to look predictably similar, there was also a demand, albeit a limited one, for something different. At one end of the market, this problem was solved by automating and modifying the mass–production car; but at the top end of the market, the wealthy vied with each other, and still do, to be the first to own the motor industry's latest *pièce de résistance*. It is said that the film director Jacques Charrier (Brigitte Bardot's ex–husband) flew to Geneva so that he could be first in the queue for the new E–type Jaguar, narrowly beating another potential customer who had flown from London. At least four owners claim to have been the first customer to take delivery of the world's most expensive car, the Rolls–Royce Camargue, which cost £37,500 when it was launched in 1973.

The post–war era of the exclusive "special" for the wealthy enthusiast began in 1952 with the appearance of one of the great classic cars of all time: the Bentley Continental, now a rare and highly coveted collectors' item. The coupé body was designed on the standard Bentley chassis by John Blatchley and was built, mostly of aluminium alloy, by Mulliners. Although the name continued until 1959, only 200 of the original Continentals were built, at a cost of £4900 each.

The Continental was followed by an even more prized "special": the Mercedes–Benz 300 SL, which was launched in 1954. It was the first production car to feature fuel–injection. However, what caught the public's imagination was the fact that the car had gull–wing doors which hinged into the roof of the car – a feature which made it different from any other car on the road. It did not seem to matter that these doors were made necessary by the structure of the frame, nor that they made getting in and out of the car an extremely inelegant business for ladies wearing skirts. The important thing was that the 300 SL was different – and costly. At launch it cost £4393 and only 1400 were ever made. Mercedes did it again in 1969 with a prototype sports coupé, the C111, which had a rotary engine as well as more practically designed gull–wing doors, but this car never went into full–scale production and very few examples were made.

Exclusivity is an essential of the playboy special, and this label could certainly be applied to the Facel Vega, a French–American co–production which combined American power units (in this case Chrysler) with European bodies – a formula which was to become increasingly popular. The ultimate Facel Vega, the Excellence, was launched in the late fifties, costing (even in those days) £6500. The eight–cylinder 6 litre engine gave the car a top speed of more than 120 mph. Only 230 examples of the Excellence were ever made and the company went out of business in 1964.

It is a sad but inescapable fact that despite the undoubted demand for the exclusive car, the companies which have attempted to supply that demand have always had great difficulty in making ends meet. One notable example is Jensen, a famous name with an impeccable pedigree dating back to 1936, when two brothers, Richard and Allan Jensen, set up in business as coachbuilders in West Bromwich, in the Midlands. After the war, Jensens used Chrysler engines

The 1947 Cisitalia coupé *(top)*, with bodywork designed by Pninfarina, was first seen at the Paris Motor Show of the same year. Cisitalia was a make produced by veteran Italian racing driver Piero Dusio, on whose cars Farina pioneered the close–coupled coupé body seen here.

Bentley Continental *(above)*, a 1952 two–door coupé with a body designed by J. P. Blatchley and built by Mulliners. One of the most beautiful and expensive cars of the period, it cost £4890 at launch. The 4·6 litre engine gave a top speed of 120 mph and the car was in production for seven years.

in their cars. The pinnacle of their achievement was reached in 1966 when the Jensen Interceptor FF was launched. This superbly sophisticated car had Ferguson four–wheel drive, Dunlop Maxaret anti–lock braking and a body styled by Vignale of Italy. Despite the wealth of technological advances represented by the FF, the company was unable to make money. Although there were determined attempts to rescue it, notably by the production of a Jensen–Healey sports car specifically intended for the extensive market of the USA's west coast, the company was finally forced into liquidation in 1976.

Like Jensen, Aston Martin has in the past been bedevilled by financial problems, but unlike Jensen, it is still in existence. The name is of course synonymous with high–performance luxury cars. Early models, which had considerable competition success, qualified as sports cars, while the later models represent the ultimate in road–going sophistication. A series of company changes since the days of David Brown (the tractor magnate) has culminated in the new Lagonda – a hotbed of electronic gadgetry which has yet to be proved roadworthy; nonetheless, there is a queue of customers more than willing to pay the asking price of over £40,000.

Another company producing cars which are both idio–syncratic and appealing to the wealthy enthusiast is that of Bristol. Unlike many of its rivals, it has remained financially stable without compromising over its product. The original Bristol, produced in 1947, was a copy of a 2 litre BMW, but in 1962 the manufacturer adopted the now familiar formula of

using a transatlantic power unit coupled to a European–styled body. The new car, the 407, was a luxury saloon which, with its modified Chrysler engine, can out–accelerate an E–type in top gear and out–accelerate a Ferrari over a standing half–mile. Although subsequent Bristols have perhaps lacked the grace and elegance of their competitors, their undoubted exclusivity places them in a very special category.

It is much more than coincidence that many of the most coveted luxury cars in the world have come from Italy, the country from which a host of famous car–makers and coachbuilders have emerged. Italian dominance in car body design parallels that of Paris in *haute couture* and Scandinavia in furniture design. Why it should be so is hard to explain. Certainly the Italian coachwork is full of innovation and has been so since the sixteenth century, when splendid carriages were built in Italy, but it is almost impossible to put into words the qualities which have been so highly developed by the Italian masters and which have created so great a demand among mass–production manufacturers, as well as by those car–buyers who can afford something very special indeed.

The names themselves are well known – Ferrari, Maserati, Lamborghini, Vignale, Ghia and, of course, Pninfarina. Battista Pninfarina, whose work is the epitome of the Italian coachbuilt car, came nearest to describing his ideal: "The interrelation between the body of a beautiful woman and that of a Farina–designed car is that both have simplicity and harmony of line, so that when they are old one can still see how beautiful they were when they were young." Such was

Farina's prestige amongst Italians that in 1961 the President of the Italian Republic granted him permission to change his name to Pninfarina, the name of the company he founded. One of his most famous cars, the 1951 Cisitalia, was displayed at the Museum of Modern Art in New York. Its elegant lines also provided the inspiration for many of the models which appeared in the later fifties.

But while Pninfarina specialised in designing elegant car bodies for others to put into production, other designers made and sold their exotics. No make of car commands quite the respect of Ferrari. The company was founded in 1940 by the Commendatore, as he is known, but concentrated for the first few years on racing cars. It was the late 1940s before a series of powerful touring cars was built, principally for the American market. Always an innovator, it was Ferrari who led the trend towards mid–engined sports coupés for the road. The first was one of the great classic cars, the Dino 246. Named after the Commendatore's son, who died of leukaemia in his twenties, the little Dino gave rise to a series of cars in which subsequent models had larger, more powerful engines. In 1972, a Spyder version was the star of the Ferrari range. But the following year Ferrari announced a sensational road car – the ultimate Ferrari road car – mid–engined with a flat 4·4 litre twelve–cylinder engine and a top speed of nearly 200 mph.

Equally fast, though lacking the distinguished ancestry, is the Lamborghini Countach – latest in that marque's range of elegant machinery. It was in 1946 that Ferruccio Lamborghini first turned his hand to making tractors. From there, he

PLAYBOY SPECIALS

progressed to tuning Fiat 500s and eventually, in 1963, to producing his first car.

The Miura, which caused a sensation at the Turin Motor Show in 1965, marked Lamborghini as a serious competitor to Ferrari on the road if not on the race–track, for Lamborghini has never raced his products. The Miura had a 4 litre engine mounted behind the seats, and the car boasted a top speed of 180 mph. The Miura was followed by the Urraco, the Jarama and the Espada and finally, in 1973, the Countach, powered by a 5 litre, V12 engine, with growling, aggressive styling that has become much beloved of pop stars, eastern potentates and, of course, all those who love speed.

Maserati, by contrast, has a somewhat more dignified image than the relatively upstart Ferrari and Lamborghini. The name was first seen on a car in 1926, when the Maserati brothers set up in business in Bologna (later to move to Modena) and built their first 1·5 litre racing car. Until the mid–sixties, the Maserati reputation was carried entirely by its successful racing cars, but since that time, the company has concentrated on high–performance luxury road cars. One of the most popular of these was the Quattroporte – a four–door saloon, powered by a 4136 cc V8 engine, which was introduced to great acclaim in 1964. The Ghibli coupé, introduced three years later, usually featured four retractable headlights and had an effortless top speed of 175 mph. It was some time before Maserati followed Ferrari and Lamborghini with a mid–engined model. Finally, in 1972, he introduced the Bora two–seater coupé, which with a top speed of over 200 mph is one of the world's fastest road cars. This model is still much in demand, despite the fact that there are few places in the world where such speeds are possible, let alone legal, on the open road.

Darling of the jet set (below), the Lamborghini Miura, named after the Spanish fighting bull and launched in 1965. Originally intended as a motor–show special, the Miura went into production and was made until 1973.

Ferrari Dino 246 (far right, top), first produced as a prototype in 1965. The little rear–engined sports car became a great favourite with the affluent public.

Maserati Ghibli (far right, centre) a classic two–door coupé with a top speed of 175 mph, in the tradition of the Italian GT (gran turismo) class.

1968 Lamborghini Espada (far right, bottom), a front–engined coupé powered by a V12 unit. An unusual feature of all cars made by Lamborghini is that the gearboxes are fitted with synchromesh on the reverse gear.

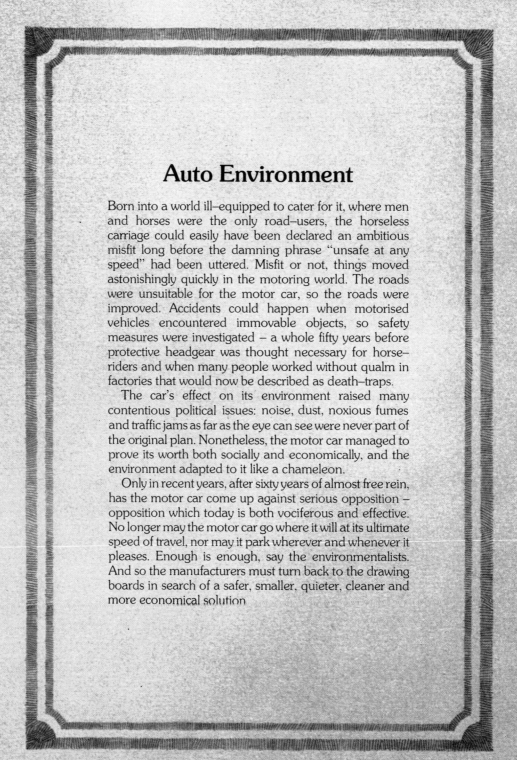

Auto Environment

Born into a world ill–equipped to cater for it, where men and horses were the only road–users, the horseless carriage could easily have been declared an ambitious misfit long before the damning phrase "unsafe at any speed" had been uttered. Misfit or not, things moved astonishingly quickly in the motoring world. The roads were unsuitable for the motor car, so the roads were improved. Accidents could happen when motorised vehicles encountered immovable objects, so safety measures were investigated – a whole fifty years before protective headgear was thought necessary for horse–riders and when many people worked without qualm in factories that would now be described as death–traps.

The car's effect on its environment raised many contentious political issues: noise, dust, noxious fumes and traffic jams as far as the eye can see were never part of the original plan. Nonetheless, the motor car managed to prove its worth both socially and economically, and the environment adapted to it like a chameleon.

Only in recent years, after sixty years of almost free rein, has the motor car come up against serious opposition – opposition which today is both vociferous and effective. No longer may the motor car go where it will at its ultimate speed of travel, nor may it park wherever and whenever it pleases. Enough is enough, say the environmentalists. And so the manufacturers must turn back to the drawing boards in search of a safer, smaller, quieter, cleaner and more economical solution

The Cost to Society

The most dramatic change brought about by the advent of the motor car in volume has been in the state of the roads. In the early days of the twentieth century, roads were merely strips of dirt compacted by vehicles. The cost of improving them to cope with the increase in motorised traffic was a contentious political issue, largely because no one was certain who should bear the cost of such improvements. Eventually, in 1909, Lloyd George introduced the Road Fund, a tax on motor vehicles that was originally intended to be used to build and maintain roads. The fund was designed to be self–financing so that motorists would be paying to provide the roads they so badly needed: however, in the event, successive governments found this novel source of revenue too attractive to allocate solely to road improvements.

A great deal needed to be done to improve the quality of roads in both Europe and North America, and there was a clear need for good, fast roads to carry long–distance traffic. The first modern motorway was opened in September 1924 between Milan and Varese in Italy. The event spurred on the road–improvement lobby in Britain and at the same time a plan for a London–to–Liverpool motorway was presented to Parliament by Lord Montagu, but was rejected. Alternative plans put to successive governments were also rejected. One particularly ambitious project was drafted by Peter Lee, then General Secretary of the Durham Miners' Association, together with an expert road engineer. The Lee plan, which would have cost £240 million, was to build 2400 miles of motorway linking major British cities; an additional advantage was that it would provide employment for a million men for fifteen months.

Even this attractive project was rejected, first by Stanley Baldwin and then by Ramsay MacDonald, although road–building was becoming recognised as a fruitful and classic way of providing employment in a period when an unacceptable number of people were out of work. Renewed impetus for the improvement of British roads came in 1933 with the announcement that Hitler was planning a motorway linking Frankfurt with Mannheim and Heidelberg as part of a system running from the North Sea and the Baltic to Switzerland. The first section, joining Frankfurt and Darmstadt, was completed and opened in May 1935.

In Britain, despite a good deal of pressure from the Liberal Party, no noticeable progress was made. In 1937 it enlisted the support of Earl Howe, a famous racing driver of the period, and in an impassioned plea to the Government, Earl Howe pointed out that in the first forty years of the age of the motor car, there had been no significant addition to the mileage of roads which had existed in the reign of Queen Victoria, although traffic density was growing at the rate of 35 per cent every five years. The Road Fund was producing £75 million for the Exchequer every year, but none of it was being spent on new roads. The British Road Federation, which represents the commercial vehicle–users, estimated that accident figures could be reduced by half if suitable roads were available.

In the United States, the first motorway–type road, the Pennsylvania Turnpike, was opened in 1940. The value of roads of this sort was quickly seen when Hitler used the German autobahn system to transport his army from one side of Germany to the other, and the publicity which this manoeuvre attracted gradually caused the British public to recognise the desirability of motorways.

Discussions continued after the war. Although in 1948 the then Minister of Transport, A. J. Barnes, announced that the Government hoped to inaugurate a series of motorways in Britain, it was not until December 1958 that the first stretch, an eight–mile section bypassing Preston, was opened.

From these beginnings, motorways spread inexorably

across Europe and America, particularly around the major industrial areas. By the end of 1959 there were 80 miles of motorway in Britain and in 1971 229 miles were completed, bringing the total mileage to 1000. The pride of British motorway–builders was, and still is, the 13 miles of elevated road north of Birmingham, so complex that it became known as "Spaghetti Junction".

However, the new roads were not built without sacrifice. To construct a motorway interchange requires sixty acres of land, all of which will belong to someone – most probably someone who believes that the motorway should be built on someone else's land, or past some other front door. Lengthy negotia–tions and tribunals, together with a cut–back in public spending, meant that motorways in Britain's crowded countryside expanded slowly whereas in other countries they were considered, for better or for worse, to be an immediate necessity. The passing of a government decree, for instance, forestalled most of the argument about the building of the "Périphérique", the Paris motorway which rings the city, carrying through traffic away from the city centre.

With a rapid increase in the density of traffic on the roads, even motorways became clogged. On the Santa Monica Freeway Interchange it is estimated that cars pass at the rate of 300 a minute and the Hollywood Harbor Freeway, also in Los Angeles, is believed to be the world's busiest motorway. For the motorist, even an empty motorway demands unceasing concentration, despite the fact that stringent speed limits have been imposed in both Europe, with the exception of West Germany, and in North America. Statistically, motorways are less dangerous than ordinary roads, but long stretches of straight road are hypnotic for the driver and schemes are currently being devised to help drivers to remain alert. In North America, many motorways are decorated with advertising billboards. In Europe, where advertising on motorways is strictly limited, the section of motorway between Chalon and Ste Menehould on the Paris–Strasbourg road has sprouted brightly painted totem poles, geometric shapes and coloured balls, intended as a visual tonic for bored, weary drivers.

Another costly item in motoring is the fight against pollution. It is by no means coincidence that Peking is believed to be the cleanest city in the world. Western commentators maintain that the main reason for this is that China has one of the lowest concentrations of motor cars per head of the population of any country in the world – although there are other contributory factors, including the absence of industrial pollution of the atmosphere. Los Angeles, on the other hand, suffered "automobile smogs" until very recently and it is regrettable that although the internal combustion engine has brought mobility to millions, it has also brought pollution.

The principal reason for this is that the internal combustion engine is in many respects inefficient. In the combustion chamber of a modern petrol or diesel engine, the fuel is only partially burned, and the noxious residue is emitted via the exhaust pipe. The outwardly visible signs of these emissions are most easily seen on buildings. York Minster, for example, in the north of England, suffered considerable erosion to its external stonework largely, it is believed, as a result of emissions from the exhausts of motor vehicles. London's St Paul's Cathedral and the cathedral in Cologne are per–manently stained brown. Particles of dust and grit cling to oily deposits on the stonework and cleaning only aggravates the problem. When the natural salts which come to the surface of the stonework are cleaned off, the softer stone underneath is exposed, and this is even more susceptible to damage.

More serious than anything which happens to buildings, however, is damage to human health. Dirt and exhaust fumes do not only fall onto roads and stonework: they pervade the atmosphere. This was recognised in the early days of the motor car when vigorous complaints were made about air pollution by those who did not own cars. Giving evidence to a parliamentary commission of the British Government an authoress, Miss Everett–Green, claimed in 1906 that "all the plants under glass were spoiled . . . and our health was injured. I had to get new typewriters. I got a new typewriter in 1902 and I had to change it again this year, it got so gritty."

The commission considered the possibility of legislating for the introduction of dustless cars, but abandoned the idea as impractical. Much of the dust was of course caused by the action of the wheels on unmade roads – which were barely suitable even for the slower and gentler passage of horse–drawn transport. Pollution of the atmosphere was an issue which aroused diametrically opposed points of view, depend–ing on where people's interests lay: obviously, motorists, would–be motorists and above all the motor industry preferred to play down the problem.

The true extent of the dangers of exhaust pollution was not fully investigated until much later. In 1971 a professor at the Brighton College of Technology estimated that in city traffic the level of carbon monoxide in the air was frequently sufficient to impair a driver's sense of judgement by up to one–fifth. At Harwell, the British Atomic Research Establishment, tests showed that exhaust pollution plays a critical part in the formation of smog, and that there was no reason why "automobile smogs" should be confined to the sunny cities of the west coast of the USA: they could happen just as easily in Britain and other Western European countries.

Some of the effects of exhaust pollution can be dramatic. Children have complained of spots, women of spoiled nylon stockings, and plants have died, having failed to adjust to the changing atmosphere. By the early 1970s pollution had become a *cause célèbre*, particularly with American environ–mentalists. At one point some Californians even took to wearing anti–pollution masks in the street.

Once the matter had become a political issue, the responsibility for "cleaning up" car engines was laid at the feet of the manufacturers, initially through the enactment of the USA's 1970 Clean Air Act. The motor industry, slowly and reluctantly, took steps to comply, and passed the costs of emission control onto their customers. There have been many attempts to solve the problem of inefficient combustion, ranging from catalytic converters, various types of filters and turbo–charging to the use of fuels with a low lead content. Ultimately the problem may provide its own solution as engine designers are forced to look to other fuel sources for the cars and commercial vehicles that are so necessary to modern life.

German officers *(below)* ponder over a model of the Berlin–Munich autobahn in 1936.

Pollution and traffic congestion *(left)* heralded by the Red Flag.

A 1920s multi-storey car park *(top left)* in the USA. Called a parking tower, it was built on a plot of ground of about the size needed for a two–car garage and was high enough to house ten cars. An endless chain, powered by an electric motor, raised and lowered the steel platforms on which the cars stood.

The New York City Police *(above)* staged a campaign in 1958 against road accidents. Brightly coloured slogans were painted on police cars carrying speedometers on their roofs to draw attention to speed limits. In 1908, the New York City Police had been the first force to use cars for traffic control.

A road safety poster *(right)* by the Belgian Ministry of Transport warns motorists of the dangers of mini–skirts in the summer of 1967: "You are distracted . . . and BANG." Similar posters were adopted by the French and Italian authorities, but none of these

countries experienced any noticeable reduction in the number of road accidents.

Parking meters *(top right)*, in Passaic, New Jersey, in 1937. The world's first parking meters were installed in Oklahoma City in 1935, but Passaic was the first town in the eastern USA to install them. Parking cost 5 cents an hour. Britain's first parking meters did not appear until 1958.

A black flag at half-mast *(above right)* in Berlin in 1953. Many towns and cities in Germany erected a black death–flag in an attempt to reduce traffic accidents. When anyone was killed on the road in the area, the flag was lowered to half–mast. The scoreboard below the flag kept a tally of the number of fatal accidents each month.

A road safety sign *(right)* in Peking photographed in 1928. The penalty for exceeding the 15 mph limit was death.

The Paris Motor Show of 1952 *(left)*, held in the Grand Palais. Motor shows have been the prime shop windows for the world's motor industry ever since the first British show in 1895 and the first American show in Boston in 1898.

"Spaghetti Junction" *(below)*, the pride of British road–builders. Completed in 1972 at a cost of more than £40 million, it is 13 miles of elevated multi–level interchange on the northern outskirts of Birmingham.

AUTO ENVIRONMENT

Safety and Economy – a Continuing Saga

From the moment it first turned a wheel, the motor car has been a potentially lethal weapon. In recognition of this, ways of making it safer have been as eagerly sought as ways of making it go faster. The first requirement was some sort of audible warning device which would let other road–users know of the car's approach and give them time to get out of the way. One of the first inventions was the bulb horn, which appeared as early as 1871 and was operated by the driver when he had a hand free. Many of the early–warning systems relied on bells, and in 1884 a Mr J. Riedel devised a system of bells which rang whenever the brakes were applied. One of the more sophisticated systems had a pedal which sounded a bell, and in 1909 an American invented the first electric horn.

Direction and stopping indicators were another vital ingredient of safety. The somewhat basic idea of a board behind the car which opened to reveal the word "STOP" when the brakes were applied was soon outdated. It was superseded by a roller blind, operated by pulling a string, which alternated the words "LEFT", "RIGHT" and "STOP". Swinging arm indicators, operated pneumatically, were being fitted to new cars by 1905.

Rear–view mirrors were another important development, but in this field there was apparently little scope for improvement. The earliest mirror on record, produced in 1896, was mounted on a ball–joint so that the driver could adjust it; not for many years was any advance made on this.

The year 1904 was the first in which bumpers appeared on a motor car, although they were already widely used on trains. Generally, car bumpers were curved, padded with rubber and mounted on springs which would absorb gentle impacts without damaging the bodywork. They were not immediately successful, largely because traffic was not yet moving sufficiently fast to make the likelihood of a collision a serious threat, but as designers began to cover the wheels (which acted well as impromptu bumpers) with mudguards, and cars started to move faster, bumpers became a necessity and were universally adopted. Only recently has there been any attempt to standardise bumper heights so that in the event of a collision they would actually meet. Incredibly, for many years, this was not considered necessary and minor collisions would often result in strings of cars being neatly hooked together by their useless bumper–bars.

Seat belts, now almost taken for granted by the industry if not always by the public, are by no means a new idea. In the very early cars, particularly those with tiller steering, it was very easy for the driver to be thrown off his seat if the car hit a bump or a pothole. In 1903, a Mr G. Pounce put forward the idea that drivers should be strapped into their seats, and in 1908 a man called Richard Radtke actually designed a prototype seat belt, although it apparently never went into production.

The earliest cars had no windscreens, but as vehicles became more powerful, goggles were no longer sufficient to protect the driver from grit and stones, let alone rain. The earliest screens were simply sheets of glass held by a wooden frame, but in 1905 an English solicitor invented what is now known as laminated glass – a single thin sheet of celluloid sandwiched between two sheets of glass and held together with transparent cement. Although this glass later went into production in France and England, it was expensive and eventually, in the 1920s, a cheaper alternative called toughened glass was developed. This was widely used on

A "pedestrian-catcher" on a French car of 1913. Wire netting stretched over a frame scooped up the jay–walker. Sixty years later British Leyland experimented with a similar device on an Austin 1800.

The **Aurora safety car** developed by Father Alfred Juliano (at the wheel) in 1958. This also featured a scoop as well as crash padding, a telescopic steering column, heavy–duty bumpers and a glass–fibre body.

A **side-impact test** on a Ford Cortina. Tests such as this helped manufacturers to develop a safety passenger–compartment, reinforced with side members to protect the occupants in oblique–impact collisions.

A **Ford Fiesta** undergoing crash testing. The car is repeatedly catapulted, at different speeds, into a solid barrier so that the amount of damage likely to result from head–on collisions can be assessed.

passenger cars until rising safety standards made its use illegal in some countries.

In the early days safety was thought of as a series of bits and pieces which could be added to the motor car to make it less hazardous. It was many years before the idea of a complete "safety" car was mooted, but such a concept was not popular with the public, the vast majority of whom had no particular desire to feel safe in their cars. They wanted cars which made them feel brave and daring – not cars which cushioned them against life's dangers. For this reason, anyone who tried to sell a safety car was regarded with a certain amount of scorn. One such man was a Roman Catholic priest, Father Alfred Juliano of Branford, Connecticut, who, in 1958, produced the Aurora "safety sedan" to his own design. Of all "safety" cars the Aurora was probably the most bizarre, with flared wings which ran from the boot to the bonnet and made the car look as though it was going backwards; however, the driver sat in a cockpit with a bubble–type windscreen, which at least had the advantage of providing better all–round vision. The car was offered for sale at $15,000 – a good deal of money to pay for a car at that time.

The world's first production safety car was the Rover 2000, launched in October 1963 to public acclaim. It was a completely new car and a courageous enterprise for Rover. The company, hitherto associated with staid if not old–fashioned cars, was looking for younger buyers. To pursue those buyers by producing a safety car was a surprising move, as safety has always been notoriously difficult to market.

What made the Rover 2000 different, and important, was that it was designed to incorporate as many safety features as possible, yet still sell at a competitive price.

On launch day the Rover 2000 cost £1264. It was a genuine 100 mph four–seater, four–door saloon with clean, angular styling reminiscent of the better Italian designs, and it boasted an overall fuel consumption of 28 mpg: all this and safety too! Many of the major safety features were incorporated in the bodywork. A steel bulkhead deflected the engine downwards in the event of a collision, instead of pushing it into the driver's lap. The steel frame of the car formed a cage which would protect the occupants in an accident even if the car rolled over, and a fireproof partition divided the fuel tank from the passenger compartment, with the tank itself mounted high enough to protect it from all but the worst impacts.

Inside the car, all vulnerable projections were thickly padded, including the backs of the front seats, so that rear–seat passengers would not suffer head injuries if thrown forward. The steering column was designed to crumple on impact.

All these features were designed to protect the car's occupants *after* an accident. However, the Rover 2000 also included other, more important, safety features that were intended to help the driver avoid the accident in the first place. Most important were the tyres. The suspension of the Rover had been designed in conjunction with the tyre manufacturers Dunlop and Pirelli, specifically to use the latest radial–ply tyres. These tyres were revolutionising road–holding in both wet and dry conditions, and on the 2000 they were fitted as standard equipment. As a result the car had exceptional stability. It also had a very efficient braking system, comprising disc brakes on all four wheels.

The Rover 2000 was the first of a new generation of cars. In Italy, Pninfarina, in conjunction with a motoring magazine, produced a prototype safety car called the Sigma, which had sliding doors and front and rear screens which were designed to fall out in one piece on impact. Volvo, a firm which sets great store by the safety of its vehicles, introduced in 1967 the 144, which had a reinforced passenger compartment, dual–circuit four–wheel disc brakes and a telescopic steering column.

For most consumers, fuel economy is a more important

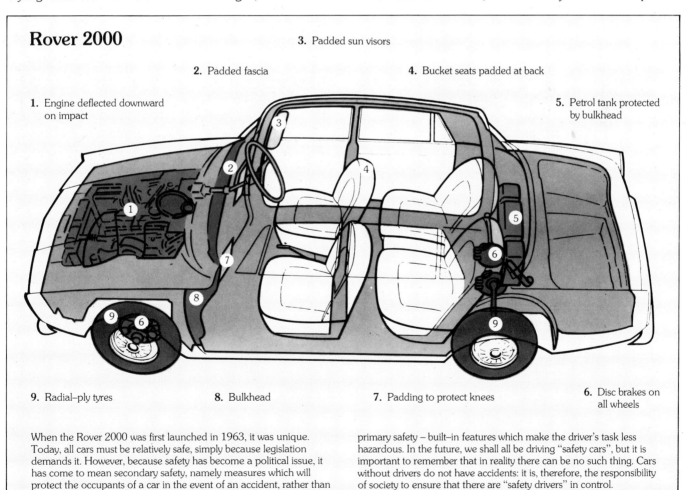

Rover 2000

1. Engine deflected downward on impact
2. Padded fascia
3. Padded sun visors
4. Bucket seats padded at back
5. Petrol tank protected by bulkhead
6. Disc brakes on all wheels
7. Padding to protect knees
8. Bulkhead
9. Radial–ply tyres

When the Rover 2000 was first launched in 1963, it was unique. Today, all cars must be relatively safe, simply because legislation demands it. However, because safety has become a political issue, it has come to mean secondary safety, namely measures which will protect the occupants of a car in the event of an accident, rather than primary safety – built-in features which make the driver's task less hazardous. In the future, we shall all be driving "safety cars", but it is important to remember that in reality there can be no such thing. Cars without drivers do not have accidents: it is, therefore, the responsibility of society to ensure that there are "safety drivers" in control.

consideration than safety in the choice of a car. As fuel crises threaten and road space for both driving and parking becomes ever more restricted, the demand for a car that will consume as little fuel as possible (preferably not petrol), occupy the minimum of space and handle easily in dense traffic has grown considerably. Some unusual vehicles have resulted.

One of the weirdest was a Phänomobil, a three–wheeler which was successfully launched in Germany in 1907 and which continued to be extremely popular until the late 1920s. The following year, another three–wheeler was produced, in Britain, by AC (the initials stood for Autocarrier) and remained in production until the First World War.

After the Second World War, a new generation of economy cars was born. Some had bubble–shaped cockpits – notably the Messerschmitt, whose canopy was rumoured to be identical to that of the German fighter plane made by the same company, and could be converted to such at a moment's notice. The original British bubble car was the Bond Minicar, which was launched in 1951. Even the modest Isle of Man boasted a "bubble", the little three–wheeler, single–seater Peel, powered by a 49 cc, two–stroke engine. With a body measuring only 53 inches long, the Peel P50 was one of the smallest cars ever made. In 1965, Peel attempted another innovation by developing the smallest car ever powered by an electric motor.

The concept of the electrically powered car is by no means new. Electric–powered vehicles had rivalled steam– and petrol–driven cars on the roads in the early days of motoring – some of them, particularly the American runabouts, being particularly practical and attractive. The London Electric Cab Company operated seventy–seven battery–powered taxis between 1897 and 1900, when the company disintegrated, and there were electric taxis in New York, Boston and other American cities at about the same time.

Electricity as a source of power for motor cars was found to have a number of advantages, the greatest being that it was clean and easy to use. But the batteries were heavy and their power output small. Thomas Edison claimed that the battery he was developing at the turn of the century would revolutionise the electric–powered vehicle. He believed that it would be lighter and more powerful, giving cars better performance and a greater range. However, his new battery, made with nickel and alkali, had few if any advantages over the lead–acid battery. Gradually, the use of battery–powered vehicles became restricted to the delivery of milk and other goods (some of the smarter London stores use battery–powered delivery vans).

Fuel shortages and pollution problems have encouraged manufacturers to look anew at the possibilities of using battery–powered cars for town motoring. In 1970 the Electricity Council in London commissioned a fleet of "Electricars" for use by the various electricity boards. At the press launch of this bold effort, a number of the cars were driven from the south coast of England to London, with an overnight stop at Crawley (the batteries were not powerful enough to complete the fifty–mile journey in one day). The principal problem was weight: although the cars could carry only two adults and a limited amount of shopping, each car weighed about a ton. One car broke down on Westminster Bridge and the driver found it too heavy to push alone.

In the USA, manufacturers have attempted to power some of their larger passenger cars with batteries. The virtuoso violinist Yehudi Menuhin, who is also a tireless con–servationist, recently bought a "Transformer I" for his own use, but as the otherwise spacious boot is full of batteries, he has had to use a conventional car for all but short journeys.

Amsterdam was the scene of a major electric–car experiment in March 1974 called the "White Car Scheme". At last, some electrically powered town cars had passed through the prototype stage and onto the road. A fleet was available for hire to members of a co–operative, who could pick them up at one station and leave them at another somewhere else in the city. The scheme eventually collapsed because there was no way of ensuring that the cars were in the right place at the right time, but the experiment was an important step forward.

The search for a viable electrically powered vehicle is one of the most active projects in the motor industry. Ford has produced the Comuta – a neat little prototype which is awaiting the advent of suitable batteries. Other manufacturers, although they have no problems over batteries for their perfect town car, have so far hesitated to make the enormous financial commitment necessary to put such a model into production.

Among the cars which could attract this type of investment is the petrol–driven Minissima, designed by Bill Towns and based on standard Mini components, but the smallest four–wheeled car on the market at present, though only in small–volume production, is the Italian Lawil, which appeared in 1976. Zagato, the Italian coachbuilders, have built a prototype city car, the Zele, which is only 77 inches long. And so the search for the ideal small car continues.

AUTO ENVIRONMENT
A Car is Born

Each new car begins with a search for a shape. In the case of a car which is to be manufactured in millions, the shape is influenced by the answers to a series of crucial questions posed by those whose responsibility it will be to sell the finished product. How many people must the car carry? How much luggage? How fast? How far? And the most crucial question of all – how much? These are not the only parameters. Engineers will already have decided essential points such as whether the engine will be at the front or the back and which wheels it will be driving. What shape and size will the engine be and what sort of fuel will it use? In addition to satisfying all these basic requirements, and many more, the designers are faced with the task of making their car just that much better than, and different from, the opposition. How to set about it?

It takes, on average, about five years for a new model to go "from board to build", although some manufacturers have achieved it in less, and some have taken much longer. First ideas appear on the sketch pads in the styling studio. These are known as "concept cars", and although few if any ever appear on the road, they are the germs from which the final product is evolved.

These concept, or "theme", cars are first submitted to treatment by a design computer (which has taken the place of the draughtsman for some of the more complicated tasks); they then begin to take shape, as "clay" models. These models

are sometimes scale models, often life–size, and frequently, for economy reasons, feature different styling ideas on each side. To make them, warmed clay is smoothed over a wooden frame and carved into shape with scalpels and other precision instruments. So realistic are these clay models that manufacturers have been known to paint them and exhibit them at motor shows, with few spectators being any the wiser.

While exterior stylists are working on the body, other teams of designers and engineers are concentrating on the interior – seats, controls, trim and colour schemes. At every stage, the cost of production is assessed. For example, gold lamé seats may look stunning, but it is doubtful whether many people could afford to buy a car that has them.

Early models of a proposed design are tested in a wind tunnel to evaluate their aerodynamic properties and determine whether the shape is suitable. As good aerodynamic styling can mean considerable savings in fuel consumption, these tests have become increasingly important in car design during the past decade.

There are also legal requirements to be considered: bumper heights, headlamps and indicators are all governed by different regulations in different countries, which makes the designer's task almost impossibly complicated. Once all these stages have been successfully passed, the machine must undergo the acid test of public opinion before being finally approved for production. The new design is usually sent anonymously to a "clinic", where members of the public are invited to give their reactions. If these are favourable, and approval has also been granted by the company's management and its financial advisers, the car is on its way.

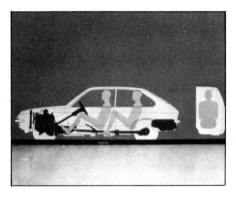

1 In the initial stages of design, full–scale drawings of the proposed new model are prepared and mounted on the walls of the design studio. These detailed working drawings show all the principal mechanical components and the layout of the passenger compartment.

2 Teams of design engineers prepare detailed full–scale drawings of each individual component of the car's body, including lights, doors, bumpers and windows. Even wing mirrors and other accessories are drawn up, actual size, so that the design can be evaluated as a whole.

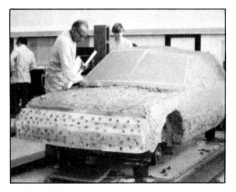

3 A wooden framework is constructed to form a base for the "clay" – a full-scale model of the new car. Technicians mould clay onto the framework and then carefully pare away the excess with knives until the model is a perfect reproduction of the design plans.

4 Completing the clay is a skilled task: at this stage the painted model has imitation glass in the windows, dummy lights, bumpers and door handles. After painting and the addition of chrome tape to the bumpers and trim the model is barely distinguishable from a real car.

5 While the clay may then be used for display and promotional use, and to assess the market appeal of the new car, design and testing continue. Moulds are made from the original clay *(above)*, and from these metal panels are formed and built up into a prototype for practical testing.

6 Nearly all modern cars are offered for sale with a range of engine sizes and body styles; consequently several different clays may be required in the development of a new car. Here the doors and windows are being fitted to a clay of a new hatchback model.

AUTO ENVIRONMENT
Cars of the Future

It is virtually impossible to predict with any degree of accuracy what the motor car will be like in the future. Many people believe that the private motor car will have ceased to exist by the early years of the twenty–first century, but this somewhat extreme long–term view does not deter the speculators.

There were always "cars of the future". Ever since the first motor car appeared, today's models have been yesterday's cars of the future. Some of them showed considerable foresight regarding the shape of things to come: more often, however, the dream car remained just that. Regrettably, we shall never know just how good most of today's designers have been at gazing into the crystal ball. What we do know, however, are the parameters which influence their guesswork.

In a world where there is considerable concern about the rate at which fuel in general, and fossil fuels in particular, are being used up, the saving of energy is of prime importance. In the early sixties General Motors completed a study which showed that a reduction of ten per cent in the drag factor (a calculation based on the airflow around the bodywork of a car) could reduce the fuel consumption of a family saloon by five per cent at 55 mph and six per cent at 70 mph. On this basis it might be assumed that the most economical vehicle would be one shaped like the shaft of an arrow – not unlike Reaction Dynamics' *Blue Flame*, in which Gary Gabelich established his world land speed record.

However, as long as the car is a passenger–carrying vehicle, there must be a compromise between the "slipperiness" of the car and its practicality. This requirement has encouraged designers to experiment with amoeba–like shapes, such as that shown by Pninfarina at the 1978 Turin Show. Otherwise, designs for cars tend to rely heavily on experience gained from the race–track, where the wedge shape first proved its efficiency. The Bertone Sibilo, which was developed from the

highly successful Stratos, is perhaps not so much a car of the next century as a car for the next decade. On the other hand, the Ford Coins is believed by its designers to be a car for the 1990s. Certainly European designers have proved that the wedge can produce sleek, elegant and economical cars – economical in terms of fuel consumption if not of production.

In the USA, automobile styling is moving in a different direction, with the emphasis less on aesthetic appeal and performance than on economy (through low speeds) and safety, which is built into the structure rather than the driving characteristics of the car. Deformable front and rear sections, substantial bumpers, roll–over bars and air bags are all part of the designers' view of the future – although even in the USA designers can dream, and representations of these dreams decorate the walls of every styling studio.

Other visions of the future include urban vehicles, which may not have drivers, and town cars that are little more than motorised shopping baskets. What fuels these will use is still a matter for conjecture, but the emphasis will certainly be economy of road space and of energy. Imaginative mass–transport schemes, such as that which proposed running passenger trains through transparent tubing suspended from buildings, are by no means an impossibility – though some way into the future. More likely to be realised is the O–bahn system developed by Mercedes–Benz in which driverless tram–like vehicles provide versatile urban transport that is controlled by a computer.

The car of the future will undoubtedly rely heavily on computer technology. There are already cars in which a computer can tell the driver his fuel consumption, average speed, elapsed time and distance covered. There would be little difficulty in adding other functions. Before long the driver will only need to ask his car to transport him to his destination: the computer will provide the route and determine his speed of travel, radar beams will prevent him running into the car in front, his lights will operate automatically and the only question in his mind will be whether he can afford such sophistication. What would Karl Benz have made of it all?

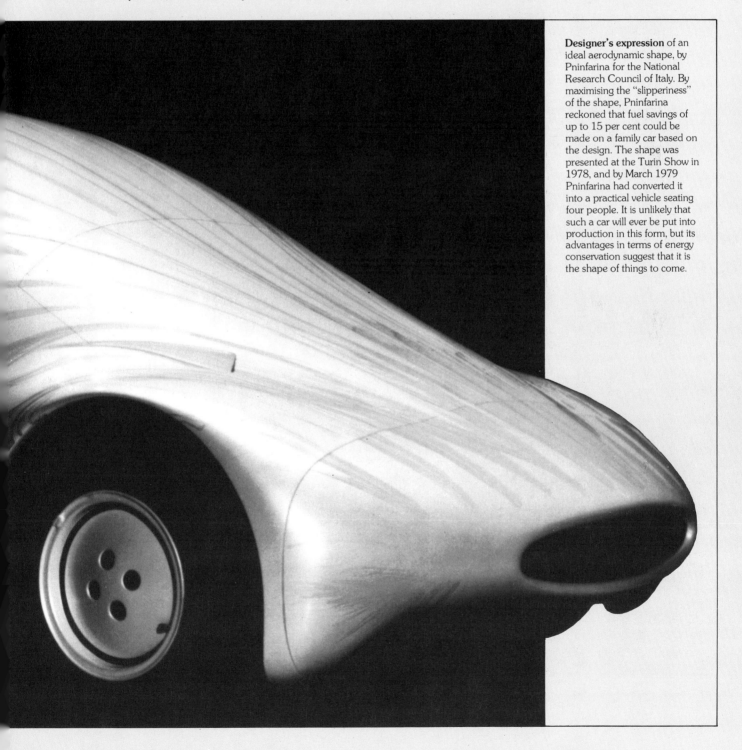

Designer's expression of an ideal aerodynamic shape, by Pninfarina for the National Research Council of Italy. By maximising the "slipperiness" of the shape, Pninfarina reckoned that fuel savings of up to 15 per cent could be made on a family car based on the design. The shape was presented at the Turin Show in 1978, and by March 1979 Pninfarina had converted it into a practical vehicle seating four people. It is unlikely that such a car will ever be put into production in this form, but its advantages in terms of energy conservation suggest that it is the shape of things to come.

Enthusiasts

To many people, the motor car is much more than a convenient way of getting from one place to another. Right from the start, there have been enthusiasts whose interest lay in collecting cars – or replicas of them. Most motor museums started life as private collections made by individuals to whom the history of the motor car was a constant source of fascination. A major upsurge of interest took place in the 1920s when even Henry Ford travelled around the United States collecting vehicles for his museum at Dearborn, Michigan.

Collecting the vehicles themselves could of course prove prohibitively expensive, unless the collector was in the millionaire class. Models were the answer for humbler mortals. It is probably true to say that as soon as man created any worthwhile object, he made a model of it. This is certainly true of ships, houses, aeroplanes and trains. Motor cars in miniature have fascinated both adults and children for years, but for most people the most satisfying models are those on which countless hours of time, care and skill have been lavished to create a finely detailed small–scale replica of the original. Today, model–makers are well served by specialist suppliers of materials and equipment for model–making, available cheaply enough for an enthusiast to build up his own private model car museum.

It is fortunate that such enthusiasts exist. The world of the motor car is a small one with only a hundred years of history behind it. The enthusiasts have ensured that this history is carefully preserved in a variety of forms and that no car, no matter how rare or how brief its man–size existence, need be lost in the mists of time.

A **German clockwork saloon** *(above left)* made in about 1920 by Bing. The Bing brothers started a model–making business in Nuremberg in 1865 and were amongst the first to make sheet–metal models of cars. On their best models the steering worked and the trim was made of polished brass. In 1915 Bing exported a million dollars' worth of models to America.

A **clockwork model** of a Mercedes Berline de Voyage saloon *(top)* built about 1910. This is one of the finest models made by the Frenchman Georges Carette, who started to make models in Germany in the 1880s. Models made by him during the early 1900s were highly prized and exported all over the world. This model, dated 1910, has hinged doors.

A **Meccano constructional car kit** *(left)* for building a sports tourer. The kit, on sale in the 1930s, included parts, a clockwork mechanism and instructions for making one of a variety of sports–car models.

A **Mercedes roadster** *(above)* built from a kit by Charles F. Davidson.

ENTHUSIASTS

Metal Models of the Past

One of the most unusual presents ever given or received must have been that given by a Jesuit missionary, Father Verbiest, to the Emperor of China, K'ang–hsi, in the late seventeenth century. It was a toy, about two feet in length, which comprised a platform carrying a primitive steam–engine which drove the platform along. It was the first powered model on record and it was to be another hundred years before engineers succeeded in inventing a practical steam–engine for road use. From that modest beginning, the model–car industry has grown to mammoth proportions and it is calculated that in the United States alone, more than $100 million per year is spent on model cars of one sort or another.

The earliest type of completed models, as opposed to kits, were known as tin toys, and those which have survived the ravages of Edwardian nurseries have become collectors' items. They appeared on the market almost before the paint was dry on the cars they represented. The models were very often built as cigarette boxes, and were not cheap, but the manufacturers of the early models soon found that they could appeal to the mass market only by keeping prices down and by using the very cheapest materials – tin, which was frequently recycled, and cardboard. However, what these early models lacked in durability they made up for in decoration.

Early American model cars were made of cast iron and tended to be tough rather than elegant, which made them more suitable as toys for children, but it was the German toy manufacturers with their highly sophisticated models who dominated the market until the start of the First World War.

Perfection in Miniature

One of the finest models ever made was the solid silver replica of a Model T Ford that the Ford Motor Company commissioned for its seventy–fifth anniversary from Garrard, the English crown jewellers. This rare specimen, a one–tenth scale model, cost $7500. Few models are so lavish, however. The most expensive and most coveted are those made by skilled craftsmen, who spend countless hours ensuring that a model is correct down to the last detail. Other models are sold in kit form, ranging from those simple enough for a child to assemble to the elaborate and costly kits sold by Pocher in Italy, which take even an expert many hours to make, and hold their price in salerooms.

The commercial importance of model cars was not lost on André Citroën, who declared that "the very first words a child should know are Mummy, Daddy and Citroën". Citroën made a great feature of toy cars; the first one was a B2 10 hp Torpedo that appeared in 1923: it had no engine and had to be pulled along on the end of a string, but later the same year a clockwork version was produced and before long as many model Citroëns were sold as real ones.

The tin–plate models were superseded in the 1930s by diecast models. These had first appeared in the USA ten years earlier under the somewhat regrettable brand–name "Tootsie-toys". Diecast toys were also extremely popular in Britain. The market leader was Meccano, founded by one of the world's greatest toy–makers, Frank Hornby, who had originally made his name with construction kits and train sets for children and adults. His first diecast cars were sold as "modelled miniatures" and were intended as accessories for the train

1939 3 litre Mercedes Benz *(top)* modelled to 1/25th scale by expert model–maker Cyril Posthumus.

A solid silver replica of a Model T Ford *(above)* made by Garrard, the English crown jewellers.

sets, but such was their success that they were relaunched twelve months later as Dinky Toys – the name which made them famous.

In common with the industry which it mirrored, the model-car business was quiet during the Second World War but was revived shortly afterwards, with great success. Household names such as Matchbox and Corgi Toys were soon to join the old faithfuls.

Popular though the little diecast toys were, and still are, the finest models have always been those built from scratch by skilled craftsmen. Probably the most celebrated of these was Henri Baignent, who once spent more than eleven thousand hours completing a working model of a Ferrari 250 for Lord Portman, the finished model being so perfect that photographs of it can easily be confused with photographs of the actual car. The instruments give accurate readings, the windscreen wipers are powered by tiny motors and there are

thirty separate lights, each system operating independently. The seats are made with leather from the original car and the entire model is only 16 inches long.

Motor racing seems to have inspired model-makers more than any other aspect of motoring, and Rex Hayes modelled a collection of cars which effectively illustrated the history of Grand Prix racing and which is on permanent display at the National Motor Museum at Beaulieu. Another expert on models and motor racing is Cyril Posthumus, whose first model was carved during the Second World War from a piece of wood he found in an army cookhouse; his second model was made from the post of a bed in which he also, at that time, used to sleep. All these model-makers and many others, including Michel Conti, Alain Petit and Gerald Wingrove, not only have great love for and knowledge of the cars they model, but are also prepared to spend as long as is necessary to perfect the details of their work.

A 1928 New Year card (*left*) from André Citroën, who believed that children who played with toy Citroëns would buy the real thing when they grew up and bought cars of their own.

Henri Baignent's model (*above*) of a Ferrari 250 GT. The radiator is made of 160 separate leaves containing 48 tubes.

Two 1/25th scale models (*below*) by Cyril Posthumus. On the left is Prince Bira's ERA, on the right a 1932 Alfa Romeo.

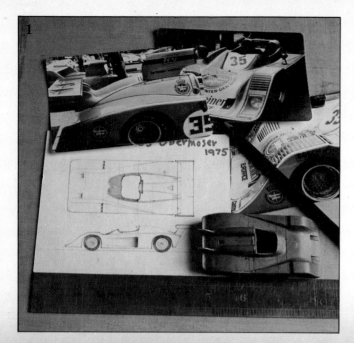

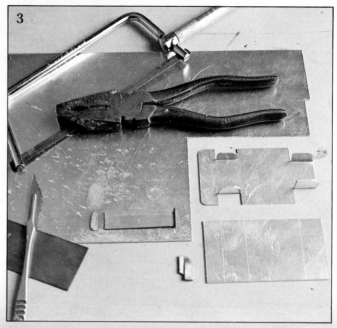

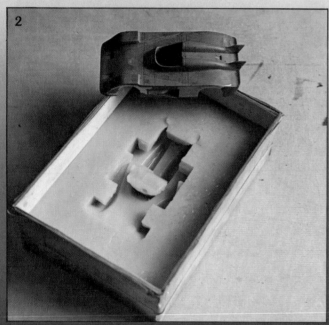

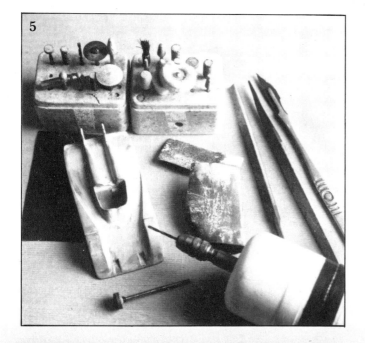

Table-top Assembly

Every model–making enthusiast has his own method of working. There are of course kits for model cars, ranging from the very simple to the highly sophisticated; alternatively, models can be built from scratch, as was the model of a 1975 Obermoser TOJ 2 litre sports car shown on the left.

Method of working

1 Scale plans and elevations of the car are drawn up from reference photos, then a master model is made using aluminium and heavy–duty filler. A slight enlargement of the proportions of the chassis is allowed to counteract mould shrinkage. Features are shaped with a file and a mini–drill, then smoothed down before structural details such as seats, body panel grooves and rear engine are added.

2 An open box with a detachable bottom is built, large enough to allow about $1\frac{1}{2}$ inches of space around the model. The inside of the box and the master model are thinly coated with linseed oil and the master placed in the box. Rubber compound, heated to 120°C, is poured into the container, covering the master to a depth of 1 inch. Once the compound has solidified, the master is peeled out.

3 A new chassis is built out of aluminium to the original plans for the production model.

4 A quantity of heavy–duty filler is worked into the mould and the chassis attached to the wet filler flush with the top of the mould. It is then left to dry naturally.

5 Once dry, the production model is removed, filed down and smoothed off. Detail is redefined with a scalpel. The axle inlets are measured and drilled. Accessories, including the rear wing and the breather box, are attached, and the model is thoroughly cleaned with spirit. The model is lightly sprayed with matt paint, allowed to dry, smoothed off and cleaned again with spirit. Then it is sprayed its final colour, using gloss paint, and once more left to dry.

6 Additional details are hand–painted with enamel colour. Wet and dry transfers are added. Finally, axles are cut to fit and wheels attached.

A range of model sports cars (below) made by the same method as the Obermoser TOJ shown above left.

Milestones in Motoring

Graham Robson

Since the day, not long past, when for the first time a horse shied away in fright from a clanking, spluttering metal contraption belching smoke and fumes, the motor car has rapidly become an indispensable part of our everyday way of life.

If the car was initially a toy for the rich and the powerful, the techniques of mass production quickly brought mobility and freedom to the mass of the working people in one of the most profound social changes of the twentieth century.

Almost as soon as it was invented the car was adopted by sportsmen and soldiers, status–seekers and artisans – a universal tool providing men and women everywhere with the means to pursue their work, take their leisure and realise their dreams. In a very real sense, the motor car has become all things to all men.

The sleek, comfortable and increasingly safe vehicle of today is far removed from its rattletrap ancestors. Its story is one of rapid evolution, spurred on by the demands of a mass market and led by the manufacturers, whose livelihood depends on their ability to woo that market. It is a story of technological change, of innovation, of creative engineering, and in this section we look more closely at some of the developments that have made the motor car into what it is today.

Contents

Design for Comfort, Safety and Economy

In modern design. the accent is on providing multi–purpose transport and many cars have seating arrangements that can be modified to suit the needs of the moment. In estate cars and hatchbacks it is normal for the rear seats to be foldable, either together or in part, and in some cars the seats can be removed completely. Many cars have front seats which can be fully reclined in order to provide sleeping accommodation and on the more expensive models seats may often be individually adjusted for height, seat angle and back–rest angle.

If a car has rear–wheel drive, it often has what is called a "live" back axle and for good roadholding this heavy component must be sprung and located properly. For "packaging" reasons, springs and dampers have to be tucked away from the loading and seating area, and on more expensive cars some form of self–levelling feature is provided. Some rear–drive cars have independent rear suspension, in which the differential is mounted on the body; front–wheel–drive cars have simple rear end assemblies.

Although cars are working tools, they must also be attractive to their potential buyers. Leather, plastic or cloth covering may be offered on seats, with carpets or rubber matting on the floor.

Modern motor cars must be more versatile than ever before in order to cope with a wide variety of tasks – from providing sporting transport to carrying heavy loads. The hatchback concept evolved gradually in the 1960s – boot lids gradually became larger and embraced the rear window, until it was often difficult to distinguish the estate car from the saloon. Outside the United States, the "hatchback" car sells in very large numbers, in cars as different as the Honda Civic and the Rover 3500.

Many details aid good aerodynamics and rearward vision. Rear windows often have electric heating wires buried in the glass, and a wipe/wash feature is sometimes fitted. To improve high–speed stability many cars have a spoiler at the rear, made of moulded rubber.

Since the mid–1960s, many new safety laws have been imposed on motor cars. To be sold in some countries they have to withstand head–on crashes at 30 mph, and severe side–impact tests. Bodies have to be reinforced at front and rear and around the passenger compartment, and may also have massive beams inside the doors.

Almost all modern cars are made in huge quantities on the basis of a welded pressed–steel body–shell. In the early days all cars had strong, separate frames carrying carefully coachbuilt bodies with wooden frames and hand–formed panels. A great deal of skilled hand–work was needed, and building costs were consequently very high. Pressed–steel panels were first used in the United States in the 1920s, and all–steel bodies became dominant in the 1930s. Later in that decade manufacturers started to combine frames with bodies, and "unit construction" shells are now almost universal. Even though modern cars have a great deal of glass, their bodies are generally very strong and torsionally rigid.

Labour costs all over the world are now so high that servicing of cars must be kept as simple as possible. Many parts are designed to be replaced rather than repaired when they develop faults, and routine work needed at regular intervals has been cut to a minimum. Many models are now designed to require servicing only at 10,000–mile intervals.

If a car can be designed to accept more than one size of engine, in several states of tune, it has a bigger potential market, so, when the new body–shell is being styled and engineered, space has to be left in the engine bay for all the units to be offered. North American and European cars often have in–line and vee–formation units in their product lines, so the bay must be both long enough and wide enough to accept them all.

However, the transmission has to be matched carefully to each engine. In general the most powerful engines are linked to higher overall gearing. This usually means that the least–powerful version is by no means the most economical, as high gearing helps fuel economy at constant–speed cruising speeds.

The small–engined versions do not always have an automatic transmission option, but almost any car with a 1·5 litre engine is offered with one. In the United States, virtually every car sold has automatic transmission, and the automatic is rapidly gaining in popularity throughout Europe.

Although the car shown has a front engine and rear–wheel drive, millions of cars are also sold with front–wheel drive.

A feature of car design and marketing for many years has been that one basic model is usually sold in many different guises. This may take the form of "badge engineering" (in which one body–shell is skilfully modified by the stylists and sold under different names), or it may mean that the same model is sold with a wide variety of engine specifications and trim/equipment packs.

The car illustrated here is the 1978 model Ford Capri, which is built in West Germany. Although all Capris have the same "3–door" body layout, they are sold with four types of four–cylinder and six–cylinder engines ranging in size from 1·3 to 3 litres, and with power outputs varying from 57 to 138 bhp. They are also available with four levels of trim and equipment, L, GL, S and Ghia, the latter being the most luxurious of all. Like almost every car in the world, a Capri can be ordered with manual or automatic transmission. All manner of extra items – from headlamp washers to retracting sun roofs, special seats to radio and tape–playing equipment – can be fitted when the car is being built. A customer rarely walks into a showroom and chooses a car which suits him exactly: the final "package" is usually tailored to his needs from a range of options.

Four–wheel brakes have been universal on cars since the 1920s, and disc brakes (which are both powerful and resistant to "fade" in hard use) have been available since the 1950s. Many fast cars now have disc brakes fitted to all four wheels but the standard "family" car usually has disc brakes on the front wheels and drum brakes on the rear.

To improve aerodynamic efficiency it is now commonplace for cars to have front spoilers to break up the air–flow on its way under the car. Great care is also now taken to control the air flowing into the cooling radiators at high speeds.

Almost every modern car has independent front suspension, which means that the front wheels are not directly linked. The most popular layout, shown here, uses combined coil–spring/damper units.

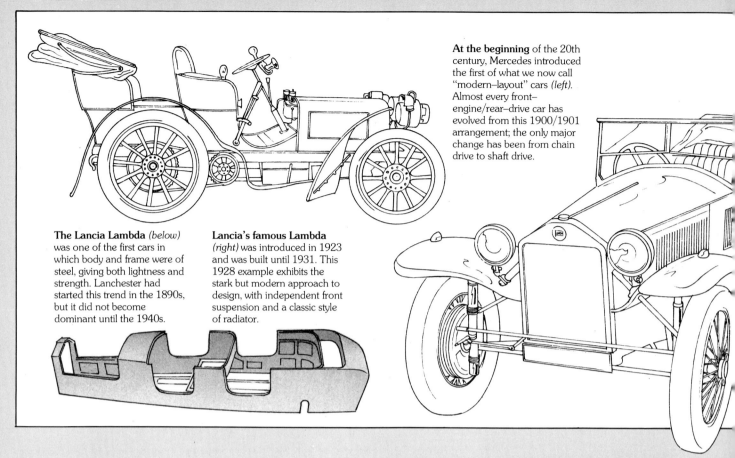

At the beginning of the 20th century, Mercedes introduced the first of what we now call "modern–layout" cars *(left)*. Almost every front–engine/rear–drive car has evolved from this 1900/1901 arrangement; the only major change has been from chain drive to shaft drive.

The Lancia Lambda *(below)* was one of the first cars in which body and frame were of steel, giving both lightness and strength. Lanchester had started this trend in the 1890s, but it did not become dominant until the 1940s.

Lancia's famous Lambda *(right)* was introduced in 1923 and was built until 1931. This 1928 example exhibits the stark but modern approach to design, with independent front suspension and a classic style of radiator.

Assembling the Component Parts

When the age of motoring began, with the successful trials of the Benz tricycle in 1885, there were no fixed ideas, or traditions, governing the way a car's components should be arranged. For simplicity's sake it was generally agreed that the rear wheels should be driven, but there was an enormous variety of engine, transmission, chassis, suspension and seating layouts.

Most early cars had their engines in the rear or tucked away under the seats, but this made them difficult to reach for servicing and repair. It was Panhard and Levassor, of France, who invented the revolutionary "*système Panhard*" in 1895, which has now become the "classic" layout. The 1895 Panhard was the first to have an engine in the nose, a gearbox behind it, and drive to its rear wheels. Since then the only real change has been for final drive by chain to be abandoned in favour of shaft drive to a rear axle which contains a differential driving shafts to each driven rear wheel.

However, although this Panhard ushered in the modern layout, it was really the Mercedes cars, first shown at the very start of the 20th century, which began to establish the general layout of modern cars. They were the first to have sleek lines, with the engine under a bonnet or hood, to have a well–raked steering column, and to have comfortable seating for four passengers.

By 1914, and the outbreak of the First World War, almost every production and racing car in the world conformed to the "*système Panhard*". The basic layout was proven, and all efforts were going into adding performance, reliability, comfort and refinement. Cars with rear–mounted or mid–mounted engines were not properly developed until the 1930s, and although front–wheel drive had been known as early as the 1900s, it was not until the late 1940s that cars began to be sold in any numbers with that layout.

In the last thirty years there has been one startling advance, inspired by the success of the original BMC Mini of 1959, by which an in–line engine (of four or even of six cylinders) is mounted transversely across the structure, and drives the front wheels.

It is only in the last generation or so that designers and stylists have come to understand that the buying public is not so much interested in a car's looks as in its practicality. Whereas cars built in the early days often found space for their passengers *after* the main mechanical layout and looks had been fixed, modern cars make all the essential engineering components subservient to the much more generous passenger space that is provided.

By providing a greater variety of body styles in recent years, cars have become much more practical and versatile. At first every car was an open tourer, and the nickname "horseless carriage" explains how this style was chosen. However, there were closed cars by the 1900s, and as the great coachbuilders began to take an interest, grand limousine, coupé and convertible bodies also became available. Estate cars, surprisingly enough, did not really become available until the 1930s, when they were often called "utilities".

Moves to combine an estate car's carrying capacity with the looks of a private car then followed, so that by the 1970s the term "hatchback" had been applied to that most practical of layouts.

In engineering terms, almost every car ever built has had four wheels (although heavy trucks often have many more than this), and *no* successful car has ever been built in which the rear wheels provided steering. It was generally agreed that the driver should be positioned near the centre of a two–way road, and since some countries drive on the left and some on the right, both right–hand–drive and left–hand–drive configurations are commonplace.

The tricycle, or tricar, is an interesting half–way stage between car and motorcycle design, but has only really survived where there is favourable licensing or taxation legislation to support it. There have been two main types in modern times, both with a single (steerable) front wheel. One type has its engine mounted directly on the front suspension, driving the front wheel, while the other (with front or with rear engine) drives the rear wheels like a conventional four–wheeled car.

Engines operated by the Otto cycle of internal combustion are normally used, operating on either the two–stroke or (much the most popular) the four–stroke cycle. In almost every case these engines are water–cooled. In the early days, before petrol engines were properly developed, cars were often built with steam engines, and in the last thirty years both gas–turbine units and Wankel rotary engines have been tried. Gas turbine engines are too costly to be viable, though Wankels now appear to be established in certain makes of car.

In general terms, modern cars are more complex, more useful and offer better performance than ever before, but they need more expert attention for repair and maintenance. They are no longer toys, but working tools.

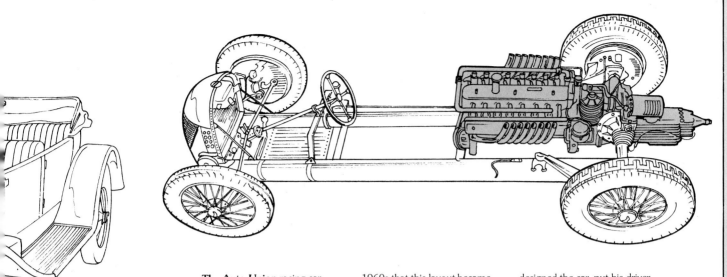

The **Auto-Union** racing car (*above*) was a great innovation in terms of engineering layout, even though it was never as successful as its great rival, the front–engined Mercedes–Benz. It was really the first successful Grand Prix car to have its engine behind the driver, although it was not until the 1960s that this layout became the norm in motor racing. This "C–Type" Auto–Union was built for the "750 kg" formula of 1934–37, in which the engine size was unlimited, but in which the car's "dry" weight (without tyres, fluids or driver) had to be less than 750 kg. Dr Ferdinand Porsche, who designed the car, put his driver farther forward than ever before, mounted the fuel tank behind him, and installed a big V16 engine bolted directly to the axle and gearbox unit. The Auto–Union was one of the first racing cars to have independent suspension units on all four wheels.

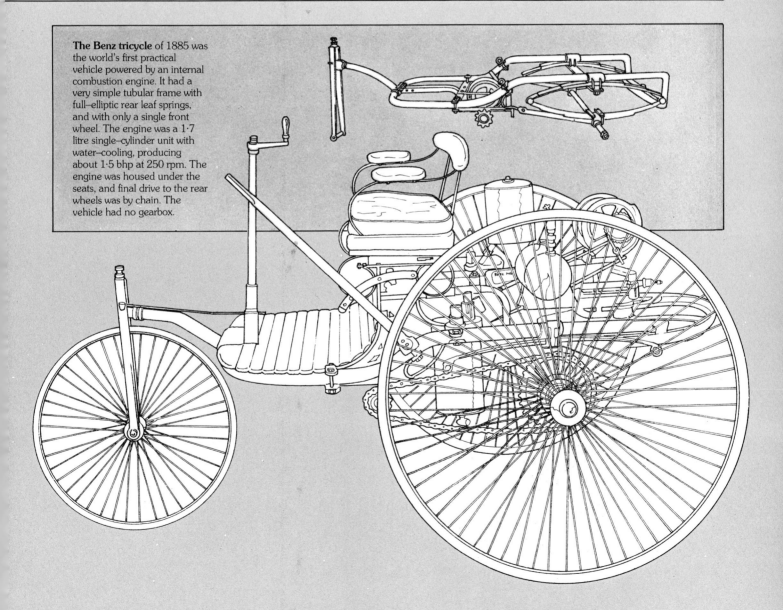

The **Benz tricycle** of 1885 was the world's first practical vehicle powered by an internal combustion engine. It had a very simple tubular frame with full–elliptic rear leaf springs, and with only a single front wheel. The engine was a 1·7 litre single–cylinder unit with water–cooling, producing about 1·5 bhp at 250 rpm. The engine was housed under the seats, and final drive to the rear wheels was by chain. The vehicle had no gearbox.

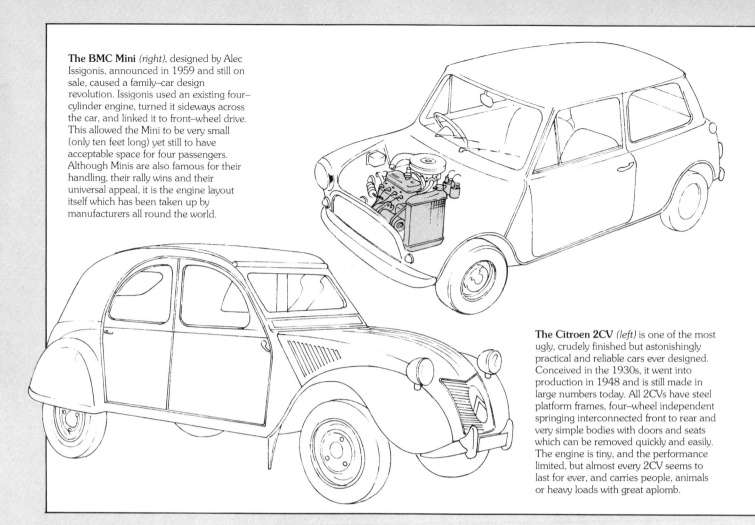

The BMC Mini *(right)*, designed by Alec Issigonis, announced in 1959 and still on sale, caused a family–car design revolution. Issigonis used an existing four–cylinder engine, turned it sideways across the car, and linked it to front–wheel drive. This allowed the Mini to be very small (only ten feet long) yet still to have acceptable space for four passengers. Although Minis are also famous for their handling, their rally wins and their universal appeal, it is the engine layout itself which has been taken up by manufacturers all round the world.

The Citroen 2CV *(left)* is one of the most ugly, crudely finished but astonishingly practical and reliable cars ever designed. Conceived in the 1930s, it went into production in 1948 and is still made in large numbers today. All 2CVs have steel platform frames, four–wheel independent springing interconnected front to rear and very simple bodies with doors and seats which can be removed quickly and easily. The engine is tiny, and the performance limited, but almost every 2CV seems to last for ever, and carries people, animals or heavy loads with great aplomb.

Combining the Chassis and Body

Whether a car was designed in the 1890s or in the 1970s, its entire layout centres around the stress–bearing chassis. Although most cars built since the end of the Second World War have been equipped with variants of the unit–construction shell, where the elements of the bodywork and the chassis frame are combined, the principles have not changed. On the one hand the structure has to be rigid enough to support the payload of passengers and their luggage: on the other, the dynamic loads – those imposed by driving, braking, cornering and by uneven surfaces – must also be absorbed in an efficient way.

When chassis frames and bodies were still separate, the bodies had to do no more than provide protection from the weather, and provide somewhere to sit. The chassis frame – which, literally, was just that, as it often looked like simple framework which might be used as a building skeleton – supported axles and suspensions, engine, transmission, brakes and all other mechanical equipment. It was quite possible for a "car" to be driven without any bodywork in place, which explains the expression "rolling chassis" – basic units manufactured in one location then delivered, often under their own power, to a coachbuilder for the bodywork to be added.

Those early frames had side members made of channel–section or even tubular steel, sometimes reinforced by wooden flitch plates cross–braced by similar steel members to give added strength.

Although engines, transmissions and axles could not be moved around, frames had to be reshaped to allow the seats to be lowered in response to the demand for sleeker, lower–profiled cars. Accordingly, frames became much more complex.

Not only did a chassis have to be very rigid to resist bending, but it also had to resist torsional stresses. By their very two–dimensional nature, separate frames were not ideally shaped for their task, and even though channel–section gave way to box–section members it was clear that still more improvement was needed. Once engineers had discovered that the frame's overall rigidity was much improved when the body was bolted to it, and once all–steel bodies had become available, it was only a short step to combine the two.

One "half–way" solution was to weld the complete floor pan to the frame – effectively a rediscovery of Lanchester's platform chassis concept – and only a little later cars were being built with their bodies completely welded to the frame. Even so, this had still not tackled the overall three–dimensional concept of stiffness and rigidity, for the layout of the traditional frame, its side–members and its reinforcements had not been disturbed.

Although Lancia, with their forward–looking Lambda (in which the sheet–steel chassis and basic touring body were combined), and Chrysler (who designed a complex structure for their hideous Airflow without a chassis) were pioneers, it was General Motors in the United States who really developed this technique.

It would be fair to call such first–generation designs as "chassis–less". In later years, as mechanical layouts changed and as the location of stress paths became more clearly understood, the traditional line of stress–bearing members began to be lost. Sills, box–section cross–members and very strong diaphragm–members began to take their share of the loads. A modern car may still have vestigial chassis rails, but is now truly "unit–construction", where every panel, including the wings and the roof panel, contributes to overall strength.

Since the late 1930s the original layout of the car – front engine, rear–wheel drive – has been successfully attacked by the two very neat concepts of front engine/front drive, and rear engine/rear drive. (No private car has ever been offered for sale with a rear engine driving the front wheels.) One big advantage of these modern layouts is that all the "powerhouse" elements can be concentrated at one end of the car. Drive shafts do not have to be routed under the passenger compartment, which allows more space to be made available for the payload. Both systems have advantages and drawbacks. Front–drive power packs are complex because the driven wheels have also to be steered; rear–engine power packs are more difficult to keep cool, and (because they are heavy) tend to unbalance the car's handling and stability.

Although four-wheel drive is necessary for cross–country vehicles, it is rarely used on private road cars. Four–wheel drive layouts are bulky, complex and expensive to design because the front wheels have to drive *and* steer.

Jensen's FF, of which 318 were built between 1966 and 1971, is the only high–performance road car ever sold with permanent four–wheel drive. Drawings *(right)* depict the 1965 prototype: production cars had more dramatic styling. The sketches show the drive layout, with front engine allied to a centre differential with drive shafts to front and rear differentials. This car had a very powerful Chrysler V8 engine, automatic transmission, and an anti–lock braking system. The side view shows that the four–wheel–drive system did not add to the height, but the plan view shows that the system had to be offset to the left to allow the front propeller shaft to fit alongside the engine.

Jensen found it very difficult to make these fast cars handle properly, and the public soon made it clear they thought rear–wheel drive was enough.

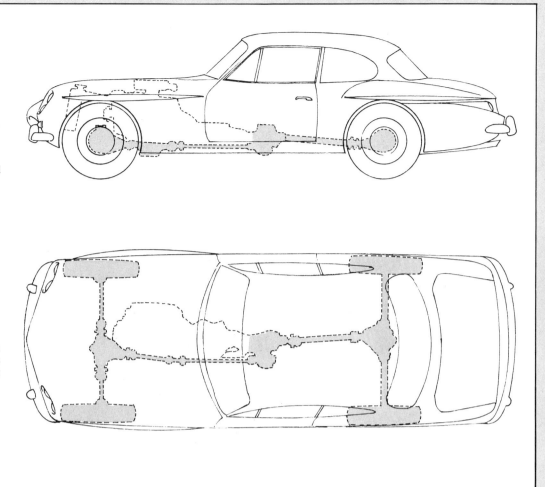

The only car to go on sale with a "space frame" chassis was the Mercedes–Benz 300SL model of 1954 to 1963, which had a top speed of up to 165 mph. Chassis stresses were absorbed by a three–dimensional lattice of tubes, which was very light but expensive to build or repair. Until 1957 this car also had a unique "gull–wing" door arrangement.

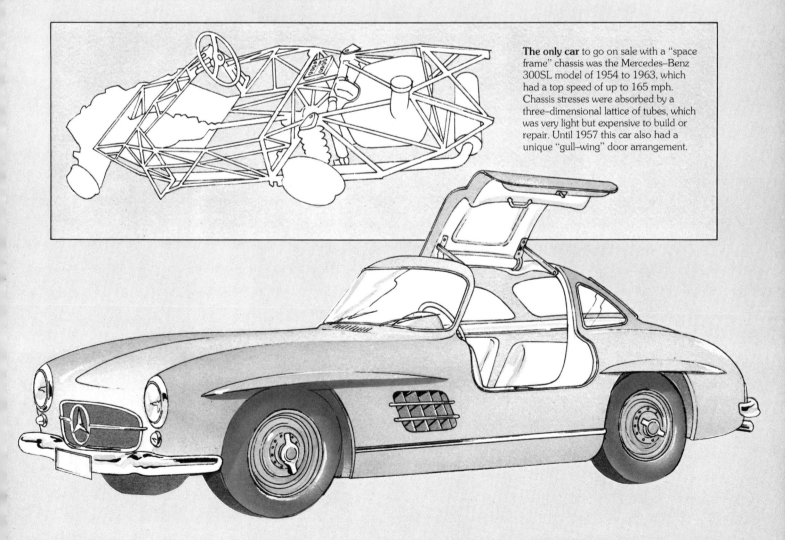

Lanchester was one of the British motor industry's pioneer concerns, responsible for many innovative features. Even in the mid–1890s, the Lanchester was many years ahead of its time, with a pressed–steel chassis forming an integral part of the body. This was inherently much stronger, but no heavier, than the crude steel–and–ash frames used by most other firms. At the same time it allowed a whole variety of coachbuilt bodies to be fitted on top of the stress–bearing structure, including *(left)* this very early example of a commercial vehicle – used at the beginning of the 20th century for delivering mail in London. It is also worth noting that the Lanchester layout, which included the siting of the engine under the seats, allowed a very stylish sloping "bonnet" to be used, which was more rakish than many of its rivals.

The estate car, or station wagon, type of body has risen to prominence and become socially acceptable since the 1930s. Early "estate cars" were just that – vehicles designed for use on private estates, for carrying staff, guns, game and dogs – and were usually based on a light commercial vehicle or light van layout. "Station wagons", like the 1930s Chevrolet *(right)*, evolved during the 1930s for carrying travellers to and from railway stations, and by the 1940s almost every popular range of cars had such an option available.

Early examples had wood–framed bodies, but all–steel shells were later developed on to which wood trim was attached for decoration. In the United States some estate bodies still have wood (or imitation wood) panelling, but this is now purely a design feature contributing nothing to body strength.

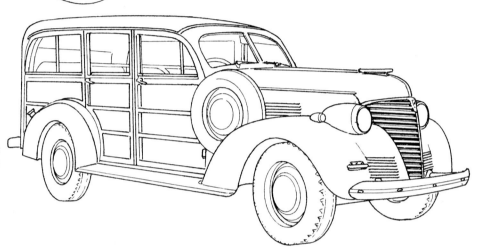

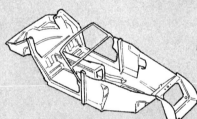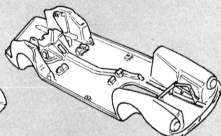

Only one production car, the original Lotus Elite announced in 1957, had an entire body–chassis unit built of reinforced glass–fibre. This was built up of three major structural mouldings, and the only metal reinforcements were in the engine bay, to support the engine and suspension, and around the windscreen, to give roll–over protection. Experience showed that the Elite was very strong, but that it was difficult to keep mechanical noise, road and wind noise, and vibration out of the passenger compartment.

The versatile Model T

When motor car bodies could be built quickly, to a simple design, with cheap and plentiful materials like hardwood and flat steel sheets, it was normal for a lot of handwork to go into the job. It was therefore possible for a manufacturer to offer many different styles based on the same chassis. Because labour was relatively cheap, this meant that a wide choice was available even on the most humble machines.

The enormously successful Model T Ford was, for many years, the cheapest car sold in North America, but it was also sold as a tourer, a saloon, a van, a two–seater and a four–seater – all with the same chassis and power unit, which could be serviced and repaired at any wayside filling station in the United States.

It also became the car to which the phrase "mass production" was first applied, and the production lines in Detroit were so arranged that the body could be dropped on to the frame from above, bolted down and the finished car driven away – all in a matter of minutes.

Bodies in the 1910s and the 1920s were usually built on wooden skeletons, to which the skin panels and the trim were nailed. At the time there was no real effort to provide a coherent style, except that each car had its own distinctive radiator. Wings were separate, there were "running boards" on each side of the body, and – until the saloon car evolved – weather protection was poor.

The Pressed Steel Revolution

While motor car design and marketing was dominated by engineers, all effort was concentrated on the chassis and running gear; the body and its fittings were regarded rather as a necessary evil. However, once marketing came under the control of level–headed merchandising experts, the emphasis was changed. In many ways it is true to say that the mechanicals were all–important in the first twenty years of the age of motoring, and that the provision of proper bodies came to prominence in the next twenty. It was this realisation, that a customer was more attracted by what he saw – seats, shape, a fine radiator and nice fittings – than by the mechanical components he probably did not understand – which brought motor car design into its proper perspective.

When cars first went on sale they sold to wealthy men who had been used to driving a fine carriage drawn by horses. That carriage would have had coachwork by companies with a great deal of craftsman–like experience in hand–building. Naturally, then, these coachbuilders turned their attention to building motor car bodies. A long–established tradition had grown up that carriage bodies (and now, therefore, car bodies) were built up on the basis of a wooden skeleton framework which estab-lished the body's basic shape. Many panels were absolutely flat, and many sections were uncompromisingly squared off; early cars lacked shape except in the scuttle area, or around the tail. All glass and side–curtains stood proudly vertical.

When style demanded more shape, and more curving of panels such as tails, doors, noses and above all wings, these shapes had to be hand–beaten, perhaps with the help of a rolling machine, then checked and laboriously rechecked against wooden master jigs defining the correct shape. It all took a great deal of time, and this, together with a steady rise in complexity and in labour costs, led to the technique of panels being stamped out in large numbers on large and powerful press tools.

To do this the required shape had to be agreed, after which the male and female press tools had to be manufactured, which was an expensive and lengthy process. While it meant that the *individual* cost of making one body panel was sharply re-duced, the high investment needed in press tools and the presses themselves made it necessary for the same model (or shape of car) to be kept in production for a long time and be built in large numbers. The cost of individuality had become high, but to get costs down it meant that many people had to be content with a car that looked similar to their neighbour's.

Such mechanisation of car body pro-duction, however, was just the start. For some time, even cars built in enormous numbers continued to have bodies based on a wooden skeleton, and there was no easy way to build these by mechanical methods. The most logical course, it seemed, was to discard hand–worked wood in favour of a metal framework – a framework which could also be produced with the aid of high–speed presses.

All cars built in any numbers today have bodies made entirely of pressed steel, but developing the technique was by no means simple. It was the Budd Corporation, in the United States, which first developed practi-cal ways of assembling the hundreds of steel panels into a complete body (by welding) and – in conjunction with the Morris company – they then brought the technique to Britain in the mid–1920s. Logically enough, the joint company set up to capitalise on the new methods was called the Pressed Steel Company.

Once all teething troubles had been overcome, it became clear that pressed steel bodies would not only be cheaper and quicker to build, but (if properly designed) they could also be rather lighter. This meant that closed coachwork could therefore be made available on small–engined cars, which had previously been crippled by the weight of hand–built wooden–framed bodies.

The search for lightness led to the limited use of light–alloy body panels, which were vulnerable to damage, or to the more

Continued over page

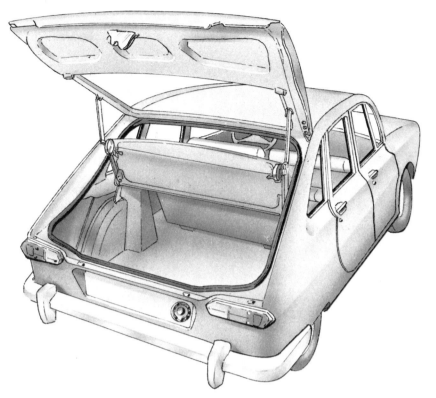

Although the conventional saloon type of bodywork, with two or four passenger doors, has been the most popular of all types for more than fifty years, the versatile "hatchback" configuration has become a serious alternative since the late 1950s. In this form a car like the Renault 16 (left) can be almost as useful as an estate car, while keeping its saloon–car looks. The requirement is to have a big rear loading door, which always incorporates the rear window, and the rear seats can invariably be folded flat to double the loading area. There is less loading space than in an estate car because a "square back" style is not provided, but a hatchback car is usually lighter and smarter–looking. Hatches usually hinge from the roof, and the best ones have a very low loading sill so that heavy objects do not have to be lifted far.

Inspired by the lead given by legislators in the United States many governments have, since the mid–1960s, been demanding that cars should be made stronger and safer, so that accidents will be less likely to cause serious injury to the car's occupants. This "ghosted" view (right) of the structure of a Volvo 240 series car shows the additions now standardised on modern cars to make them stronger. The front and rear structure is designed to crumple progressively in head–on or rear collisions, though the main passenger compartment stays intact. "Energy–absorbing" bumpers deal with low–speed taps. So that the car does not crumple if it rolls over, the panels round screen and door openings are very strong. The door beams protect passengers from side impacts.

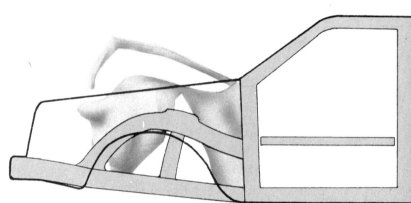

widespread use of fabric–covered bodies. In this application the fabric was tightly stretched over a framework, and treated with a preparation causing the fibres to tighten even more. This worked very well except that the fabric was vulnerable to damage and deterioration. It was, however, both light and cheap, and was popular in the 1920s and early 1930s.

There was a short–lived vogue for what are known as "Weymann" bodies, named after their inventor, the Frenchman Charles Weymann. Wooden–framed bodies had a marked tendency to "work", i.e., to squeak and generally lose their rigidity. Weymann bodies solved this problem by having their wood sections held apart by metal brackets, and were often fabric–covered.

Once the production techniques of building bodies entirely from pressed–steel panels, all welded together, had spread all over the world, cars split into three distinct types. Real mass–production saloon and convertible shells were made by the pressed–steel method. Expensive and relatively exclusive cars continued to be built by craftsmen, with a great deal of

hand–work and special attention to detail. In between, cars built at the rate of only hundreds or thousands a year were built with bodies produced on a semi–batch production basis, still using wooden framing, still using some hand–work, but also using steel panels wherever possible.

It was soon noticed that welded–up pressed–steel bodies were very rigid, and as experience and design expertise built up it was found that they could be made to be even stronger and still remain light in weight. It was also obvious that such a body could add remarkably to the overall behaviour of a chassis, and it was therefore logical to find ways of welding the two assemblies together. It was also at about this time that the pioneering techniques invented by Lanchester, of the platform chassis, where the steel floor was not only welded to the chassis but became an integral part of the layout, were also revived.

The first unit–construction shells were really nothing more than bodies welded to conventional frames, but engineers soon found ways to take weight and complication out of the combination without losing

strength or (equally as important) losing refinement. For many years unit–construction bodies had full length "chassis" rails running under the floor pans, but later designs used strong box–section sills under the doors in their place. Computer–aided design, developed in more recent years, has allowed many alternatives to be investigated at the initial design stage, so that all a body's panels and sections (including the potentially strong pillars, panels across the nose, scuttle and behind the seats) play a part in providing beam and torsional stiffness.

A consequence of this sort of complication is that bodies have become more complex and therefore very costly to design, develop and tool up for mass production. It also means that they must be kept in production for longer periods so that a return on the investment is guaranteed.

When a new car is being designed (and even before engineering begins) decisions are made about the variety and styles of bodies to be offered.

If, for instance, it is thought that two–door, four–door, estate, van and coupé

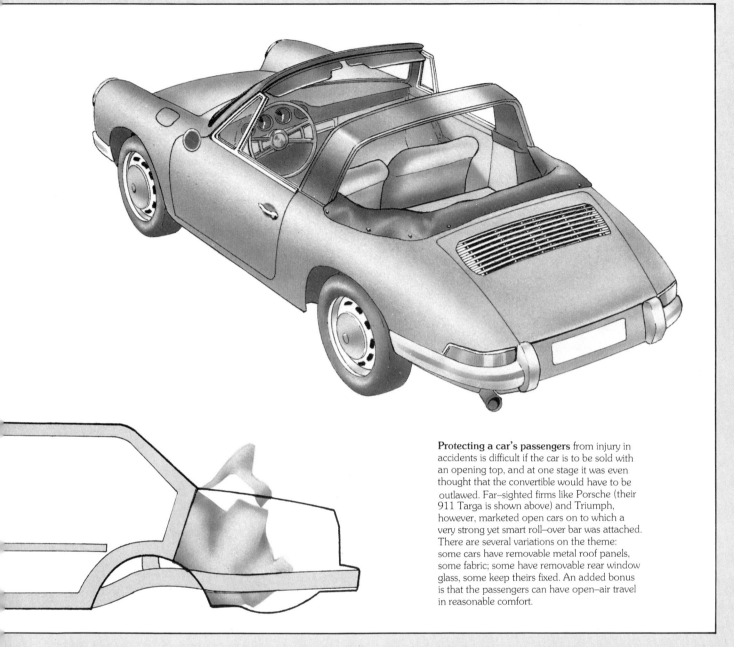

Protecting a car's passengers from injury in accidents is difficult if the car is to be sold with an opening top, and at one stage it was even thought that the convertible would have to be outlawed. Far–sighted firms like Porsche (their 911 Targa is shown above) and Triumph, however, marketed open cars on to which a very strong yet smart roll–over bar was attached. There are several variations on the theme: some cars have removable metal roof panels, some fabric; some have removable rear window glass, some keep theirs fixed. An added bonus is that the passengers can have open–air travel in reasonable comfort.

versions of a new car are to be sold, the body design must take account of this at the outset, so that all types can be made on the same production lines.

Although a few very expensive cars are still built using the age–old hand–building methods of body construction, almost every production shell is built of pressed–steel, and most designs feature unit–construction. Even open–topped sports cars, which live on in spite of earlier fears that they would eventually be outlawed, are built in this way.

The feasible alternatives to the use of steel in bodies are light alloy (usually based on aluminium), glass–fibre or moulded plastics. Aluminium alloys are extensively used where the need for light weight and for high resistance to corrosion outweighs that of lowest cost. A light alloy panel is inescapably more expensive to produce than a steel panel (and more difficult, as aluminium is soft and not as easy to weld to its neighbouring panel) and generally not as rigid when pressed into complex shapes.

Moulded plastics produce light and accurate panels, but are even more costly in tooling terms than those required for pressed–steel. Although plastics are not yet used for many exterior panels of a car, they find a place at the nose and the tail, and form an ideal basis for the many trim and decorative panels used inside the machine.

Glass–fibre construction has a particular and useful part to play in the modern motor car industry. Bodies made from this material do not need enormously costly tools, and the latest techniques mean that excessive amounts of hand–work are no longer required. Nevertheless, too much time is needed to allow the shells, or panels to "cure" once they have been produced, and this automatically limits the number of bodies or sections that can be made in a working day. Glass–fibre techniques, how–ever, are much more productive than hand–building methods, and for cars built at a rate of thousands rather than millions a year they may be ideal.

Another innovation was the popular "hatchback" body, which provides the practicality of an estate car with (often) the good looks of a saloon. When combined with folding rear seats, it can, if needed, give

a really useful loading area to a family car. Because of the large hole exposed by the hatch, the body must be even more sturdily engineered than usual around the tail, and the location of the spare wheel and fuel tank needs careful thought.

The most significant development of the 1960s and 1970s was the proliferation of safety legislation. From many countries, usually led (in time) by the United States, has come a flood of laws designed to protect the driving public from injury in accidents. Car bodies now have to with–stand controlled crash tests – forwards, backwards and obliquely – into concrete barriers; they must be capable of rolling over without the shell collapsing, and they must be able to resist assault from the side. In most cases this has meant that extra panels, bars and sections have had to be added, and in most cases bumpers have become much more massive, complex and shock–absorbing. Safety recommendations now apply not only to the frame and shell itself, but also to the seats, to the safety belts restraining the passengers and to the glass fitted to windscreens.

The driving force
Almost every modern petrol engine with spark ignition uses the **four-stroke cycle** *(top)*, still known as the "Otto" cycle after the inventor of the first viable engine of the 19th century. The four strokes occupy two complete revolutions of the crankshaft and are, respectively: *Induction*, where fuel/air mixture is drawn into the cylinder by the descending piston; *Compression*, where the valves are closed and the mixture is compressed; *Combustion*, where an ignition spark explodes the mixture, driving the piston down to produce the unit's power, and *Exhaust*, where the exhaust valve is open, and where the spent mixture is expelled into the atmosphere.

The two-stroke cycle *(centre)* was developed so that engines could be dramatically simplified: there are no valves to be opened or closed. The combustion process occupies only one crankshaft revolution (in other words, there are only two strokes), and the sequence is: *Piston* ascending, compressing fuel/air mixture above it, and drawing fresh mixture into the crankcase below it; *Combustion*, where the compressed mixture is exploded and pushes the piston down, compressing the crankcase mixture at the same time; *Exhaust* and mixture transfer, where spent mixture is exhausted above the piston, while part–compressed fresh charge is transferred from crankcase to combustion chamber by transfer ports. This process is less efficient than the four–stroke cycle and more wasteful of fuel.

The Wankel engine is the only rotary unit to be sold in large quantities, although it is not an entirely "pure" rotary or vibration–free system. Wankels operate on the four–stroke cycle (Induction, Compression, Combustion, Exhaust), and the triangular–shaped rotor effectively carries the cylinder or chamber shape around with it.

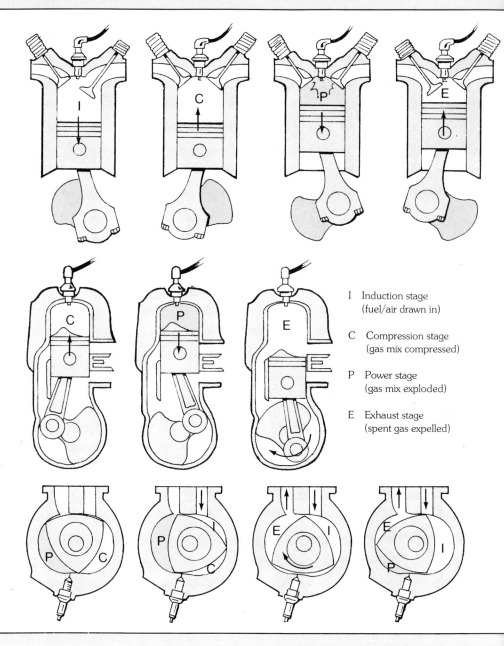

I   Induction stage (fuel/air drawn in)

C   Compression stage (gas mix compressed)

P   Power stage (gas mix exploded)

E   Exhaust stage (spent gas expelled)

The Search for a Power Source

Without an engine there could be no motor car or – literally – "horseless carriage", and it was the feverish search for a viable engine which held back the development of motor cars in the 19th century. Until the 1860s all travel had to be by courtesy of the horse (either by riding the horses or using them to pull carriages) or by train, where the motive power was the steam engine.

Attempts were first made to power road vehicles with steam engines, but these – while reliable and even potentially powerful – were very large, heavy and inefficient. It was soon clear that without major advances in steam–engine design they could not be made practical for use in small private cars. The search, therefore, turned to internal (as opposed to external) combustion units.

In the early 1860s Etienne Lenoir (who had patented the world's first internal combustion engine, powered by coal gas) invented a crude surface–type carburettor, which allowed volatile liquid fuel to be vaporised and burned in one of his engines.

A few years later Dr Nikolaus August Otto invented the engine that has been immor–talised with his name. This had poppet valves which opened and remained closed as appropriate to allow fuel/air mixture to enter and spent gases to be exhausted from the cylinder.

However, Otto himself had little to do with the application of "his" cycle to car engines. It was Karl Benz (in 1884–85) who began the marriage of a crude scaled–down gas–type engine to a primitive tricycle, and it was Daimler, in 1883, who patented a high-speed (750 rpm) enclosed crank four-stroke liquid–fuel engine. From these tentative beginnings a vast industry was born.

Within a few years, almost every car engine was using Daimler's ideas. Early examples were single–cylinder units, often air–cooled, but water–cooling, twins, three–cylinder and four–cylinder units soon followed. By the beginning of the 20th century almost every basic engine layout – in–line, 'V–formation and horizontally-opposed – had been tried. Air–cooling

began to lose ground as power outputs (and therefore waste heat) continued to rise, and the more compact, complex and advanced V8 and V12 units were made available in North America once the production techniques of making and machining large castings were developed.

Layouts soon settled on the "con-ventional" side–valve arrangement, which meant that although combustion–chamber shapes were not ideal, the valve gear itself was very simple. Because one of the less–satisfactory components in early engines was the cylinder–head gasket, many engines of the 1900s and 1910s had cylinder heads in unit with the cylinder block, the combined casting being bolted down to a separate crankcase. In general crankshafts were made without counter–balance weights, but as engine rotating speeds were still low (and six–cylinder engines, which have inherently good balance, were common), this was not thought to be a serious failing. Connecting–rod bearings were usually cast directly to the rods themselves. Most engines had only a single up–draught carburettor, and both inlet and exhaust

Continued over page

206

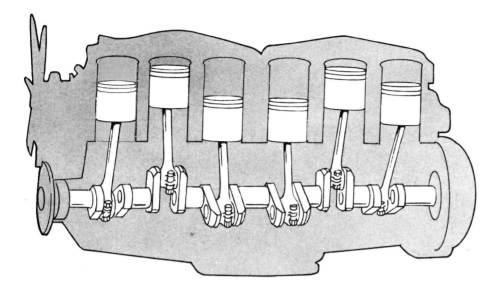

The legendary Rolls-Royce Silver Ghost engine *(left)*, built from 1907 to 1925, brought silence and refinement to motor car engineering for the very first time. There was nothing radically new about the in–line six–cylinder layout, but it was beautifully made and lovingly assembled. In many ways a "Ghost" unit was typical of Edwardian design, with a capacity of more than seven litres, non–detachable cylinder heads, side valves which could be extracted after valve caps had been removed, a crankshaft without balance weights, and magneto ignition. The seven–bearing crankshaft and other details were typical of Royce's methods.

American engineers quickly took to motor car manufacture and began to look for ways of making powerful, efficient and compact engines. Cadillac soon settled on an up–to–the–minute V8 layout, and made it so carefully that they could boast of complete interchangeability at a time when many car parts were still being hand–made and hand–matched to other units.

Even so, there was much in the Cadillac design which was in the mainstream of engine layout. Most engines of the 1900s had long strokes and narrow cylinder bores. Almost invariably they had valves mounted at the side of the cylinders, in a line, operated by a single camshaft. In the case

of the Cadillac, and most other V–engines, one camshaft was placed in the base of the V and operated valves in both cylinder banks. Valves were closed by springs, and tappets (situated at the bottom of the valves) could be adjusted for length.

The advantage of the V8 engine, as shown in this drawing, is that it can be almost as compact as an in–line unit and virtually no longer than an in–line unit with half the number of cylinders. For reasons of dynamic balance, all V8 engines have cylinder banks inclined at an included angle of 90 degrees. V12 units use a 60–degree 'V', or, in certain rare instances, a 120–degree 'V' layout.

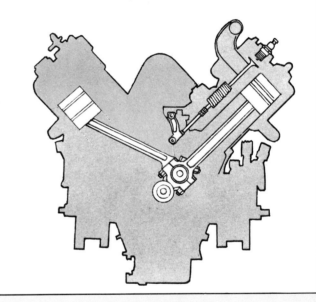

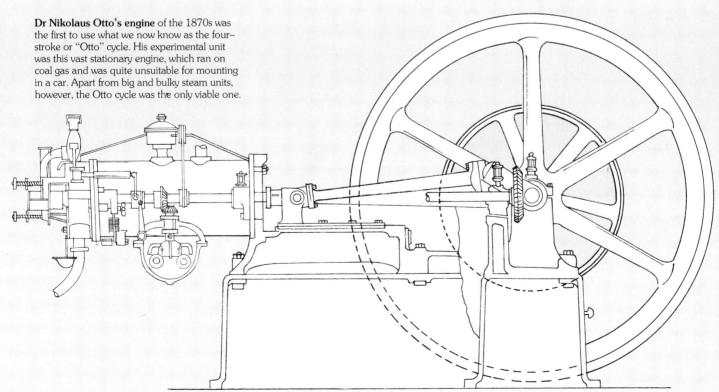

Dr Nikolaus Otto's engine of the 1870s was the first to use what we now know as the four–stroke or "Otto" cycle. His experimental unit was this vast stationary engine, which ran on coal gas and was quite unsuitable for mounting in a car. Apart from big and bulky steam units, however, the Otto cycle was the only viable one.

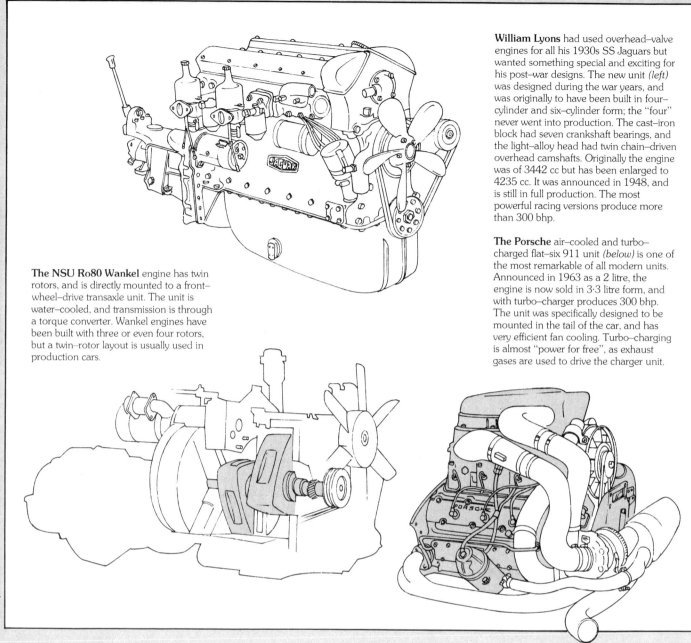

William Lyons had used overhead–valve engines for all his 1930s SS Jaguars but wanted something special and exciting for his post–war designs. The new unit *(left)* was designed during the war years, and was originally to have been built in four–cylinder and six–cylinder form; the "four" never went into production. The cast–iron block had seven crankshaft bearings, and the light–alloy head had twin chain–driven overhead camshafts. Originally the engine was of 3442 cc but has been enlarged to 4235 cc. It was announced in 1948, and is still in full production. The most powerful racing versions produce more than 300 bhp.

The Porsche air–cooled and turbo–charged flat–six 911 unit *(below)* is one of the most remarkable of all modern units. Announced in 1963 as a 2 litre, the engine is now sold in 3·3 litre form, and with turbo–charger produces 300 bhp. The unit was specifically designed to be mounted in the tail of the car, and has very efficient fan cooling. Turbo–charging is almost "power for free", as exhaust gases are used to drive the charger unit.

The NSU Ro80 Wankel engine has twin rotors, and is directly mounted to a front–wheel–drive transaxle unit. The unit is water–cooled, and transmission is through a torque converter. Wankel engines have been built with three or even four rotors, but a twin–rotor layout is usually used in production cars.

manifolds were usually crudely cast and shaped. The science of air flow, and of mixture distribution to cylinders, was by no means understood.

The search for power, and for finding it without making the engines even bigger and heavier, meant that operating efficiency had to be improved. Before long the merits of overhead valves (valves pointing down towards the pistons) and the combustion space profiles they required became known, and by the 1930s all but the very cheapest engines were based on this layout. High–performance engines needed valve gear which operated precisely as intended, which meant that the camshaft profile had to be as close to the valve stem as possible. It was Mercedes and Peugeot who made overhead camshaft layouts fashionable and successful in Grand Prix racing, and by the 1920s such engines were also to be found in high–performance road cars.

By the end of the 1920s, therefore, the general layout of motor car engines had become established. Cars with steam engines (like the Stanley, of the United States) had their adherents, but the engines

were usually bulky, complicated and un–economical. Most engines were now being built with cast–iron blocks and heads, though light alloy was favoured where high combustion temperatures had to be accommodated.

From time to time fashion, perhaps linked to new taxes in certain countries, made a new engine layout popular. For many years, for instance, there was no satisfactory way of mounting the engines flexibly in the frames, so four–cylinder engines (which have untamable vibrations) were not very popular for the more refined cars; this situation changed rapidly in the 1930s after rubber engine mountings had been developed.

A straight–six was always popular, and the more up–market manufacturers then reasoned that if six was good, eight could be even better. Many cars – in Europe and especially in North America – were sold with straight–eight engines, which were beautifully smooth, although long, and some tended to suffer from rather weak and spindly crankshafts.

It was because of these limitations that

'V'–formation engines came to maturity. In this way it was possible to combine a large number of cylinders (and greater displacement) without the penalty of an over–long unit. V8 engines had been built when motoring was still struggling for respectability, but it was Cadillac who first put such a design into fully–tooled quantity production. A few years later they were followed by Packard's introduction of the world's first production–line V12 unit.

After that there was only one step which could be taken in the interests of great prestige – to produce a V16 unit – and such engines were sold in small numbers by Cadillac and Marmon, in the United States, though both the original designs were announced as the North American continent plunged into the economic depression. Later in the 1930s, however, Cadillac relaunched a V16, this time with side valves and a 135–degree angle between cylinder banks; the "ideal" V16 angle is 45 degrees.

In Britain, the annual taxation on cars was based on the piston area of the engine, which explains why many British engines of the inter–war period had long cylinder

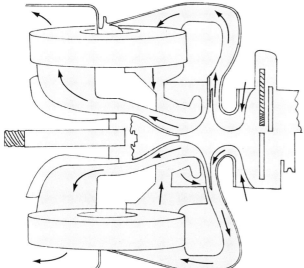

The gas–turbine engine *(left)* became a practical proposition for aircraft use at the end of the 1930s, but it was not until 1950 that Rover built the very first gas–turbine–powered car. The gas–turbine principle is very simple, with a continuous–flow combustion process, but as temperatures are very high and turbine rotating speeds are also very high this means that costly materials have to be used. Air enters from the atmosphere, is compressed (here by a centrifugal compressor), then expands fast as fuel is injected into the stream and burnt, driving the power turbine as it makes its way back to the atmosphere. The compressor is powered by a compressor turbine, driven by the hot gases. In this installation there are ceramic heat exchangers to extract waste heat from the exhaust and pass it to the inlet air.

Legislation has been introduced in many countries since the middle of the 1960s forcing car manufacturers to limit the noxious gases emitted by their engines. This process began in the United States, where cities like Los Angeles had begun to suffer badly from the effects of photometric smog caused by the exhaust gas emissions from millions of private cars. Analysis of exhaust gases showed that unburnt hydrocarbons, carbon monoxide and oxides of nitrogen were all undesirable elements, and the new laws now limit the content of such gases which can be expelled into the atmosphere. To make this possible, engines now have to complete the combustion process inside the cylinders (or extract the last unlawful traces in catalytic converters in their exhaust systems), and a great deal of research has gone into the best way to achieve this. Honda, with their CVCC engines *(right)*, meet the latest regulations by effectively using two inlet passages, and a pre–chamber rather like those used for so long in diesel units. Rich mixture is allowed to enter the engine through the small valve near the plug, and fresh air enters through the normal inlet valve. The sparking plug ignites the mixture in the pre–chamber, which then expands into the principal chamber and completes the burning in a most efficient (and complete) manner; it is then exhausted in the usual manner. Honda's view is that conventional engines do not have the best layout, and that their way is the most logical. The valve–gear arrangement is complex and therefore expensive in that an extra valve has to be operated, but Honda claim that the lower cost involved in the fuel metering and exhaust clean–up process adequately compensates for this. Many other engines resort to carefully preset (and sealed) carburettors, or to the use of fuel injection with exhaust gas being recirculated to inlet ports, in an effort to achieve "clean" power.

strokes and narrow bores. It was in Britain – perhaps more than in other countries – that the concept of building one type of engine in several sizes first came to full maturity, and where it was usual for there to be related four–cylinder and six–cylinder engines machined in the same factory.

Before the Second World War no radically different type of engine came along to challenge the piston engine; indeed the Otto cycle still reigns supreme as the motor industry enters the 1980s – more than a century after the original Otto engine was built. During that war, however, the British took an important lead as the first nation to build aircraft with gas–turbine "jet" engines. While the pure jet principle was not a practical idea for private cars, it was thought that perhaps an offshoot of the "prop–jet" (where the turbine power was harnessed to turning a shaft instead of providing pure thrust) might suffice. Several companies began to build prototypes, but Rover was the first to have an automotive–type engine running, in 1948, and the first to show such a car, in 1950. Like everyone else in the field (which included Fiat, Renault, BMC and Chrysler) they found that the engines were very costly to build, and were not at all economical. Over the years, millions of man–hours were sunk into solving these problems – but without real success. Complex heat exchangers helped to minimise fuel consumption (by transferring wasted exhaust heat to the inlet charge of air), but no way has yet been found of building turbine units at normal prices.

The Wankel rotary unit, developed by Felix Wankel, has however had a limited success. It is not entirely vibration–free (there is still an eccentric "crankshaft" in the design) and not at all cheap to build, but NSU in Germany, and – to a much greater degree – Mazda in Japan, have both successfully marketed cars with twin–rotor units. Such engines are fast becoming reliable, but are apparently not easy to "clean up" in exhaust emission terms.

In all this discussion, it is easy to ignore the way the compression–ignition, or "Diesel" engine, has almost completely taken over from spark–ignition engines in commercial vehicles, and for stationary use. Diesels use direct fuel injection into the cylinders at the precise moment when the air has been compressed to its limit, at which time spontaneous combustion takes place. Diesels are not as powerful as their spark–ignited equivalents, and usually have to be built with much heavier parts; their exhaust emission is often very "dirty", even though their fuel consumption potential can be very good. An increasing number of cars are now being sold with diesel engines.

In the 1970s the question of exhaust emissions became dominant in the field of engine design. The legal requirement to limit emissions originated in the United States, but has spread to most industrialised countries in the world. In general, the only technical advance in engine design in the last ten years has been with "clean air" exhausts in mind, and although specific power outputs continue to rise slowly, the immediate future holds more promise of improvements in fuel consumption than in horsepower. More and more engines are turning to fuel injection, which can be precisely set, rather than carburettors, in an attempt to improve efficiency and running economy.

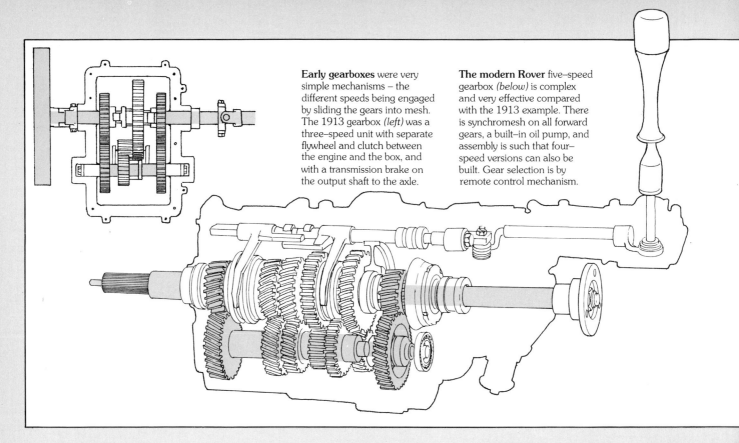

Early gearboxes were very simple mechanisms – the different speeds being engaged by sliding the gears into mesh. The 1913 gearbox *(left)* was a three–speed unit with separate flywheel and clutch between the engine and the box, and with a transmission brake on the output shaft to the axle.

The modern Rover five–speed gearbox *(below)* is complex and very effective compared with the 1913 example. There is synchromesh on all forward gears, a built–in oil pump, and assembly is such that four–speed versions can also be built. Gear selection is by remote control mechanism.

Power to the Road Wheels

No car powered by the internal combustion engine can get by without a gearbox to provide it with different ratios for different requirements. Only where steam engines were fitted, and where there was so much torque delivery at very low engine speeds, was a gearbox not needed. In every modern car, a low ratio is needed to allow slow–speed driving, and for climbing hills, while a high ratio is needed for high–speed cruising. Depending on the speed range of the car, the total number of forward gears may be three, four or (more often in modern cars) five. A separate reverse gear is always provided.

When cars were first being developed, their speed range was so limited (maximum speed was often no more than 10 mph), and their load–carrying capacity so small, that only one gear was needed. It was Panhard, with the *"système Panhard"* layout of front engine, central gearbox and rear axle, who first began to evolve the type of manual gearbox we still find familiar in cars of today.

At first all the gears were exposed underneath the car, so that they were liberally sprayed with water, grit and road filth, but enclosing cases and lubricant were soon provided. All early manual gearboxes were similar in concept to those used on contemporary industrial machines – on which ratios were changed by sliding gear wheels into and out of mesh. Because this had to be done when the car was moving, it meant that gears were usually revolving at different speeds when they were forced into mesh. To disconnect the engine from the transmission, a friction–drive clutch was provided. At first a cone arrangement was common, but later the more normal flat

disc, clamped between driven plates, became the standard format.

Drive was introduced at one end of the mid–mounted gearbox, and taken out of the other end. Top gear was "direct" drive, but intermediate gears had to make use of two sets of gear trains, mounted on one or more layshafts. Before the First World War many cars had final drive by chain, which meant that output from the gearbox was by a cross–shaft to sprockets outside the main frame members, and which were in line with similar sprockets mounted on the back axle itself. When the "Hotchkiss" drive (shaft drive to a differential gear in the back axle itself) became common, drive was by shaft from the back of the transmission.

Up to the 1920s, most cars had their gearboxes separately mounted in the frame and driven by a short shaft from the engine, but soon it became normal for the box to be bolted direct to the clutch housing and the engine castings themselves.

Gearbox design since then has advanced in stages. First, it was agreed that to engage the gears by sliding them into mesh with each other was crude, and this was replaced by the method of having gears in constant engagement, by having dog clutches on the gear shafts themselves, and by sliding these face dog arrangements into engagement as necessary. Nevertheless, the art of double–declutching – using engine speed and clutch to match speeds to a particular phase of the changing process – was needed to ensure silent changes, and considerable driving skill was still needed.

To make the process easier, General Motors invented "synchromesh" – a friction–cone addition to the dog–clutch arrangement which successfully matched gear wheel and dog–clutch speeds before actual engagement occurred. This feature was made available on 1929 Cadillacs and Buicks, and within a few years had spread to

almost every production car in the world. Synchromesh has been refined in detail over the years, and is now normally fitted to all forward gears, but its principle has not changed.

During the 1930s in particular, and to a lesser extent in post–war years, there was a rash of free–wheel fittings, and other items, all intended to make gear changing easier, but all disappeared in favour of the more sophisticated component.

To cut down engine speeds at high road speeds, and to improve fuel economy, "overdrive", though this cannot, of course, many years. These are often separate transmission cases, and "gear up" the normal top gear. The most advanced designs have epicyclic gearing, and changes can be smoothly made without the clutch being depressed and the drive disengaged. Many modern cars now have five–speed gearboxes, in which fifth is a geared–up "overdrive", though this cannot, of course, be engaged without using the clutch.

Automatic gearboxes – those in which ratios were changed by electrical/hydraulic or mechanical means without action being needed by the driver – have been understood from the dawn of motoring, but practical units did not become available until the 1930s. Central to the designs was the fluid coupling, refined as the more efficient torque converter, in which there was no direct mechanical link between engine and gearbox. Changing is inspired by speed–sensitive servos, which in modern systems take account of engine speed, road speed and the torque input from the converter.

Almost every modern American car now built has an automatic transmission, usually with three forward speeds. Only DAF, with their ingenious belt–driven arrangement, has been able to offer an idealised step–less transmission system.

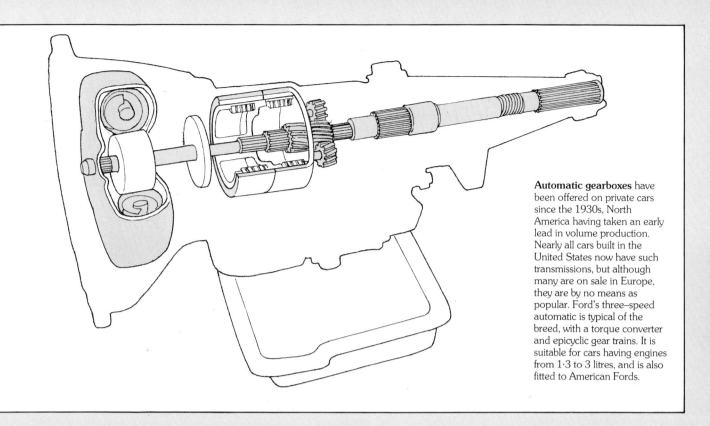

Automatic gearboxes have been offered on private cars since the 1930s, North America having taken an early lead in volume production. Nearly all cars built in the United States now have such transmissions, but although many are on sale in Europe, they are by no means as popular. Ford's three–speed automatic is typical of the breed, with a torque converter and epicyclic gear trains. It is suitable for cars having engines from 1·3 to 3 litres, and is also fitted to American Fords.

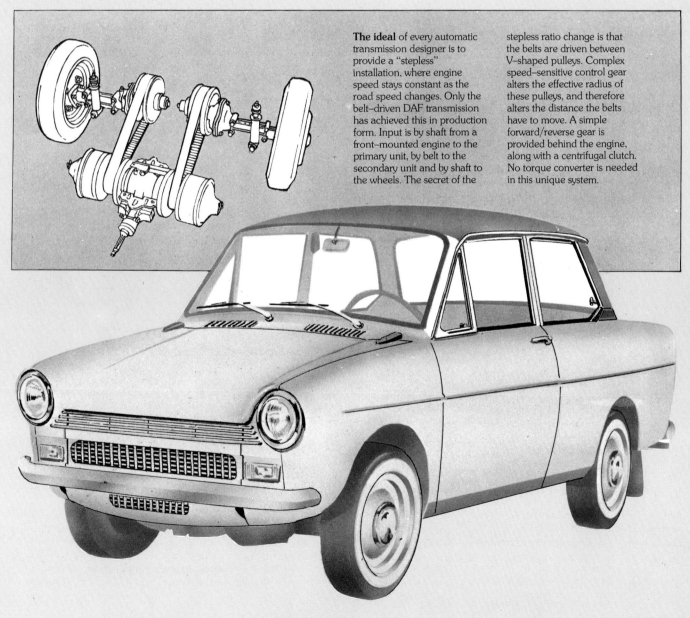

The ideal of every automatic transmission designer is to provide a "stepless" installation, where engine speed stays constant as the road speed changes. Only the belt–driven DAF transmission has achieved this in production form. Input is by shaft from a front–mounted engine to the primary unit, by belt to the secondary unit and by shaft to the wheels. The secret of the stepless ratio change is that the belts are driven between V–shaped pulleys. Complex speed–sensitive control gear alters the effective radius of these pulleys, and therefore alters the distance the belts have to move. A simple forward/reverse gear is provided behind the engine, along with a centrifugal clutch. No torque converter is needed in this unique system.

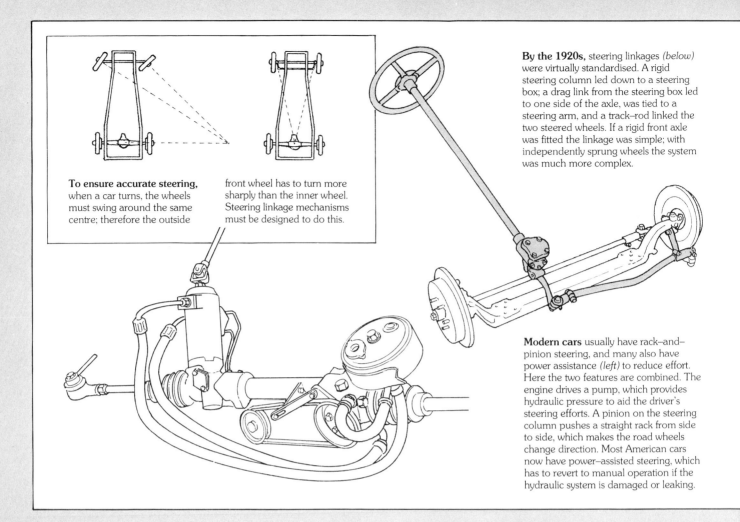

To ensure accurate steering, when a car turns, the wheels must swing around the same centre; therefore the outside front wheel has to turn more sharply than the inner wheel. Steering linkage mechanisms must be designed to do this.

By the 1920s, steering linkages *(below)* were virtually standardised. A rigid steering column led down to a steering box; a drag link from the steering box led to one side of the axle, was tied to a steering arm, and a track–rod linked the two steered wheels. If a rigid front axle was fitted the linkage was simple; with independently sprung wheels the system was much more complex.

Modern cars usually have rack–and–pinion steering, and many also have power assistance *(left)* to reduce effort. Here the two features are combined. The engine drives a pump, which provides hydraulic pressure to aid the driver's steering efforts. A pinion on the steering column pushes a straight rack from side to side, which makes the road wheels change direction. Most American cars now have power–assisted steering, which has to revert to manual operation if the hydraulic system is damaged or leaking.

Steering and Suspension Systems

No matter how fast or slow the car is, nor how new or old, the principal requirements for suspension and steering are the same. Wheels must be allowed to rise and fall to accommodate bumps or holes in the road without unduly disturbing the car and its occupants, while the front wheels must be arranged to change direction at the driver's wishes to allow the car to be taken along a winding road.

As one would expect, at first a car's suspension system was simple and crude. Using principles established on horse–drawn carriages in the previous century (and also, incidentally, on railway carriages and engines), many had their rigid axles sprung by stiff half–elliptic leaf springs, though many cars (including the famous "curved dash" Oldsmobile) used more complex arrangements. Springs, in the early days, were so stiff that no form of damping was needed to control the movement of the axles.

As motor car engineering progressed, cars became faster and ever faster, and the occupants came to demand more and more driving comfort. Almost by definition, this meant that more axle movement had to be provided, and that springs had to be softened. Soft springs, uncontrolled, did little for a car's roadholding, and were particularly bad for the steering, so it became necessary to add dampers. These

use friction in one way or another to discourage movement. Early dampers had levers linked to axle and chassis respectively, rubbing one friction surface against another. More modern units use the frictional properties of fluid being forced through small holes, either in lever–arm or telescopic form.

Although most cars still have rigid back axles (with or without drive shafts inside them), all modern cars have independent front suspension, which means that each front wheel can move up and down independent of its partner. The wheels are tied to the structure, body or frame by links. This became necessary because of the serious effects of high speeds and bumpy roads on cars with rigid front axles.

During the 1940s and 1950s an enormous variety of suspension systems was developed. The movement of wheels and axles came to be controlled by leaf springs, coil springs, torsion bars, rubber in torsion and in compression, by hydraulic means, by high–pressure gases and by a combination of these. All proved to be effective in one way or another, but some have become less popular than others because of their high cost and complication.

The MacPherson strut system has been adopted by many manufacturers because it is simple (it uses coil springs combined with telescopic damper units – both of which are cheap to make, and consistently effective) and because it is compact and spreads the loads around the structure to minimise the reinforcements needed to absorb them.

Sophistication used to be popular, as a means to selling cars; cost effectiveness and actual performance is now thought to be more important.

For this reason, although independent suspension is agreed to be necessary at the front of a car, clever design often makes it unnecessary at the rear. In cars where the space problem of a rigid axle moving up and down under the floor is not thought to be critical, it is often retained; in small cars, where every cubic inch counts, independent rear suspension is often tucked into the corner of the structure.

Today, steering mechanisms are thoroughly understood. The complex requirements of front wheels which have to move up and down *and* be steered from side to side are fully resolved and computer analysis now helps linkages to be idealised.

When front wheels were linked by a rigid axle, the linkage was simple enough, but independent suspension means that steering and tie–rods have to swing in arcs along with suspension members. Safety considerations (necessitating a system which does not push the column back into the car in case of accidents) affect the layout of the steering, which is usually bolted up to the cross–member of the car.

Many modern cars use a rack–and–pinion system, which is mechanically efficient and occupies the least possible space. But a growing number of cars, particularly those of American manufacture, now back up the rack–and–pinion system with power assistance.

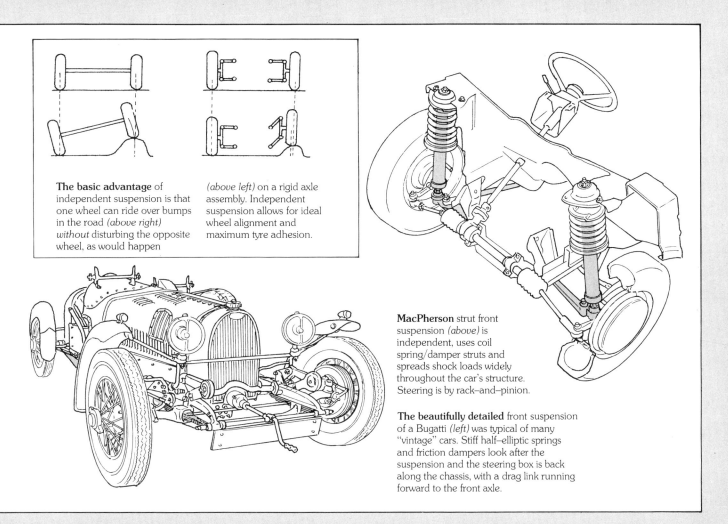

The basic advantage of independent suspension is that one wheel can ride over bumps in the road *(above right) without* disturbing the opposite wheel, as would happen *(above left)* on a rigid axle assembly. Independent suspension allows for ideal wheel alignment and maximum tyre adhesion.

MacPherson strut front suspension *(above)* is independent, uses coil spring/damper struts and spreads shock loads widely throughout the car's structure. Steering is by rack–and–pinion.

The beautifully detailed front suspension of a Bugatti *(left)* was typical of many "vintage" cars. Stiff half–elliptic springs and friction dampers look after the suspension and the steering box is back along the chassis, with a drag link running forward to the front axle.

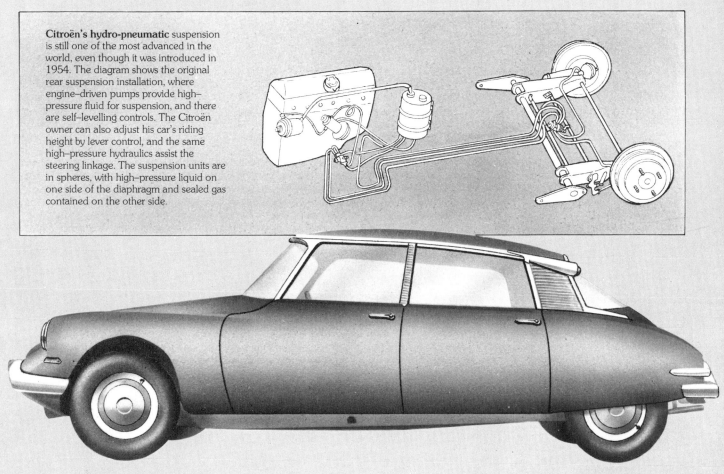

Citroën's hydro-pneumatic suspension is still one of the most advanced in the world, even though it was introduced in 1954. The diagram shows the original rear suspension installation, where engine–driven pumps provide high–pressure fluid for suspension, and there are self–levelling controls. The Citroën owner can also adjust his car's riding height by lever control, and the same high–pressure hydraulics assist the steering linkage. The suspension units are in spheres, with high–pressure liquid on one side of the diaphragm and sealed gas contained on the other side.

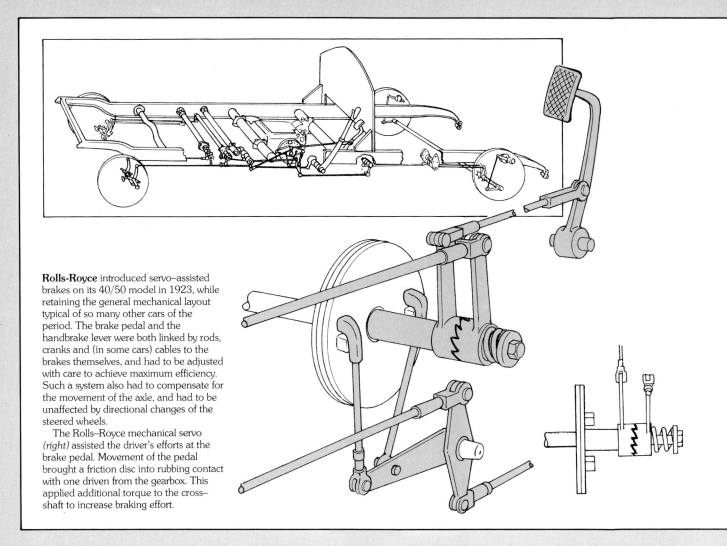

Rolls-Royce introduced servo–assisted brakes on its 40/50 model in 1923, while retaining the general mechanical layout typical of so many other cars of the period. The brake pedal and the handbrake lever were both linked by rods, cranks and (in some cars) cables to the brakes themselves, and had to be adjusted with care to achieve maximum efficiency. Such a system also had to compensate for the movement of the axle, and had to be unaffected by directional changes of the steered wheels.

The Rolls–Royce mechanical servo *(right)* assisted the driver's efforts at the brake pedal. Movement of the pedal brought a friction disc into rubbing contact with one driven from the gearbox. This applied additional torque to the cross–shaft to increase braking effort.

Stopping Power

The "other half" of performance is the braking system: without brakes it would be quite impossible to use a car. When the car was invented, early models had to be stopped by pressing a spoon–shaped lever against the tyre treads, but this was very inefficient, particularly if the tyres them–selves were slippery. Brakes were so poor that cars habitually carried a "sprag" or wedging system to insert in the wheels or transmission to prevent the car from run–ning away when parked on hills.

Although the principle of disc brakes was understood right from the start (and was, of course, in use on pedal cycles for many years before it was applied to motor cars), production cars in the developing motor industry were equipped with drum brakes. These, at first, were fitted only to the rear wheels, or to the transmission, and could be applied either by having friction segments pushing out to the inner surface of a drum to slow it down or by having segments clamping down on the outside of drums; the one was called "internal expanding", the other "external contracting". Once again, experience in wet and muddy conditions soon showed that the internal system was much the most satisfactory, and it was soon standardised.

In many cases, there was a separate footbrake and handbrake system, each operated by its own set of rods, cranks and cables. The footbrake often operated on a transmission brake fixed to the drive shaft, while the handbrake operated drums fixed to the rear wheels or axle. Later, the systems were standardised.

Front–wheel brakes were not standar–dised for many years, partly because of the very real difficulty of working out a rod and cable linkage to front wheels which had to be steered, and partly because they were not needed until vehicle performance rose considerably. By the mid–1920s, however, four–wheel braking was usually found on all new models.

Servo–assistance was first offered by Hispano–Suiza (and later by Rolls–Royce, using the Hispano invention), where the operation of the brake pedal allowed a friction disc, driven from the gearbox, to rub against another in the braking system, thus helping the driver's own efforts. Later, in North America, the vacuum servo system was developed for the same purpose, where engine manifold vacuum could be arranged to pull a piston inside a chamber, which helped move the cylinders in a normal pedal–operated braking system.

Mechanical brake linkages began to give way to hydraulic layouts in the 1920s, once satisfactory ways of sealing the lines had been developed. The operating cylinders themselves were quite costly, but the actual hydraulic "plumbing" was very simple, and such layouts are always now used in modern cars.

The major modern development in braking systems has been the disc brake. This uses an old principle in a new way, where the friction pads are clamped together in a pincer–like movement onto a rotating disc. This is a very efficient method, as although the disc becomes very hot, it can also get rid of that heat rapidly, and (with the appropriate pads and materials) fade, or deterioration in the braking performance, can virtually be eliminated.

Study of braking shows that the front brakes have to do the most work (the harder the brakes are applied, the more of the car's weight is thrown forward onto the front wheels), so drum brakes are often still specified for rear wheels. This also helps to make a good handbrake installation pos–sible, which is otherwise rather difficult. On very high–performance cars, however, where the brakes must literally be as good as possible, disc brakes are fitted to all four wheels. Depending on the suspension being used, some cars have their brakes (drums or discs) mounted "inboard", which is to say that they are mounted at the inner end of drive shafts, clamped to transmission or similar cases.

To eliminate rear wheel locking when weight transfer takes place, many cars have pressure–limiting valves in their hydraulic circuits. On cheaper cars these usually have fixed settings; on others, links to the rear suspension allow the setting to be increased for heavy loads.

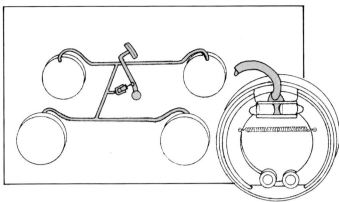

The basic elements of a hydraulic braking system *(left)* are that the brake pedal and cylinder are linked to each wheel brake, and to what is known as the "slave" cylinder, by pipes full of hydraulic fluid.

The principle is simple; when the foot pedal is depressed, the piston in the cylinder pushes fluid into each of the wheel cylinders, whose pistons then move to actuate the brake shoes. The adoption of hydraulic systems was delayed for many years due to the difficulty in evolving satisfactory piston seals. Many cars now have vacuum servo assistance to boost the braking; this uses engine manifold vacuum to help move the pedal master cylinder piston, and can be arranged either to improve the braking or to reduce efforts required.

Disc brakes *(right)* were first used in quantity on fast fighter aircraft during the Second World War, and were used with spectacular success by Jaguar on their C–Type sports–racing cars in 1952. In a drum brake the friction surfaces are pushed outwards to make contact with metal drums, but because they are not ideally cooled the systems can overheat and cause fading. The big advantage of disc brakes is that the friction pads are pushed inward to clamp onto discs which are always exposed to draughts of cooling air. They are much less liable to fade, and now find a home on at least the front wheels of almost every modern car.

Although on the racing Jaguar installation it was not at all easy to change brake pads, on current disc calipers a set of new pads can be installed in a few minutes. In addition – to make them even more impervious to fade – discs fitted to big and fast cars are often ventilated to allow air to circulate behind the rubbing surface.

It is not at all easy to arrange for a successful handbrake linkage on a disc brake layout, which is one of several reasons why they are not often used on rear wheels. In this case a small drum brake, operated by the handbrake lever, is often installed in the hub of a disc casting.

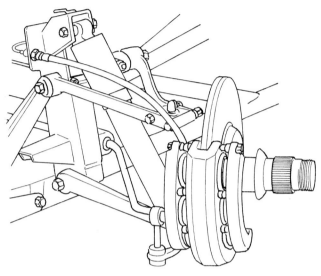

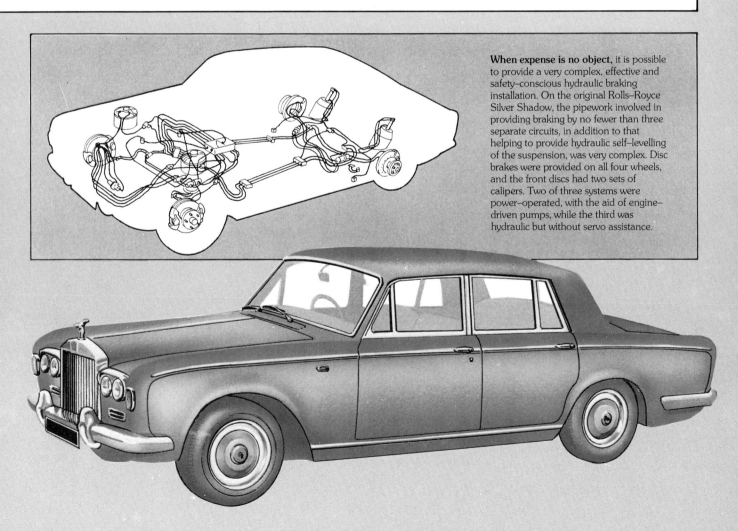

When expense is no object, it is possible to provide a very complex, effective and safety–conscious hydraulic braking installation. On the original Rolls–Royce Silver Shadow, the pipework involved in providing braking by no fewer than three separate circuits, in addition to that helping to provide hydraulic self–levelling of the suspension, was very complex. Disc brakes were provided on all four wheels, and the front discs had two sets of calipers. Two of three systems were power–operated, with the aid of engine–driven pumps, while the third was hydraulic but without servo assistance.

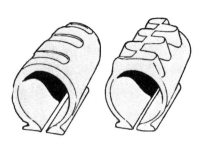

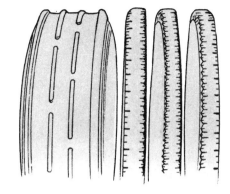

The earliest tyres *(above)* had virtually no tread – a feature which was later provided to give grip on the loose and uneven road surfaces. Simple transverse cuts, to give a cogging effect, or heavy studs to dig into the road were thought to be sufficient.

A modern tyre *(above right)* is not only much more sophisticated in construction, but needs no inner tube, and has a very detailed tread pattern to give wet and dry grip and to disperse surface water.

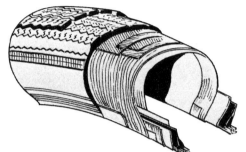

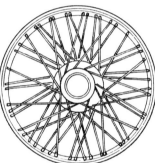

One very clever 1960s idea *(above)* from Pirelli was to provide treads that could be removed when the main carcass had been deflated. The theory was that one tyre, say, could have smooth and winter–type treads as appropriate. The tyre, however, did not go into production.

Almost every modern tyre *(left)* has what is called radial ply construction. This keeps the tread very stable on the road and ensures a long service life.

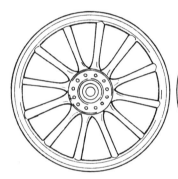

"Artillery"–style wheel, common until the 1920s, often with wooden spokes.

Wire spoke wheels, with single centre lock fixing, still popular on sports cars today.

The sculptured pressed steel wheel is cheaper to make but is still visually attractive.

Modern wire wheels, stronger than before, and sometimes with multi–bolt fixings.

Wheel, Tyre and Dashboard Design

In the field of component design and appearance, no less than in major assemblies, there has often been spectacular progress over the years. First of all an item is made to work, then to work well, next to work perfectly and finally to be made to look good as well. Wheels, tyres, lights, instruments, seats and many other interior fittings are all immeasurably more effective than they were in the early 1900s.

The question of style is one which has already been discussed. However, in modern times almost every styling feature has to be prepared with function well to the fore, and with the implications of primary or secondary safety already considered.

Nowhere is this more obvious than in the art and science (for there is something of both in the business) of designing new tyres. When motor cars were first invented they had solid tyres with no aids to traction or braking. The first pneumatic tyres, which owed much to the Dunlop inventions, were fragile and unreliable components, and it

was not for many years that the problems of finding wet–road grip, and of dispersing surface water, began to be understood.

Tyres, mainly made of natural or synthetic rubber, are filled with high–pressure air so that they can help cushion the car and its occupants against road shocks. The wheel rims themselves, and the covers, must all be airtight, so that none of this air is lost over a period of time, thus reducing the pressure. Rubber compounds are chosen to provide an airtight seal, and to give maximum grip in traction, braking, steering and cornering.

Although advances in rubber–compound technology continue to occur, the most significant changes over the years have been in the shape of the tyres and the way in which their carcasses are built up. Early tyres, as illustrated, were at least as high as they were wide, had simple textile carcass construction and provided a very hard ride due to their narrow rim base and thick–wall construction. They were also of rigid "beaded edge" pattern.

Over the years, for a given purpose and weight of car, tyres have tended to become much fatter and squatter. The rims on

which they are mounted have become wider and wider, which has not only allowed the resulting larger tyres to develop more grip by having more rubber on the ground, but has also allowed them to become more efficient absorbers of shocks set up by road disturbances.

Expressed in figures, early tyres had what is known as 100 per cent height/width profiles, whereas almost every modern tyre has a profile less than 78 per cent; many are down to 70 per cent, and really fast cars sometimes even have 50 per cent tyres. Covers fitted to racing cars sometimes have ratios as low as 25 per cent.

Such low profiles do not always bring benefits without drawbacks. Designers find that squat tyres are more difficult to match to the rest of the suspension, and there are sometimes difficulties in finding space for them inside the wheel arches of small cars.

In the beginning, tyres had to have separate thin–walled rubber "inner tubes" to retain the air, but by the 1950s it was possible to make the side walls of the covers themselves airtight – and so the "tubeless" tyre was born.

The construction of tyres is much more

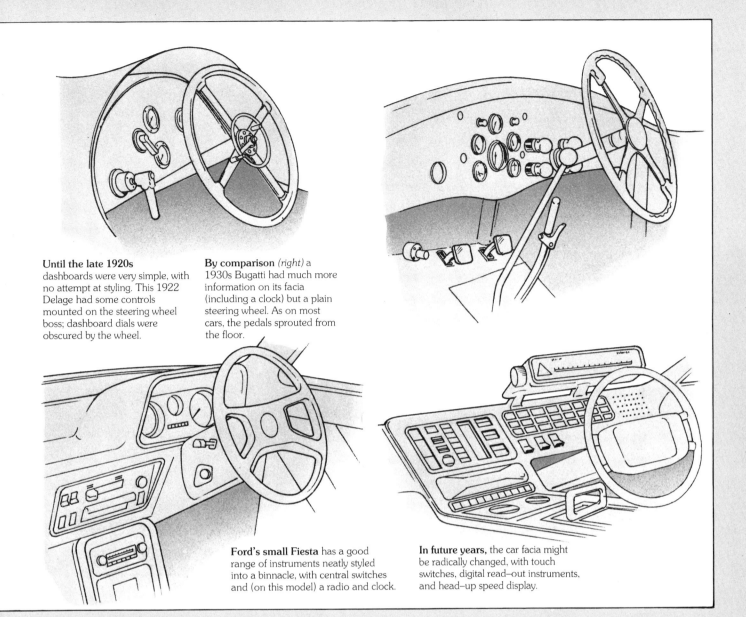

Until the late 1920s dashboards were very simple, with no attempt at styling. This 1922 Delage had some controls mounted on the steering wheel boss; dashboard dials were obscured by the wheel.

By comparison *(right)* a 1930s Bugatti had much more information on its facia (including a clock) but a plain steering wheel. As on most cars, the pedals sprouted from the floor.

Ford's small Fiesta has a good range of instruments neatly styled into a binnacle, with central switches and (on this model) a radio and clock.

In future years, the car facia might be radically changed, with touch switches, digital read–out instruments, and head–up speed display.

complex than might at first appear. The great advance since the 1950s has been the evolution of the "radial ply" tyre, where the main tread–supporting bands, immediately under the rubber in contact with the road, are laid around, rather than across, the carcass. This has had important benefits to stability, roadholding, tyre behaviour and to the long–life potential of a given tyre. Although radials are more expensive to manufacture than the now obsolete "cross–ply" type, they are more cost effective to the customer in the long run. There is a running discussion on the merits of textile or steel–wire–based radial plys – the one gives a more refined ride, the other better stability and performance; the debate continues.

Tread design began merely to let a cover have some sort of gripping or cogging effect on the road surface, but before long it was found that suitable treads could allow more grip to be developed on wet roads. In recent years, treads have often been asymmetrical, to allow the outside to work in a different way from that part nearest the inside of the car, and many are now laid out so that they actively expel the water running into the main channels from the road. The search

for refinement is now such that treads often have random cuts around their circumference so that noise and vibration are minimised.

The advance in wheel design has mainly been with an eye to appearance. The early type of "artillery" wheel (so called because gun carriages usually had this type) was strictly utilitarian, and often had wooden spokes; many early cars had wheels fixed to the axles, and detachable rims. Wire spoke wheels, sometimes with Rudge centre–lock fixings, sometimes bolted to hubs, became popular in the 1920s and 1930s, but the pressed–steel wheel, often very simply styled and usually with a decorative finish, became normal on most cars from the end of the 1930s.

Wire spoke wheels have lost much of their appeal nowadays, because it is often difficult to keep the individual spokes tight, and they have been replaced in the status stakes either by carefully sculptured pressed–steel wheels, or expensive and attractive cast–alloy wheels, sometimes with centre–lock fixing.

To a stylist, one of the most important features of a car is the facia and in–

strumentation, which the motorist has to look at all the time he is in the car. Early cars had a strictly utilitarian panel, haphazardly inhabited by dials and switches. By the end of the 1920s the space was usually well filled, particularly on expensive cars, and by the 1930s the stylists began to bring some sense of integration to the layout. Now instruments, switches, ventilation controls, radio and other in–car–entertainment fittings, stowage space and the inevitable ashtray are neatly grouped together.

Safety considerations have had much to do with the evolution of steering wheel shapes, panel padding, control disposition and instrument lighting in recent years. It is now generally agreed that there is an ideal place for most individual controls, and some firms go in for one corporate layout on all their models.

In future, modern electronics techniques and features already found in aircraft may find a home in new cars. The object will be to make the driver's job as easy as possible, and on–board computers may work out fuel consumption, inform the driver of the distance to his destination, and even remind him when a service is due.

Acknowledgements

General credits
Author and publishers would like to thank the following for their help in textual research: Brian Adcock of Vauxhall Motors; BL Cars; Stuart Bladon, Deputy Editor of *Autocar*; John Bolster and the publishers Weidenfeld & Nicolson for permission to quote extracts from *The Upper Crust*; Alan Booker, customising specialist; *Custom Car* magazine; Andrew Farmer, model–maker; G. N. Georgano; Walter Hayes and the Ford Motor Company; Cyril Posthumus; Tony Ronald of Renault (UK) Limited; Mrs Vera Russell and the staff of the National Motor Museum, Beaulieu; Roger Stower, archivist at Aston Martin; Volkswagen (UK) Limited; and Gerald Wingrove.

Artists' credits
Chapter titles and illustration on page 17: Cecil Vieweg/Artist Partners

Double–page spreads and illustration on page 176: Brian Sanders/ Artist Partners

"Milestones in Motoring": David Parr and Kuo Kang Chen/Studio Briggs; page 197, Jeremy Banks/Studio Briggs

Retouching: Gordon Briggs/Studio Briggs; Combined Graphic Services

Photographic credits
Photographs are credited by descending order of the base line of each photograph. Where two or more photographs lie on the same base line, credits read left to right. In some instances, the last–named credit on a page may apply to more than one photograph.

The National Motor Museum, Beaulieu, has been abbreviated in the credits to NMM.

1 Peter Roberts; 2 Miss J. M. MacBey (private collection), Cyril Posthumus, Dr J. Renfrew (private collection); 3 Dr J. Renfrew (private collection); 4 Kobal Collection, Dr J. Renfrew (private collection), Peter Roberts; 6 Brown Brothers, NMM; 6–7 NMM; 7 Ford Motor Company, NMM; 8 Associated Press; 8–9 NMM; 9 Aerofilms; 12–13 NMM; 12 Ann Ronan Picture Library; 13 Peter Roberts, NMM; 14 The Mansell Collection, Central Office of Information, The Mansell Collection, Peter Newark's Western Americana; 15 NMM, NMM, Peter Roberts; 16 NMM; 18 The National Automotive History Collection Detroit Public Library, NMM; 19 General Motors, Oldsmobile Division; 20–21 Ford Motor Company, England; 22 Mr M. E. Mager (private collection); 22–23 Peter Roberts; 23 Mr M. E. Mager (private collection), Mrs Sheila Crampton (private collection); 26 Peter Roberts; 26–27 NMM; 27 Peter Roberts, Cyril Posthumus; 30–31 Mrs S. Reeves (private collection); 30 NMM; 31 NMM; 32 René Dazy, NMM; 33 NMM; 34 NMM; 34–35 NMM; 35 NMM; 36 NMM; 36–37 NMM; 37 NMM; 40 NMM; 41 NMM; 42 NMM; 43 Peter Roberts; 46–47 Chris Jones; 48–49 Chris Jones/Foto Alvarez; 48 Chris Jones; 49 Chris Jones, Chris Jones/Daimler Benz; 50–51 Citroën; 52 NMM, Camera Press; 53 Syndication International, Fox Photos; 56–57 NMM; 56 NMM; 57 Peter Roberts; 58 John Frost Collection; 58–59 The Mansell Collection; 60 Radio Times Hulton Picture Library; 61 Peter Roberts, René Dazy; 64 Radio Times Hulton Picture Library, Popperfoto, Radio Times Hulton Picture Library; 65 Radio Times Hulton Picture Library; 66 Central Press; 67 Mr V. Stevenson (private collection), Peter Roberts; 70 Peter Roberts; 70–71 NMM; 71 NMM; 72 (insert) Popperfoto, (insert) NMM, NMM; 73 NMM; 74 Brown Brothers, Peter Roberts; 75 Ford Archives/Henry Ford Museum, Michigan, NMM, NMM, Peter Roberts; 78 NMM, 79 NMM; 82–83 Ronald Grant Archive; 82 Culver Pictures Inc.; 83 Ronald Grant Archive, Peter Newark's Western Americana; 84 John Kobal Collection, National Film Archive/Rank; 85 Kobal Collection/Walt Disney Productions, Kobal Collection/Walt Disney Productions, National Film Archive/United Artists; 86 Kobal Collection; 87 National Film Archive/MGM, Culver Pictures Inc.; 90 Culver Pictures Inc., Culver Pictures Inc., National Film Archive/Twentieth Century Fox; 91 Culver Pictures Inc.; 94–95 Cyril Posthumus; 95 Cyril Posthumus; 96–97 Kevin MacDonnell; 96 (insert) Louis Klemantaski; 97 Peter Roberts; 100–101 Phipps Photographic; 100 Cyril Posthumus, Andrew Farmer; 101 Andrew Farmer; 102–103 Radio Times Hulton Picture Library; 102 Louis Klemantaski; 103 NMM, Silverstone Circuits/Geoffrey Goddard; 104 Peter Roberts, Cyril Posthumus; 105 Andrew Farmer, Andrew Farmer, Nicholas Eddison; 106–107 Nurburgring GmbH; 107 Nurburgring GmbH/Karl Heinz Luckell; 108 NMM, LAT Photographic; 109 Louis Klemantaski, LAT Photographic; 110 Peter Roberts; 110–111 Peter Roberts; 112 Peter Roberts; 113 Brands Hatch Circuit; 114–115 Popperfoto; 115 (top insert) NMM, (bottom insert) Sport and General; 118 Brown Brothers, Henry Ford Museum, Dearborn, Michigan; 119 Peter Newark's Western Americana, Ann Ronan Picture Library, Ford Motor Company, England; 120 Ford Motor Company, England; 120–121 Ford Motor Company, England; 121 Ford Motor Company, England, Peter Roberts/Ford Archives, Dearborn, Michigan, Culver Pictures Inc.; 122 Ford Motor Company, England; 122–123 Culver Pictures Inc.; 124 Mary Evans Picture Library; 124–125 Cyril Posthumus, Mary Evans Picture Library; 128–129 Ullstein; 129 Peter Roberts, Peter Roberts, Peter Roberts, VW; 130–131 John Topham Picture Library; 130 Popperfoto; 132 NMM; 133 John Frost Collection, NMM; 134–135 Leyland; 134 Fox Photos, Leyland Historic Photos; 135 Leyland, Leyland Historic Photos; 136–137 United Press International; 137 Datsun, Toyota; 140 NMM; 141 Cyril Posthumus, Aston Martin; 144 Camera Press; 144–145 Peter Roberts; 145 George Hall, Peter Roberts; 148 Mike Key, *Custom Car* magazine, Ford Motor Company, England; 149 *Custom Car* magazine; 150 David Messer; 151 David Messer, David Messer, Daily Telegraph Colour Library/Roy Strong, David Messer; 154–155 Petersen Publishing Company; 155 Syndication International; 156–157 *Custom Car* magazine; 157 *Custom Car* magazine; 158–159 Camera Press/James Pickerell; 158 Camera Press/James Pickerell; 159 Colin Taylor, Camera Press/Thomas A. Wilkie; 160 Petersen Publishing Company; 161 All–Sport, Peter Roberts, NMM; 164–165 Peter Roberts; 165 Peter Roberts; 166–167 United Press International, NMM; 170 Carrozzeria Pninfarina, Peter Roberts; 171 Peter Roberts; 172–173 Black Starr/John Launois, NMM; 173 Ferrari, Maserati, Lamborghini; 177 Ullstein; 178 Mary Evans Picture Library, United Press International, Popperfoto, Popperfoto, Popperfoto, Popperfoto, Mary Evans Picture Library; 179 NMM, Aerofilms; 180 René Dazy, Peter Roberts, Ford Motor Company; 182 ANP; 183 Vauxhall Motors Limited; 184–185 Carrozzeria Pninfarina; 188 Victoria and Albert Museum; 189 Victoria and Albert Museum, David Messer; 190 Cyril Posthumus, Citroën, Ford Motor Company, England; 190–191 Cyril Posthumus; 191 Daily Telegraph Colour Library; 192 David Messer; 192–193 Andrew Farmer; 193 David Messer; 194–195 Camera Press.

Index

Throughout the index, page numbers set in Roman type (42, 137) refer to the main text; page numbers set in italic type (*42, 137*) refer to material which includes illustrations or captions; page numbers set in bold type (**42, 137**) refer to material in the final section, "Milestones in Motoring".

INDEX

INDEX